CATHY BEYER
DORIS PIKE
LORETTA McGOVERN

Surviving Unemployment

A FAMILY HANDBOOK FOR WEATHERING HARD TIMES

HENRY HOLT AND COMPANY · NEW YORK

Henry Holt and Company, Inc.
Publishers since 1866
115 West 18th Street
New York, New York 10011

Henry Holt® is a registered trademark
of Henry Holt and Company, Inc.

Published in Canada by Fitzhenry & Whiteside Ltd.,
195 Allstate Parkway, Markham, Ontario L3R 4T8.

Library of Congress Cataloging-in-Publication Data
Beyer, Cathy.
Surviving unemployment: a family handbook for weathering hard
times / Cathy Beyer, Doris Pike, and Loretta McGovern.—1st ed.
p.   cm.
Includes index.
1. Unemployment—United States.   2. Unemployment—
United States—Psychological aspects.   3. Vocational guidance—
United States.   4. Work and family—United States.   I. Pike, Doris.
II. McGovern, Loretta.   III. Title.
HD5724.B45   1993
331.13'7'0240694—dc20   92-32402
                                                                         CIP

ISBN 0-8050-2050-0
ISBN 0-8050-2051-9 (An Owl Book: pbk.)

Henry Holt books are available for special promotions and premiums.
For details contact: Director, Special Markets.

First Owl Book Edition—1993

Designed by Victoria Hartman

Printed in the United States of America
All first editions are printed on acid-free paper.∞

10 9 8 7 6 5 4 3 2
10 9 8 7 6 5 4 3 2
pbk.

CONTENTS

FOREWORD
How to Avoid Feeling Deprived

Open Letter to Readers
of *Surviving Unemployment*

A decade ago I enjoyed prime rib at the Ritz-Carlton and purchased toys for nieces and nephews from F. A. O. Schwarz. My attitude has since undergone a complete reversal.

Today, when excess would not stand between us and our goals, my husband, Jim, and I enjoy being frugal. In general, we both prefer low-cost meals, used acquisitions, and free entertainment. This attitude reversal lies at the heart of why neither Jim nor I have ever felt deprived while sustaining our lifestyle for so many years.

The feeling of deprivation will undermine any effort to pursue long-term discipline. Dieters will fail as long as they hate low-calorie food. Would-be athletes will fail as long as they hate exertion. Wannabe tightwads will fail as long as they view frugality as a lifestyle they must endure or were forced into by circumstance.

To overcome the feeling of deprivation, consider the following three points: First, recognize that you are engaging in the discipline out of choice. You decide to give up something so that you can have something else. If you think, "I eat leftovers because I *have* to," you view yourself as being deprived. Think instead, "I eat leftovers because curbing my food bill is something I *can* do to reach my goal." This attitude adjustment is like the question, "Is this glass half empty or half full?" When you recognize that you are making a choice, your attitude changes from deprivation to empowerment.

Second, as you cut back, give up expenses, starting with the ones that provide the least value for dollars spent. The order of elimination will differ from tightwad to tightwad. For example, in the beginning Jim and I ate out frequently. After a less-than-spectacular meal of stuffed lobster we agreed to give up restaurant meals altogether. We did not enjoy them enough for the cost. During one of my speaking engagements a woman told me her husband was a chef and loved to eat out. In their case they probably received sufficient value from restaurant meals to continue going out. They needed to find other things to give up first.

View giving up extras as transferring funds from one area of your life to another. To assess your priorities, constantly ask yourself if you received sufficient value for the money you spent. When it costs $20 to take the kids to a fast-food meal, is it ten times better than the $2 home-cooked meal? Is the convenience worth $18? People commonly make the mistake of spending money on smaller items that are low on their priority list and, as a result, cannot afford the big things high on their list.

Third, do not compare your economic situation to someone else's. If you are trying to lose weight, it can be frustrating to watch a thin person eat twice as much as you. Having a slow metabolism just means you have to work harder.

If your income is less than someone else's you will have to eliminate more from your priority list to achieve the same goal. Jim and I knew that we had to work harder than our parents and grandparents to afford a similar home. We had nothing to gain by bemoaning today's higher interest rates.

Wringing your hands over economic inequities merely wastes emotional energy that could be better used in a positive way to achieve your goal. Accept the givens in your situation and work with them.

Feeling empowered by recognizing you are choosing to scale down to reach a goal, eliminating expenses in order of least value received, and accepting the givens in your personal economic situation are the steps of "beginner tightwaddery." Beyond this there is a higher plane of enlightenment . . . "the Zen of advanced tightwaddery." You progress to a state of mind where you develop an aversion to "stupid expenditures" as defined within your personal value system. They become symbols of darkness that have been placed in your path to thwart your efforts—hence my seemingly irrational disdain for Jell-O pudding snack packs.

Likewise, you come to equate aspects of frugality (which our culture regards as deprivation) as symbols for past or future achievements. You know you have gotten it when you discover you prefer refrigerator stew to prime rib, not because it tastes better, but because more than merely feeding your body, it nourishes your soul. You know these symbols represent a larger lifestyle that will enable you to acquire (or has enabled you to acquire) the things that are genuinely important to you.

Amy Dacyczyn, a.k.a. The Frugal Zealot,
author of *The Tightwad Gazette* newsletter

PREFACE

During the mid-eighties, when the rest of the country was prospering, my family was a victim of the recession in Texas. Referring to the casualties of the Texas oil crisis at that time, a February 1986 issue of *Business Week* stated, "The rest of the world may be cheering, but the recent break in oil prices is reverberating like a death rattle throughout major segments of the industry."

Consolidation of the U.S. oil industry continued throughout the eighties. Oil companies were leveraged to the hilt, and the major oil companies used their massive financial clout to pick up bargain-priced, debt-strapped independents. Yet analysts remained optimistic. This positive forecasting appeared to be endemic. In the same *Business Week* article, a financial analyst was quoted as saying, "I don't see any evidence of bank failures." In fact, it was at this time that the seeds of the bank failures were being sown. In 1990 over 200 banks failed, compared with only ten the decade before.

While the government employed the word *recession* to describe the economic downturn, those whose jobs were threatened began to whisper the dreaded word *depression*. This recalls the statement made by Harry S Truman, "A recession is when your neighbor loses his job. A depression is when you lose yours." This discrepancy in terminology arose from a decline in certain occupations while others flourished. In the midst of an overall recession, we will continue to see industry-specific depressions.

By 1986 every family on our block had suffered a job loss or major salary cut. Nearly every house on the street had either been on the market or gone through foreclosure. The stress on families in the neighborhood resulted in more than one broken marriage. Watching friends lose jobs and walk away from their homes was difficult, but most distressing was the breakup of families.

My husband, Bill, did not escape the Texas scourge. A petroleum geologist, he was laid off in 1986 for the second time since moving to Houston in 1982. That he had made the only significant find in his department during the previous years, that he had graduated from Ivy League Dartmouth College and had gone on to get his master's in geology, and that he possessed excellent communication skills could not save his paycheck or his career. There were no jobs to be had.

Bill and I learned about unemployment the hard way: we lived through it, more than once. According to a poll from a November 1990 issue of *Newsweek*, most chief wage earners would not move to a new location, sell their car, sell their home, ask their spouse to get a job, or seek financial aid from their parents if they lost their job. Eighty-three percent of them would not expect to move in with their parents. Reading that survey, I smiled, because Bill and I chose to do most things on that list.

When Bill lost his job in May of 1986, the unemployment rate for petroleum geologists was over 25 percent. Transferring into another field was his only hope of finding work, and the only opportunities were in hazardous waste investigation and cleanup in the Northeast. The day after he received the pink slip, we put our house on the market. We used unemployment checks to buy plane tickets for Bill on the red-eye to Boston so he could start a job search while staying with his parents in neighboring Wakefield. I stayed in Houston with our daughter that summer. Luckily we sold our house, losing all of our equity but owing nothing on the mortgage. My daughter and I, along with the pets, joined Bill at his parents' home in October. It wasn't until March that he found a job, and it was the end of May before we could rent a house.

We managed to weather unemployment with our credit intact and some savings left in the bank. At the time we went through unemployment, we didn't realize how sound our decisions were or how well we fared. Looking back now, it's hard to believe we ever got through it.

The purpose of this handbook is to save other people from groping in the dark to survive unemployment. I'm hoping this book will help hold families together.

Cathy Beyer

INTRODUCTION
Job Security Is an Oxymoron

When growth in the country resumes, it will not be in the giant industries that formerly provided the foundation of American capitalism. New careers will be cultivated in fields emerging from this current recession: biotechnology, health care, new software services, communication services, and environmental technology. The demand for products and services from these areas has continued on a path of steady growth, even as other industries have declined.

Comfortable midsize companies, less burdened by manpower and overhead, are the most promising sectors of the economy in the nineties. These modest organizations are setting the pace for companies to come. Gone are the excesses of the eighties, replaced by sensible moderation. Recovery, when it comes, will reflect this new attitude. The recession of the early nineties had an enormous effect on every structure in our economy. Banks collapsed, the construction bubble burst, and manufacturing imploded, all taking with them millions of jobs—jobs that will never be recovered.

No longer can one be assured a position as a "company man." No longer can one afford to be lulled by the parental posturing of top management. The key to career survival in the future is self-reliance. Each new job must be approached with the zealous entrepreneurial spirit of the self-employed, and life must be managed accordingly. In visionary mode, we must be on the alert for those signals that predict changes in the industries we depend on to employ us and anticipate that there will always be industry recessions. Industry recessions are a fact of life. The miracle growth industries will appear every few years instead of generations apart.

And as those industries prosper, they will provide business opportunities to an army of satellite companies and services. "Job-keepers" will need to be ever vigilant toward the opportunities on the horizon and the requirements needed to fill those positions. To thrive will mean never to be complacent.

Unfortunately, experts predict that any resulting productivity will not replace the jobs that have been lost in manufacturing, defense, and financial services, for instance, and that these areas will continue to shed jobs like old skin. The heights of prosperity reached in the eighties might never be seen again. The good news is that the broader range of growth indicated in the birth of services and aligned products may sustain a stronger economy longer than a few supercharged industries could.

A spiraling plunge in oil prices in 1986 nearly crippled Texas, where unemployment reached 8.9 percent. Its job base was debilitated when oil, construction, and finance, the very industries responsible for its prosperity, hit the skids. The experience shattered Texas to its very roots, and rebuilding is extremely slow. To recover, Texas had to undergo surgical restructuring.

Progress began with a new foundation built on emerging industries. Wholesale and retail trade, business services, computers, petrochemicals, corporate relocations, and industrial activity on the Mexican border are propelling the state to recovery. This time the climb to greater prosperity is being made inch by careful inch. A disabled banking system continues to burden business, and the evolution of one industry is offset by the demise of another.

Similarly, the "Massachusetts miracle," built more on expectations than on reality, disintegrated. Analysts predict Massachusetts' journey to economic health will be a long and difficult trip. The road map to recovery appears to be research and development combined with free trade.

Never again should America's work force ride the crest of the wave, thinking it will go on forever—at least, not without a safety net. No longer should American workers blindly accept the corporate bill of goods. Every worker should be cautioned against finding just one niche and staying with it indefinitely. Nothing lasts. Staying tuned to changes in technology and checking the balance of your position against the progress of the company or industry that employs you are vital. Staying awake on the job has a whole new meaning.

Although there is not going to be a roaring economic rebound, there are ways to be well positioned for the future. The global environmental market offers a wide range of opportunities for firms to provide services and products for testing, cleanup, conservation, and control. Revenues in this billion-dollar industry have already shown a growth rate of 30 percent despite the recession. Stricter government regulations on environmental issues worldwide, especially in the European Community, Mexico, and Australia, have created a burgeoning demand for new products and services. Environmental technology requires expertise in high-tech equipment and skills in engineering, chemistry, and other sciences.

After spending billions on hardware, companies are searching for software that is easier to use or operates with greater efficiency on existing machinery. The fastest-growing segment of the "new tech" industry, according to statistics from the Employment and Training Administration, is computer programming and software services. These niche-market businesses will activate occupations in technical computer service, systems analysis, programming, operations and systems research, data entry and composing, electronic technology, and specialties in communications and public relations.

Jack Curphy of Curphy & Malkin Associates, a Los Angeles firm specializing in high-tech and data-processing job placement in states west of and including Colorado, says that 1991 was the worst job market in his twenty-two years in the industry. Although 1992 saw some improvement, the recovery is moving at a snail's pace. "The real problem now lies in the fact that companies have become more selective. They have time to wait for just the right person," Curphy states. "In the past, criteria were easier to meet. If a candidate met eight out of ten requirements, he or she was still highly desirable. Now companies demand that we do not send applicants who do not fulfill 100 percent of their needs." Future jobs, Curphy adds, "appear to be in the biotechnical and biomedical fields."

The "graying" of America provides employment opportunities in health care. Health care costs will continue to be covered by ever-expanding government programs that may at some future date include a national health care plan. At present many senior citizens requiring care have been more fortunate financially than younger generations in this recessionary period. Many sold their properties before the decline in real estate values, and some have managed to maintain solid savings and investments. Additionally, this group has a strong lobby for increasing government responsibility toward medical care. Therefore the health care industry is likely to create a steady stream of new jobs for home health aides, medical assistants, physical therapists, and medical record technicians. Spin-off businesses include computer supplies and medical equipment.

While job growth at hospitals is expected to stay flat in an effort to keep costs down, treatment provided outside hospitals, including home health care and nursing homes, is on the rise. Careers in biotechnology will expand considerably in the near future. Since biotech production requires fewer people, however, growth in this exciting new field will never reach the heights obtained by computer and electronic manufacturing.

IN THE MEANTIME

The true state of the economy remains a mystery. Government claims the recession is on the decline. Controversy rages over when the recession will end. If and when the end is officially declared, the unemployed might well ask, "By whose standard of measurement?"

There will always be industry-specific depressions, regardless of the nation's status of economic recovery. Occupations will continually face elimination in affected sectors as the economy changes. Two factors will escalate the occurrence of these industry-specific depressions: the inability of our country to exercise exclusive control over our economy, since it is influenced by world conditions, and the speed of technological changes, which inevitably eliminate jobs.

As companies try to ward off decline by streamlining management teams, unemployment in careers within certain industries has risen above the national unemployment level. Retailers are reeling from the plunge in sales, manufacturing continues to crumble, banks everywhere are closing, and headline-making scions of business are declaring bankruptcy. America's professionals are staring helplessly at their own mortality.

Dan Lacey, former editor of *Workplace Trends*, commented, "More than 70 percent of the layoffs we track are white-collar workers, but when you consider that from 1989 to mid-1992, 1.25 million workers were victims of permanent corporate staff cuts—not layoffs, but cuts—it means that one in every 100 working Americans has been directly hit." He added, "Everyone in America has tasted this experience. Someone in their family or neighborhood was hit. When you consider that virtually everyone in America has been affected, you begin to understand the enormity of this problem."

In 1991 over 7.7 million families faced the devastating effects of unemployment. In a July 1992 issue of *Time*, writer John Greenwald reported, "The axe just keeps falling on the beleaguered American worker." During a recovery period in 1992, an additional 375,000 jobs were lost as businesses continued to scale down. During this same period Amoco, Unocal, Mobil, Hughes Aircraft, and Aetna continued to pare down on salaried jobs. The top ten defense firms cut more than 80,000 jobs in 1991, over 60,000 in 1992, and some project even more cuts through 1994. "Staying lean," Greenwald writes, "has become embedded in the corporate consciousness. . . . Corporate America has shed an average of 1,500 positions a day." In this continuing recession many families will face their first encounter with loss of income and could lose their homes, cars, positions in the community, and, ultimately, each other.

Traditionally, white-collar workers have viewed employment as their socioeconomic right. College graduates believe their degrees guarantee job security. To them, unemployment is a badge of dishonor. Embarrassed by having to face creditors, friends, and family members, unemployed professionals experience isolation and depression.

As unemployment sweeps the nation, toppling in its wake those once considered invincible, a handbook written by someone who survived the experience should be an invaluable tool. The purpose of this book is to provide the reader with the guidelines Cathy and Bill Beyer discovered to keep them together when unemployment threatened the quality of their lives—not once, but three times.

They know that unemployment strikes at the heart of the family. Weathering unemployment taught them methods of survival included here as strategies for coping with finances, with finding transportation, food, and clothing, and with one another. *Surviving Unemployment* is for those who fear unemployment or those who are actually facing unemployment for the first time. This book addresses aspects of unemployment that no one ever talks about. It provides support for those who are unprepared, both financially and emotionally.

The advice a worker and family usually get about unemployment is analogous to the pep talk your great-grandmother gave to Grandma on her wedding night: "Just close your eyes, try not to complain, and hope it will be over soon." *Surviving Unemployment* will guide you through the period of time between jobs, using anecdotes of composite families who have been there and giving advice for reaching appropriate sources of assistance. This book helps not only the individual who lost a job but the whole family.

Unemployment is perhaps the most devastating experience a family will face outside of the disability or death of an immediate family member. *Surviving Unemployment* will show families how they can work through this experience together.

Surviving Unemployment

1

CAUTION, DETOUR AHEAD:
Facing Job Loss

Dismissed, discharged, terminated, laid off, let go, fired, retired. . . . No matter how you say it, your job is gone. Life is a journey, and employment paves the highway you travel on. Ambitions fuel your sense of purpose, of hope, and propel you forward. Losing a job is like being forced off the main highway and onto an unmarked detour.

Tony C. works as vice president of mortgages in a mid-size bank. For the last several months his bank has been negotiating for a merger with another, larger financial institution. Already beset with problems at home, Tony works even harder and longer hours hoping to lock in his position once the merger goes through.

Family finances are strained to the limit because Susan, Tony's wife, couldn't return to teaching after their daughter, Natalie, was born. Natalie suffers from severe epileptic seizures and requires full-time care. Therefore their health insurance through the bank's plan is critical for covering Natalie's expensive medical care. When she turns 3 (in five months), doctors advise surgery to reduce or eliminate Natalie's seizures. Tony and Susan also have a son, Nicholas (4½), who attends preschool.

1

Despite the rumors and the staff's well-founded suspicions about impending layoffs, the bank's president assures Tony he has nothing to worry about, lulling him into a false sense of security. Most of his coworkers are waiting for the other shoe to drop.

SOFT SHOULDERS MAY MEAN HARD TIMES

Early warning signs of layoffs or of a pending termination give you the time to prepare for a detour in your career. By monitoring the economic health of the company you work for, you can gauge the likelihood of layoffs in your department. Assessing both your relationship with coworkers and your recent achievements on the job helps you to measure the strength of your position within the company. If you have already been forced off the road, knowing how and why it happened will help to alleviate your doubts and fears and prepare you for your next job.

Guide for Gauging Your Company's Economic Health

1. *Work force reductions:* Recent hiring freeze; reducing the work force through attrition; offers of voluntary separation or early retirement.
2. *Merger mania:* Rumors of corporate acquisitions or mergers, which result in duplication of positions.
3. *Lost contracts:* Loss of major contracts; no replacement for a major contract that is ending.
4. *Mushrooming meetings:* Escalation of managerial meetings; rumors of financial problems; official reassurances that no one's job is endangered. (This should set off alarm bells. Many companies won't own up to impending layoffs for fear of losing the staff they intend to retain.)

Appraising Personal Standing at Work

1. *Technological trends:* Are you keeping up with technological changes in your field? Are you continuing to evolve with the company?
2. *Performance appraisals:* Are you making a direct contribution to the company's bottom line? Are you busy all day without achieving concrete results?
3. *Job satisfaction:* Do you hate your job? Has it affected your performance at work? Has it affected working relationships?
4. *Office politics:* Are you included in important meetings and discussions? Have you been shut out from the inner circle? Are you involved in important projects? Do coworkers seek your opinion?

Laura F. is a divorced mother of two boys, Brian (11) and Matthew (16). For seven years she owned and operated a midsize advertising agency. She was very proud of the success she had achieved and envisioned a handsome legacy to pass on to her sons.

After her divorce Laura wasn't sure she could successfully hold a job, much less run her own business, but within two years after she opened, she was earning a comfortable living and the future looked bright. Recently she considered buying a larger, more elaborate house. The decision was based on acquiring a major account she was pitching and was fairly confident she would land. The new business would add several thousand dollars to her income.

Then the bottom dropped out of her American dream. Not only did she not get the major account (budget cutbacks forced the company to jettison its new campaign), but several of her other clients also fell victim to the recession. The deepest cuts were made in advertising budgets.

Laura tried to hold out by first augmenting revenues with her own savings to pay the bills, then by cutting her expenses to the bone. This meant laying off loyal employees who were sure to have a hard time finding new jobs in their depressed field. Although in her heart she felt the layoffs were untenable, she was left with no other alternative.

Caught in a Catch-22 situation, Laura didn't have the staff to serve her remaining clients in the manner to which they had become accustomed, and they too beat a hasty exit. Her business folded, leaving her with little savings, no unemployment benefits (as a self-employed person who chose not to carry insurance against the contingency of unemployment), and no child support payments from her former husband, who ceased sending checks when her business began to flourish.

Laura failed to see the handwriting on the wall. In her euphoria over her success in a time when the country was riding high, she never factored in the inevitable fall that follows. She truly believed the recession wouldn't touch her enough to notice, that advertising budgets were so sacrosanct in our consumer world, they would survive the knife even in bad times.

The omens were all around her—reports from her clients of hiring freezes, intended mergers, and layoffs—but she made no preparation for the possible effects on her own business. She vowed if she got another chance, she would never make the same mistakes again.

ROAD UNDER REPAIR

Unless you've been there before, it's hard to predict your reaction to losing your job. Anger, tears, panic, shame, sometimes even relief are all normal responses. Emotions aren't something you can preprogram, but awareness of what you might experience may prepare you to cope better.

- *Anger:* An overwhelming sense of complete betrayal.
- *Anticipation or acceptance:* A sense of relief (and release) from the uncertainty of termination.

- *Shock or disbelief:* Inability to grasp a fait accompli.
- *Self-doubts:* Asking "Where did I go wrong?" rather than evaluating all the elements that led to termination.
- *Desire to escape:* Making a hasty exit before negotiating properly for severance packages and other benefits due.
- *Delight:* Having someone do for you what you really wanted to do yourself but didn't have the nerve.
- *Sorrow:* Grief over losing the privilege of working on important projects or losing relationships with coworkers.
- *Shame or humiliation:* Feeling worthless, too embarrassed to tell anyone.
- *Crying:* As common among men as among women.

Joseph P. is 55 years old. He is a scientist with a Ph.D. and has worked in the defense industry for nearly thirty years. For the last fifteen years he has been with a small company, a think tank for research and development.

Married for twenty-eight years, Joseph and his wife, Barbara, have four children, three living on their own, the fourth just starting college. As an only child, Joseph also cares for his aging, widowed mother, whose only source of income is her Social Security check.

Life has gone according to plan for Joseph and Barbara. They were able to educate three of their children and have every expectation of doing the same for the fourth. They live in a spacious two-story house in an upscale neighborhood. Each drives a late-model car. Recently they bought a lakefront cottage to which Joe dreams of retiring to fish and sail the boat he intends to buy. The son of a bricklayer, he is grateful that his family didn't have to cope with the hardships of his youth.

Joseph anticipates that he can retire in seven years when he is 62. Their youngest child will have completed college by then, and most of their extraordinary expenses will be behind them. With the proceeds from the sale of their house, his pension funds, and IRAs, Joseph and Barbara feel they will be well set enough to indulge themselves in some world travel and to live comfortably.

Joseph had managed to escape the massive cuts made in the defense industry in the late seventies. From that he harbors the belief that his educational background and his status in the industry make him too valuable to lose. In the past year since the rumors about layoffs began to circulate, he has assumed he will once again survive the cut. He truly believes his company will recognize and reward his expertise and dedication to his job at the cost of family time.

Then comes the day Joseph is invited to his boss's office "for a little chat" about early retirement. When the conversation was finished, Joseph knew he had no other option but to take what he was offered and leave. In twenty minutes Joseph's whole life fell apart. This blow to the very center of his universe propels Joseph into an emotional spin that decimates his ability to cope with what is to follow.

EMERGENCIES AAA WON'T HANDLE

Despite the range of emotions you are bound to experience and can't control, you can keep a rein on how you respond to the news. This is not the time to burn bridges.

The company that pink-slips you today may be the first to hire you back when business picks up. In any case you will need a decent reference from this employer. Also, your boss or someone in the department may change jobs and could be in a position to hire you when you apply for your next dream job. Steer clear of the following road hazards:

- *Violence:* Arguing and shouting undermines any efforts on your part to solicit assistance or to negotiate on your own behalf. Wait until you cool off before scheduling your termination interview.
- *Sabotage:* Stealing files or office equipment, "accidentally" destroying expensive equipment, or messing up com-

puter programs may quench your momentary thirst for revenge but would wreak more havoc on your reputation and your future than on the company.

- *Intrigue:* Rallying coworkers to walk with you, badmouthing the company, or writing poison-pen memos to company executives, stockholders, or important clients will only backfire. Executives and coworkers move around, and they may be in a position to evaluate or even hire you for a future job. Above all, you will need a good reference. No matter how attractive conspiring against others may sound now, recognize that you are in a state of shock and will regret these actions when you are more rational.

- *Self-destruction:* The idea of drinking until you are numb may sound inviting, but alcohol is a depressant and will only exacerbate your despondency. You need all your wits about you to cope. A raging hangover is the last thing you want.

If you feel overwhelmed to the point of despair, or even suicidal, call someone for help immediately. A friend, a pastor or a rabbi, or a counselor at a mental health clinic can lend a sympathetic hand and get you back on course. See chapter 14, "Am I Blue?" for where to get support when you have nowhere else to turn.

BON VOYAGE

Your termination interview could make or break you over the next few months. This is where you begin to negotiate for the best deal you can get under the circumstances. Be assertive but deferential, firm but flexible, and most of all, never, never let them see you sweat.

Learn why you lost your job: a merger? new management? financial difficulty? change of market direction? Ask your boss to include this explanation in your reference letter so a potential employer will see that your dismissal was through no fault of your own. If it was, you had better find out why and beg mercy from your former boss not to make that information public on the promise that you will clean up your act.

Ask for positive comments on what aspects of your work were good, and add them to your updated résumé. Try to negotiate alternatives to losing your job, such as counseling, job sharing, or staying on as a consultant or on a per-project basis.

Unless you have a guarantee in your contract or in your company manual, your employer is not obligated to give you a severance package. Yet your boss's guilt and insecurities over firing employees can sometimes work to your advantage. Hold out for a severance package if you have exhausted all other options for staying on. (See chapter 3, "Bridge over Troubled Water," and appendix A for suggestions on how to negotiate your "golden parachute" and for other resources to consult.)

Get a letter of recommendation in your hand before leaving the premises. Some employers have the best of intentions but don't follow through.

Immediately collect copies of your evaluations. This will document your performance in case of negative reports resulting from any antagonism your boss may feel over your negotiations for a severance package or other benefits.

Remove personal files, books, and equipment, including your business card file and Rolodex. You will need this information for your job search. Make copies if you are not allowed to remove the originals.

AND HOW WAS YOUR DAY TODAY, DEAR?

Delivering the unpleasant news to your family is difficult, so difficult that some go to elaborate lengths to hide it.

Richard and Anne K. have been married for three years. A talented graphic artist, Richard had been working for the same printing company since he graduated from college five years ago. The company is aggressive and efficiently managed, and Richard had every expectation of having a job there until he chose to move on.

Thanks to the generosity of both sets of their parents and mainly cash wedding gifts, Richard and Anne had enough for the minimum down payment on a small home. Their grand plan called for a baby in three years and for Anne to give up her job as a women's fashion buyer in a department store after the baby is born.

Anne became pregnant right on schedule, and Richard was delighted when she agreed to give up her job to become a full-time wife and mother. Although a contemporary man in most ways, he nurtured the primal desire to be the sole breadwinner, taking care of his family the way his father does. Richard's eternal optimism and mischievous sense of humor strike Anne's parents as indications of a laissez-faire attitude, thus a detriment to his potential earning power. Richard is aware of their attitude, which both amuses and annoys him at the same time.

With the increasing use of desktop publishing for brochures, newsletters, catalogues, and annual reports—the mainstays of Richard's company—the need for his services steadily declined. Whereas, at one time almost every job that came in required artwork, clients were submitting their orders camera ready for printing. As the last in, Richard was the first out when the company decided to whittle away at his department.

Richard saw it coming, so he was not surprised when it happened. Neither was he devastated. He was sure he would get another job quickly. Since he believes there are a wealth of places other than printing houses that could use his talent and expertise—advertising agencies or in-house departments, commercial art studios, department stores, publishing firms, and television studios—he decides not to tell Anne about losing his job until he gets another. He doesn't want to worry her in this late stage of her pregnancy, and knowing that Anne will immediately share the news with her mother, he also doesn't want to provide any more fuel for his in-laws' already negative opinion of him.

When Richard's search proves fruitless after two weeks and Anne reminds him that she will be giving notice to her boss soon, he realizes he has to tell her the truth. (He had been maintaining his same schedule of leaving and returning home to keep Anne from suspecting what he was up to.) Anne is furious when she finds out, not because he lost his job but because he didn't tell her immediately. She feels betrayed and hurt that he didn't trust her enough to rally round him when he should have needed her the most.

Procrastinating only makes the task harder. Break the news to your mate immediately. If necessary, use a euphemism to soften the blow, such as, "Sweetheart, I'm still trying for the gold watch but I definitely got the sack," or "I've got good news and bad news. The good is I finally got that extended vacation I always wanted; the bad is I was laid off," or "I may be dressed in slacks today, but I'm wearing a pink slip."

You probably won't have to say a word. One look at your face, at your hunched shoulders, your red eyes, your movements (as though you've been sucker-punched), and your loved one will know exactly what happened.

Be prepared! Your mate may be more devastated than you. The intensity of his or her emotions may surprise you—the anger, the indignity, the sorrow, the humiliation, and most of all, the fear. Try not to view this as a criticism of you but as a testimony to her or his feelings of protectiveness toward you and the family.

Often parents try to shield their children from bad news or from facts they think the kids are not ready for yet. Being up front about your job loss is a little like explaining the facts of life to your kids—better to tell them yourself before they get the wrong version from their friends.

Kids have a right to know. Increased tension in the household affects them too. If you don't explain that you are upset about losing your job and are preoccupied with finding another, they are likely to think they caused the problems, did something bad to make everyone so unhappy. Spend a little extra time with toddlers and infants, who cannot understand what's happening but may react to increased stress within the household. Use a reassuring voice. In fact, comforting them may relax you.

Family support is vital to bolster the wavering self-esteem that comes with job loss. How the mate deals with the situation could affect the relationship on a permanent basis. Lack of understanding and sympathy could make a good relationship falter and destroy one already in jeopardy.

SHIFTING GEARS

Find a safe place to vent emotions. Your mate may be the most obvious choice, but a calm, detached third person may serve you both better. Don't discount seeking professional counseling. Having an unbiased listener helps you sort out your feelings and form a constructive outlook on the future. (See chapter 14, "Am I Blue?")

If you already planned a vacation, particularly if it's prepaid, go ahead and take it. R&R may be just what you need to let go and rev yourself up for your job search. Just don't get carried away and allow R&R to slide into procrastination. Two weeks of "vegging out" should be the maximum.

If office space at your former company is part of your severance package, don't allow yourself to get sucked into finishing up old projects (unless that was part of the deal). Use the time, place, and available resources to promote yourself.

I'LL TAKE THE HIGH ROAD

A detour could take you through desolate wilderness but could end in a fabulous place where you've never been. Your destination could be a better place than where you were originally going. Admittedly, unknown territory is intimidating, even frightening. Ask a country boy lost in New York or a New Yorker lost in the Beartooth Wilderness. Equipped with proper directions, both can find their way.

Try to view your period of unemployment as a new adventure. Accept it as an opportunity to sharpen your skills and challenge yourself. The toll it takes may well be canceled out by your newfound strengths.

STEP BY STEP

In summary, the ten basic steps to take on the heels of losing your job are:

1. Tell your family immediately.
2. Evaluate reasons for job loss.
3. Deal with emotions.
4. Prepare for departure.
5. Negotiate severance package.
6. File for unemployment compensation or other benefits due you.
7. Take a vacation or at least a step back to prepare for the task at hand.
8. Plan your strategy.
9. Go forward with confidence.
10. Read this book for guidance on how to get by until you land your next job.

CHARTING YOUR COURSE:
Planning Your Finances

Y ou may not have been aware at the time, but your job
defined the way you lived. The salary you received or the
check you drew from your business each week dictated what
kind of house you lived in, where you shopped for your
clothes, or where your kids went to school. An increase in the
weekly check could mean a trip to Bermuda instead of a week
at the Jersey shore.

Now that your job (or business) is gone, your life is bound
to veer off in a different direction, but don't just go with the
flow. Chart a new course. Begin by taking stock of where you
were and where you are.

THE GUIDING LIGHT

Imagine yourself an entrepreneur and your new business
is your life. Now is the time to streamline your spending and
prioritize expenditures to meet the financial needs of your
new enterprise. Ask your staff (family) to work together to
launch your new venture.

First, assess your financial worth. Creative bookkeeping is
not allowed; this is a reality check. As with any good explorer
embarking on a new trail, you will need the proper tools.

(You may want to consult *The Price Waterhouse Book of Personal Financial Planning*, by Stanley H. Breitbard and Donna Sammons Carpenter [Henry Holt, 1990] or the *Personal Financial Planning Handbook*, by Jonathan Pond [Dell, 1991] to guide you.) Your compass kit should include all of your financial records from the last full year you were employed: credit card bills that list the items you bought; paycheck stubs and other income records; checkbook ledgers; bank statements and passbooks; tax returns; car expenses; tuitions; day-care costs; and insurance policies (health, life, automobile, homeowners/rental).

Simply stated, there are two categories to inventory: expenses and assets. Each breaks down to several subcategories, all of which need to be examined and reevaluated.

Outline your history of spending under two headings:

1. Fixed expenses such as mortgage payments or rent, taxes, car payments, and utilities.
2. Those with flexibility (variable expenses) such as groceries, clothing, gifts, cable TV, hobbies, long-distance phone calls, personal care (haircuts, gym fees, etc.), kids' allowances, charitable donations, vacations, entertainment, and recreation.

Now go over all assets, starting with the most liquid such as savings accounts, stocks, bonds, insurance policies, severance package, veteran's and/or unemployment benefits, as well as the less tangible such as access to loans—secured (home equity) or unsecured (charge cards and bank overdraft privileges). List any financial assistance, public or private, that may be available to you now or in the future such as family loans, food stamps, or energy assistance programs.

WITHDRAWAL SYMPTOMS

When listing your assets, there are two schools of thought about whether you should include your Individual Retirement Account (IRA), 401(k) or Keogh if you are under 59½ years old. Some experts advise that withdrawing that money early is too costly and shouldn't be considered unless you have no other alternative. Not only would you have to pay full taxes on the money withdrawn, you would also be charged a 10 percent penalty. Therefore, a $2,000 early withdrawal could cost you $1,100.

Other financial advisers feel that you shouldn't think twice about using these funds as a way to bail out in hard times, particularly if you are only in your thirties or forties. Although the penalties are stiff, you need the cash now and can begin again to protect your old age after you get back to work.

There are some exceptions to the 10 percent penalty for early withdrawal from IRA and Keogh funds: If the holder has set up a series of roughly equal payments tied to life expectancy; if the holder is suffering from a mental or physical disability that is expected to last for more than a year or may be fatal; if the holder has died. A fourth exception applies only to Keogh funds: to pay otherwise nondeductible catastrophic medical bills in excess of 7.5 percent of your adjusted gross income.

Early withdrawal from 401(k) plans may be made (but only from the employee's contribution, not the matching portion from the employer) if you have "an immediate and heavy financial need" and no other resources are "reasonably available" to you. Examples of immediate and heavy financial need as outlined by the Internal Revenue Code are for medical expenses for you or your family, to prevent your eviction from or foreclosure on your principal residence, and payment of tuition for postsecondary education for you or your dependents.

The employee must be able to document the lack of other reasonably available resources such as insurance reimbursement, nontaxable loans from other plans, commercial loans, or liquidation of nonessential assets. Hardship distributions from 401(k) plans are still subject, however, to the 10 percent tax on top of regular income tax. Those over 55 who have taken early retirement may be able to withdraw from company-sponsored retirement plans without penalty, but they still have to pay taxes on the amounts withdrawn.

To avoid the 10 percent penalty, you may be allowed to make a loan against your 401(k). The employer who administers the account must give consent. Guidelines for early withdrawal or loans are outlined in the Internal Revenue Code, which may be obtained at your local IRS office.

PLAYING OUT YOUR CARDS

By studying the lists you have compiled, you should be able to determine how your total expenses compare with anticipated income and how long your money will last at that level of expense. More than likely a crystal-clear message to adjust expenditures to accommodate your reduced income will appear.

You may be out of work for two weeks or two years. Even the economic pundits can't agree on how long the recession-cum-depression will last. Prepare for the likelihood of at least six months of unemployment. Make your budget accordingly. This could range from the "we-can-live-without-that" concession to a bare-bones austerity plan. Take heart! You may find your discretionary expense list will afford you opportunities to reduce costs without requiring a total abandonment of your normal standard of living.

HONEY, LET'S SHRINK THE BUDGET

Deciding where and how to cut the budget should be a family affair, since everyone is affected by the revised spending plan. Making an edict that "We are going on an economy kick" invites belligerence, particularly from the younger members of the family.

Laura's boys, Brian and Matthew, had rarely, if ever, been asked to make sacrifices. She knows that her change in economics, now that her advertising agency has folded, will drastically alter their lifestyle, maybe even their self-esteem. No more $80 Reeboks or costly Nintendo cartridges. No more generous allowances, which is sure to curtail their activities with their friends.

A divorced mother who has been the sole support of her sons for several years, Laura exuded self-reliance and strength. Now she needs her children's cooperation and support. She needs them to be aware of her current status and how they will be affected, so she asks them to participate in her financial reevaluation. She is hoping that allowing the boys their say in where expenses should be cut will reduce their resentment and promote the "we're in this together" camaraderie so critical during this time.

They promise to be fair and sensitive to each other's feelings when making suggestions to cut back. Therefore, Laura's request that the boys give up the large quantities of gum and candy bars they consume daily was much more well received when she offered to give up smoking in return. The boys quickly agreed, since they had been begging her to give up her cigarettes for a long time.

The family calculates how much they could save in a month just by saying no to smoking, chewing, and chocolate bars: one pack of cigarettes a day at $2.25 $\times$ 30 = $67.50; thirty packs of gum at 50 cents = $15.00; sixty candy bars at 50 cents = $30.00. Total projected monthly savings = $112.50, not to mention the doctors' and dentists' bills that could result from these less-than-desirable habits.

Once the pact is made, suggestions for cutting down are hurled fast and furiously among them, some reasonable (using leftovers for a second meal, unheard of in their home before), some off the wall (cementing the grass over and painting it green to save on gas for the lawn mower), but all offered with good intentions. With great reservation, Laura offers to give up her twice-weekly aerobics sessions if Matthew would store away his golf clubs temporarily. They agree that walking or jogging would be a good way of getting their exercise for free. They set up a twice-weekly jogging schedule. They insist that Brian join in too, giving them the added benefit of some family time, often missed when they were all so busy with their separate schedules.

Brian and Matthew make personal budgets, charting expenses and alternatives for earning money. The process lets them exercise a sense of control over their finances.

LIVING WELL WITH LESS

As the saying goes, "Less is often more." This applies particularly well to credit cards. The fewer we have, the more likely that we won't succumb to indiscriminate spending, thus leaving us with more money in our pockets.

The last thing you want to do at this point is add to your debt. After selecting one or two credit cards for emergencies (an oil company card and one major bank card), put the rest under lock and key. If you don't trust your self-control, cut up the remaining cards. Don't cancel your credit on those accounts, however, as it may be difficult to qualify again in the future. Be strict with yourself when defining emergencies. New skis shouldn't qualify.

THE BUCK STOPS HERE

Some other ways of reducing expenses without having to change your lifestyle to any great degree are:

- Switch to a less expensive telephone service.
- Go to a dental school for oral health care.
- Turn on your dishwasher only when it's full.
- Do one large wash instead of two small ones.
- Use washers and dryers at night when rates are cheaper.
- Turn off lights and TVs when you leave the room.

- Close off unused rooms to conserve fuel.
- Don't use the fireplace—it sucks heat up the chimney.
- Decide in advance everything you need from the refrigerator to cut down on opening and closing the door.
- Use the toaster oven instead of the electric range oven whenever possible.
- Fold clothes as soon as the dryer stops to limit ironing.
- Dry clothes outside on sunny days.
- Brown-bag lunches.
- Reuse plastic bags.
- Buy food and household supplies in bulk whenever possible and split with friends or family if the initial outlay is too heavy.
- Buy used instead of new whenever possible.
- Wait for a sale before buying anything that isn't needed immediately.
- Buy out of season (coats in the summer; garden tools in winter).
- Buy salvage items from insurance adjusters' offices. Items recovered from thefts that the insureds with 100-percent coverage are not required to accept back can be purchased for 10 to 25 percent of original cost. This includes washers, dryers, televisions, furniture, and more. Most adjusters' offices will send a periodic listing of items available to their mailing lists. Call fire and theft adjusters in your area (listed in the Yellow Pages) to see if or how you can get on the list.
- Check salvage stores before making purchases. They buy whole stocks left over from disasters, many of which are barely touched by the fire or flood from which they were salvaged.
- Read your mail carefully—stuffers in utility bills or statements often advise on new money-saving programs.

Any one of these suggestions may sound to you as effective as putting a Band-Aid on a severed artery, but implementing all together could constitute a tourniquet for expenses. According to *The Tightwad Gazette*, there are three basic methods to save money:

1. Buy it cheaper.
2. Make it last longer.
3. Use it less.

As an example, *The Tightwad* suggests: (1) Switch to a less expensive brand of coffee and purchase with a coupon; or (2) Make your coffee go further by reusing your grounds with half as much fresh grounds added to the old ones; or (3) Decide to drink half as much coffee. With a $5.12 cost for the original brand of coffee, you could save $3.94 per month by using strategy one or as much as $4.53 per month by combining strategies one and three.

The Tightwad Gazette is published by a Maine woman, Amy Dacyczyn, who claims her family of six lives the good life on less than $30,000 a year while managing to buy the farmhouse of their dreams and two cars. Living by what they term their tightwad strategies, they assert they want for nothing. In her monthly publication she shares her shopping secrets to promote "thrift as a viable alternative lifestyle." Subscriptions to *The Tightwad Gazette* may be obtained by sending $12 to RR 1 Box 3570, Leeds, ME 04263-9710.

GIVE-AND-TAKE

Native Americans had the right idea long before European settlers ever touched this country's shores. With no convenience stores on every corner, trading one commodity for the other was common practice.

Bartering is enjoying a resurgence in popularity, not necessarily because of the recession. Many are recognizing that bartering eases demands on the family's cash flow, and almost anyone can do it. This time-honored tradition is an ideal illustration of Mutual Assistance Programs (MAPs).

To enhance the new financial course they have plotted, Anne and Richard develop some MAPs to help them through the maze of problems bound to crop up until Richard finds another job. They invite friends, family, and neighbors, who are also having a hard time making ends meet, to participate.

Richard arranges with a neighbor to care for her children two days a week while she works, in exchange for her babysitting his child while he looks for a job.

Anne arranges with a neighbor to alternate doing minor errands. One week she picks up the cleaning, returns books to the library, or drops off shoes for repair for both of them, and the next, her neighbor does the same for her. In addition to saving on gasoline, the arrangement gives Anne more time on the weekends, freeing her from these chores to spend time with her family.

Bartering is a value-added resource, a means of saving money while helping one another and creating a greater sense of well-being and belonging. Authors Edgar Cahn and Jonathan Rowe refer to this practice in their book *Time Dollars* as the "ancient precurrency practice of mutual aid." In their opinion, communities are energized by neighbors acting like neighbors and extended family.

Reflecting American ingenuity at its finest, trade networks are springing up throughout the country and are well on their way to big business. The cost for joining is minimal, but the rewards are reputed to be considerable.

Trade networks offer everything from auto repairs to major surgery on partial or full barter. As a member, you build up barter credits according to how many avail themselves of your products or services. These credits are in turn applied to those products or services that you select. In essence the network operates as a bank, recording your "deposits" and "charges." You even get a monthly statement.

Even though no money changes hands, some bartering is still subject to taxation. Trade revenue is taxable as personal income if purchases are made for personal use. Trade income spent for legitimate business expense items is normally tax-deductible.If exchanges are not commercial in nature, they may be deemed tax-exempt.

Two of the larger trade networks in operation are ITEX Barter Systems, Inc., with executive offices at One Lincoln Center, Portland, OR 97208-2309 (telephone 503-244-4673); and National Barter Corporation, 3909 S. Maryland Pkwy., #402, Las Vegas, NV 89109 (1-800-523-2047).

CUTTING OUT IS CUTTING DOWN

Cutting down is not only economically advisable, it is fashionable and necessary to save the environment. When urging the younger members of the household to cooperate, conservation is the best argument. An occasional reminder that we are helping to save the planet may make everyone more conscientious about turning off lights, TVs, and stereos.

WHO GETS WHAT WHEN

One basic rule for survival during tight times is not making payments on postponable bills. Only you can determine which of your creditors will wait the longest without initiating collection action. As much as you wish to protect your credit rating, keeping food on the table, the lights on, and the house warm must take priority.

Establish a priority list on who gets paid first and who can wait. To do so, you've got to do some homework. Creditors must be approached by phone, letter, or personal visits to determine how cooperative they will be. (See the sample letter on page 23.) If you own your home with a mortgage, your lender may be able to provide "forbearance" by accepting partial payments. On secured debts your creditors may allow you to defer payments by paying only interest for a period of

LETTER TO CREDITORS

(Date)

(Name of contact person)
(Title)
(Name of business)
(Street address)
(City, state, ZIP code)

RE: Account # (your number)

Dear (contact person):

- describe
  situation

Your records show that I currently owe a balance of (amount) on my account. I am presently out of work, though I am confident that with my expertise and experience I will soon find new employment.

- request
  payment
  alternatives

In the meantime, I have some difficulties meeting my prior level of financial obligations. I respectfully request an interim payment arrangement until I can restore my income.

- inquire about
  necessary
  documentation

May I have an appointment with you to discuss possible options? I will call you on (day) morning to arrange a convenient meeting time. Please let me know then what documentation you will require to expedite a new arrangement.

- state
  intention
  to cooperate

My credit rating has always been a source of pride to me. Preserving that rating is very important. Thank you for your understanding and cooperation.

Sincerely,

(Your name)
(Your address)
(Your city, state, ZIP code)
(Your telephone number)

time. On unsecured debts you could pay minimum only. (See chapter 10, "Obscene Phone Calls.")

Expect the unexpected when negotiating for time. Your conservative banker may be more sympathetic than your neighborhood cleaner. Of course, all of these deferred payments will catch up with you down the road, but hopefully at a time when you have a new job and can better afford to pay.

UNCLE SAM STILL WANTS YOU

Even though your income is cut way back, you still have to file a tax return. H&R Block can survive without you: do it yourself. You probably qualify to use Form 1040A, a simple two-page form. File early if you expect a refund.

Be sure to file both state and federal quarterly estimated returns if you are collecting jobless benefits. These benefits are taxable, and your taxes are not deducted from the amount you receive. Failure to file quarterly could result in exorbitant interest charges compounded daily. (See chapter 3, "Bridge over Troubled Water.")

There are any number of self-help books for filing tax returns. Most recommended for the 1040A filers is *J. K. Lasser's Your 60-Minute Tax Return*. *J. K. Lasser's Your Income Tax* is considered the most authoritative of the guides and offers buyers a free twenty-four-hour hot line if you need human consultation. Both books are published by Prentice-Hall and updated annually. The IRS also offers a number of publications (free) and an information line (1-800-829-1040). Call 1-800-TAX-FORM to request publications. IRS Publication #505 gives information on estimated taxes and withholdings.

Remember to keep a record of all expenses for job hunting. If you are looking for a new job in the same field, all expenses are deductible, such as employment agency fees, transportation costs, résumé printing, postage, meals (if seeking a job in another state), dues for professional organizations, and trade magazines. When required for the job, educational expenses are also deductible. Be sure to keep all receipts in case of an audit. For more information, call 1-800-829-3676 and ask for Publication #17, *Your Federal Income Tax*.

SWEETENING THE POT

You have been out of work for three or four months and there is no new job in sight. Money is getting scarcer and scarcer. Time to make the doughnuts or take on any other temporary job to help beef up your bottom line.

Consider the endless possibilities available for making extra cash, up to and including renting out a room. This in no way should dent your pride; your boarder could well be a former bank president.

From Maine to Texas the long-term unemployed are digging in their heels and finding ways to supplement income, both mundane and imaginative. Look for income enhancers that do not require additional training, are not too time-consuming (to allow sufficient time to look for a job in your field), and most significant at this point, supply regular, immediate income.

If you can free-lance in your field, all the better. The extra money is the short-term benefit, but the boost to your self-confidence and the new contacts you make are even more beneficial to both your psyche and your future prospects.

Put a new twist on the free-lance/consultant angle. Promote yourself as an "employee on lease," or go one step further and round up a stable of other unemployed workers with diverse capabilities to offer to companies looking for temporary assistance. Before doing so, check on the extent of your liability and responsibilities, such as whether you need to have workers' compensation or other kinds of insurance. Also determine whether you are responsible for deducting taxes from fees paid to your employees on lease or if they can be construed as consultants, responsible for paying their own taxes.

If field-related jobs are unavailable, let your entrepreneurial spirit rise to the surface. One 60-year-old executive recruiter who couldn't recruit a job for herself for over a year became a jack-of-all-trades. She ferried neighbors to the airport, house-sat, took care of dogs, watered plants, baby-sat, and rented out space in her driveway. In between she filled in at the town library and coordinated seminars. Not exactly the road to easy retirement, but it paid the bills.

Be very wary of work-at-home schemes that promise to "help you earn money in your spare time," particularly when you are required to send payment for "start-up costs." More often than not, the information you receive in return is how to rip off someone else in a similar way.

> Laura is faced with a $2,000 bill for a badly needed new roof. She needs quick cash. She considers pawning some of her valuables but is too embarrassed to go to a pawnshop alone and too ashamed to ask anyone to go with her.
>
> With no other alternative, she skulks through the doorway with the triple gold balls hanging above, clutching her valuables to her chest, and feeling she has fallen as far as she can go. She looks around expecting to see shady characters trying to unload items of indeterminate ownership. Instead, she sees upscale professionals reluctantly relinquishing (temporarily) their Rolexes for enough cash to catch up on their BMW payments.
>
> Laura owns several pieces of jewelry that were appraised by her jeweler for a total of $5,000. She had already investigated and discovered she could expect between 40 and 50 percent of appraised value from a pawnbroker. She accepts the $2,000 offered with the confidence that her jewelry would still be there waiting for her to redeem for the agreed term.

Officially, pawnbrokers are called collateral loan companies. Today most look like high-end jewelry stores. They encourage clients to redeem. One pawnbroker reports that his best customer made eighty-nine loans on the same fifteen items in a year and a half.

Pawning your valuables is merely another viable alternative to getting a loan. The requirements are simple: no waiting days (or weeks) to be approved, no complicated forms to fill out. Just present an item of value and proper identification, haggle a bit, and more than likely you and the pawnbroker will settle on a figure. This is in essence a loan for four months at around 5 percent per month. Your item of value is your collateral.

SINK OR SWIM

In treacherous waters, even the strongest swimmers need life preservers. Buckle yours on tight and dive in. With a little luck and a lot of planning, you'll rise to the surface.

BRIDGE OVER
TROUBLED WATER:
Unemployment Benefits

During this roller-coaster ride of personal devastation mixed with anger and frustration, marching yourself into the unemployment office may be the last thing you want to do. You're not alone. Most of the people you will encounter as you wait your turn would also prefer to be anywhere else than there.

What may be comforting is that few are there because of any fault of their own. Losing a job in tough economic times is something beyond your control, like a natural disaster. Like the little Dutch boy who stuck his finger into a crack in the dam, you can't stem the tide by yourself.

Unemployment compensation is a form of insurance established by the federal government to protect you and others like you who are the victims of a bad economy or a business in trouble. You have as much right to avail yourself of these benefits as filing a claim against your homeowner's insurance for a damaged roof.

Taking your place in the unemployment line is by no means a reflection on your ability. In a way, it's almost a badge of honor, a worker's Purple Heart for injuries sustained in the line of duty. Filing your claim as quickly as possible is the best way to begin tending your wounds.

The money for unemployment insurance comes from taxes paid by employers. No deductions are made from a worker's paycheck. Benefit payments to the eligible unemployed are about half the average pay earned during the base period, defined as the fifty-two weeks prior to the date a claim is filed.

WHO QUALIFIES—THE WHITE AREA

If you worked for someone other than yourself, lost your job through no fault of your own, earned more than $1,200 during the fifty-two weeks before you were discharged, are ready to take a full-time job, are actively seeking work, and are a U.S. citizen or otherwise legally eligible to work in the United States, you probably qualify for unemployment insurance.

WHO DOESN'T—THE BLACK AREA

Those generally not eligible to collect unemployment benefits are employees of churches and certain religious organizations; worker trainees in a program administered by a nonprofit or public institution; real estate brokers or insurance agents who work on a commission basis only; consultants working in an independently established occupation who are not under direct control of regular employees or not performing work considered in the usual course of business; certain employees of state and local governments such as elected officials and those in policy-making and advising positions; members of a legislative body or of the judiciary; and others. Who does and does not qualify is outlined in the Employment Security Law, copies of which are available for review in most libraries or at your local Employment and Training Administration office.

THE GRAY AREA

Under certain conditions, independent consultants or sub-contractors may in fact be eligible for unemployment benefits. For example, someone who worked under the direct supervision of company employees, performed work considered to be part of that company's usual course of business, and occupied his/her primary office within the company may have a legitimate claim as an employee of that company, ergo eligible for unemployment benefits.

Those who quit their jobs are generally not eligible for unemployment compensation, but there are exceptions. Sometimes, when an employee feels compelled to quit because of significant changes in the job description ("more than a reasonable employee has to accept"), to protect health and safety, or to escape from racial and/or sexual harassment, that employee may qualify for unemployment compensation.

"DISCHARGED FOR CAUSE"

Most unemployment compensation statutes deny benefits to anyone who is discharged for misconduct, generally known as "discharging for cause." Misconduct, however, is subject to interpretation and does not necessarily let the employer off the hook for unemployment benefits. In fact, this is the subject of most unemployment compensation hearings.

Incompetence is not misconduct. Making mistakes or lacking the necessary job skills is not misconduct. But if the employee has demonstrated an ability to perform in the past and stops performing competently, that is misconduct. Negligence is not misconduct. Having three on-the-job accidents in five months, for example, is not cause for dismissal if there is no evidence of a conscious disregard of the employer's interests; nor is an accident as a result of preoccupation with a personal problem.

Examples of Misconduct

- Deliberate damage to equipment; willful failure to follow safety rules and regulations
- Unreasonable or excessive use of obscene language in violation of employer's rules
- Excessive and unjustified absences and tardiness; failure to inform supervisor
- Lying; stealing; using equipment without permission of supervisor
- Failure to obey reasonable rules and follow reasonable orders
- Unjustified assault on coworker or supervisor
- Spending too much time socializing at work after being told not to
- Refusal to work on weekends

Not Interpreted as Misconduct

- Incompetence; genuine inability to do the work
- Accidents; negligence; errors that are not the result of reckless conduct
- Isolated incident using obscene language
- Justified absences and tardiness
- Age; physical condition; illness; pregnancy
- Failure to obey unreasonable rules and follow unreasonable orders
- Justified assault on coworker; self-defense
- Associating with coworkers or marrying coworker in violation of employer's rules
- Refusal to work on employee's Sabbath day

PROCEDURE FOR FILING A CLAIM IN A DISPUTE

Go in person to your local state unemployment office. Take at least two forms of identification, your Social Security card, and the names and addresses of every employer worked for within the prior two years. Do not reveal at that time that you were fired. To the unemployment agency, "fired" automatically signals "fired for cause" and could delay action on your case. Merely say you were laid off.

The unemployment agency will contact your employer for the other side of the story, weigh both sides, and ultimately make a judgment as to your eligibility. If you come out the loser, you can request a hearing. Pay strict attention to the deadline imposed for making an appeal. When you are allowed twelve days, for example, those are twelve calendar days, not business days, and begin from the date on the notice, not when you receive it.

If you were fired for cause, the burden of proof is on the employer, meaning that he or she must prove that you were guilty of misconduct. If you quit, you must prove you had a very good reason for doing so. If there is a dispute over whether you quit or were fired, the burden is on the employer to prove that you quit and not for good cause.

Ideally you should have an attorney to represent you, even though you won't yet be going to court. Generally your case at this point will be reviewed by a hearing officer. Still, your chances of prevailing will be much better, since the attorney will know how to present your case efficiently and in the best light. (See chapter 11, "Equal Justice," for how to obtain an attorney at little or no out-of-pocket cost.) Should the hearing officer decide against you, you can appeal again but may be given only one calendar week to file, so act quickly.

When Richard lost his job with the printing company, he assumed that his discharge was part of the cost-cutting policy initiated in his office. Therefore he was shocked when he was informed by the unemployment office that he was not eligible for benefits, based on his boss's claim that Richard had been discharged for cause. Richard's boss, Tom Carlson, asserted that Richard would repeatedly refuse to work on weekends. If true, this could be construed as justified cause for dismissal and thus could exclude Richard from eligibility for unemployment benefits.

Richard filed for and was granted a hearing. He told the hearing officer that Mr. Carlson would consistently ask him to work on Saturdays despite his repeated explanation that, as a Jew, Saturday is his Sabbath, his day of worship and rest. When Richard offered to work with Mr. Carlson on any Sunday, his boss said that was impossible since that was the day he attended church with his family.

The burden of proof was on Mr. Carlson. He conceded that the bad economy had prompted him to make some cuts in his organization but that Richard was included in the sweep principally because he considered Richard "arbitrary and uncooperative" for refusing to work on Saturdays. He argued that Richard was "using his religion as an excuse when in fact he was not a practicing Jew who attended services." When pressed, Mr. Carlson could not pinpoint any times other than Saturdays that Richard refused to work overtime.

After hearing both sides of the issue, the hearing officer declared Mr. Carlson had failed to prove that Richard was guilty of misconduct on the job. Richard's willingness to work overtime any other time except Saturdays demonstrated his good faith. The hearing officer pointed out that under the law, Richard has the right to observe and honor his religion in any way he sees fit. Richard's application for unemployment benefits was approved.

FILING A CLAIM NOT IN DISPUTE

File during your first week of total or partial unemployment. To delay may cost you benefits. In some states a filing schedule has been established according to the last digit in your Social Security number. Save yourself a trip by checking first to see if that system is in place at your local unemployment office. When applying, you will need proof of your Social Security number, the names and addresses of all employers for whom you worked during the fifty-two weeks prior to filing, and a wage stub, W-2 form, or some other record of salary.

If you move out of state, you may file an interstate claim. Immediately report to the nearest unemployment insurance office in the state to which you moved. Call in advance to check on interstate claim procedures.

Pregnancy does not disqualify a woman from collecting UI benefits as long as she meets all the eligibility requirements for collecting, including being available for full-time work and conducting an active work search.

Sometimes the active-work-search rule will be waived for claimants who need retraining to find a new job. This could mean up to eighteen weeks of additional UI benefits while the claimant is in training.

Trade Adjustment Assistance (TAA) is available to workers who lose their jobs or whose hours or wages are reduced as a result of business lost to increased imports. Through TAA, you may be eligible for training, a job-search allowance, a relocation allowance, and other reemployment services. You may also receive weekly trade readjustment allowances (TRA) following the exhaustion of your unemployment benefits.

CAUSES FOR DISQUALIFICATION

Those who give may also take away. You may be disqualified from receiving unemployment benefits if your unemployment insurance office discovers you:

- Left your job voluntarily without good cause
- Were fired from your job because of deliberate misconduct
- Were suspended from your job because you broke company rules

- Left your job because you were convicted of a felony or misdemeanor
- Are not able and available to work full time or are not looking for a full-time job
- Are attending school other than an approved vocational or industrial training course
- Participated in a work stoppage due to a labor dispute

As with any decision contrary to your interest made by your UI office, you may request a hearing.

PAYBACKS ARE HELL

In the interest of complete fairness, your former boss has the same right of appeal as you. Should he or she prevail in a dispute over benefits, you may have to repay any you have collected thus far.

April 15 comes every year, even for the unemployed. Your UI benefits are taxable, but your UI office does not deduct your taxes from each check as your boss did. You are responsible for paying your own taxes. You must file quarterly estimated statements to avoid paying penalties and interest charges to both the state and federal governments. You could end up with a whopper of a tax bill if you don't pay quarterly.

In January you will receive an IRS Form 1099-G showing the total amount of unemployment benefits you received. For more information on UI benefit taxes, see IRS Publication #905, *Income Tax Information on Unemployment Compensation.*

BAILING OUT WITH A "GOLDEN PARACHUTE"

Accepting a severance package sometimes precludes your collecting unemployment benefits. This generally occurs when you resign "voluntarily," in exchange for a more generous package, aware that you are about to be laid off anyway.

Check with your local employment office to ask whether and how your eligibility would be affected before making your final decision. Don't take the word of the first person you speak to. Check and recheck; verify with a supervisor. If the answer appears to be "No benefits" in the one case, ask for options and alternatives. Few bureaucrats offer this information voluntarily.

Your decision should be based on accurate information. The last thing you need right now is another surprise.

You may qualify for a severance package unless you have been discharged for cause. Even then, companies will offer something just to rid themselves of "undesirable" employees. Negotiate for as much as you can get before accepting your severance package. (Refer to the "Severance Package Checklist" in appendix A.)

By subtly demonstrating to your employer that you are aware of your rights, you establish a position of strength. Put your emotions aside. You may be harboring great resentment toward your boss, but don't let that get in the way of locking in the best deal for yourself. Don't get sold on the "standard package." There is no such thing.

When pressed, many companies will give a variety of benefits including allowing you to use the company car you've been driving or to buy it at reduced cost, hiring you as a consultant for various projects, accelerating vesting for retirement or stock-option programs, providing outplacement services, or allowing the use of an office and clerical staff for a period of time. Extension of day care for your child(ren), if that has been a company perk, is also an option, as is additional compensation for vacation days earned but not used.

Most companies generally pay one week's salary for each year of service. However, two or three weeks' salary for each year is not uncommon in certain situations. Executives usually get even more. Lump-sum or periodic payment is another aspect of severance to be considered. Taking the money all at once guarantees the cash in your hand.

Periodic payments carry the risk that if the company goes

broke, so could you, but extra advantages such as continuation of full benefits (health, etc.) for a few more months and added credits to your retirement program may make the limited gamble worthwhile. If you opt for the periodic plan, make sure your payments continue through the expiration of the agreed term even if you find a new job. Try to complete any needed medical and dental treatment while you are still covered by the company.

Once you have come to terms, get it in writing. Ask for a written explanation for termination—such as "the company was experiencing financial difficulty and had to make cuts"; "a merger"; "new management"; or "changing marketing direction"—so you can document for your next employer that you were discharged through no fault of your own. Also request a letter of reference.

Some severance-pay arrangements are covered in the Employee Retirement Income Security Act (ERISA), a copy of which may be obtained at your local library or Employment and Training Administration office.

Check with your former employer on whether taxes were deducted from your severance payments. Services provided as part of the package may also be subject to additional taxation. Your local IRS office is the best free source for this information.

SHAKING THE TREE

You are your own best advocate. If you don't ask, you don't get, and the more you know and persist, the better your chances of getting a fair shake.

MOTHER HUBBARD'S BARE CUPBOARD:
Putting Food on the Table

W ith a wise reassessment of your family's eating habits, you can save yourself from Mother Hubbard's fate. Her depleted larder should have tipped her off that the time had come to start fresh and lean, two key words when it comes to food and economics.

SKIMMING THE FAT

Think how many items you automatically pick up each time you go to the market—cookies, cakes, potato chips, candy, ice cream, sugar cereals. The list goes on and on. Add up the cost *and* the grams of fat, not to mention the sugar. Eliminating these types of items from your shopping basket is not deprivation, it's just good sense. You are not only saving money but preserving your family's health.

The nineties is a decade of moderation, and diet falls significantly within this principle. Any nutritionist worth his or her moderate salt urges avoiding extremes in diets: to use sodium, sugars, and alcohol in moderation; cut way back on fats of any type, particularly saturated fats; and eat plenty of vegetables, fruits, and grain products. Whole grains, vegetables, fruits, and pasta are the staples of a healthy diet and are very affordable. In essence, as you trim the fat from your diet, you can trim the fat from your food budget.

A lean diet is not the same as skimping. It's choosing quality over quantity. Eating too much is just as harmful as eating too little. "An apple a day keeps the doctor away" may be a cliché, but the meaning is clear. A nutritious diet can and does cut down on visits to the doctor—no small expense these days, particularly without the buffer of medical coverage.

Four months have passed since Laura had to shut down her advertising agency, and she still hasn't found a job. With money getting tighter, she asks her sons, Brian and Matthew, to help her take a long, hard look at their daily eating habits to determine where they can save some money. Because of their conflicting time schedules, Laura had been buying a great deal of prepackaged instant foods that each could prepare quickly for one and without fuss. When times were "normal," no one thought twice about the additional cost of these prepackaged items, nor about the $15 to $20 spent on snack foods, de rigueur for people on the run, or so they thought.

After cutting out the "fat" from their normal grocery list and making appropriate substitutions, they found that they could easily save anywhere from $20 to $40 a week, depending on how ambitious they wanted to be in the kitchen. Each pledged to give at least three hours a week as chief chef, making nutritious meals from scratch and packing up individual servings for the freezer.

They began to plan menus a week in advance but with enough flexibility to take advantage of local and seasonal specials. They took into consideration the overall likes and dislikes of the family as well as individual idiosyncrasies. To provide a better guarantee that they would stick to this new eating regimen, they selected foods that were appetizing and appealing to the whole family.

For purposes of health as well as the budget, meat would be included for only two of the week's seven meals. Chicken, turkey, pastas, soups, salads, and occasionally fish (a take-it-or-leave-it item for the boys) filled out the rest of the menu. The boys promised not to sneer at leftovers anymore when Laura promised to come up with some ingenious methods for their reuse. Fresh and dried fruits, air-popped popcorn, and pretzels replaced ice cream, pies, potato chips, cookies, and taco chips as desserts and snacks.

Planning is one thing, executing is another, so Laura expressed her need for moral support when doing the marketing, at least initially. The boys agreed it would be best that the three go together to help each other avoid temptations.

They decided to do their major marketing in a single trip, using a list and sticking to it—no more impulse buying. They would use discount coupons only for items on their list and only when the discounted cost was less than house brands. (Most experts agree that while house brands are generally priced at about 15 percent less than nationally advertised brands, there is little or no discernible difference in quality between the two. Often the house brand is produced by a nationally known company in the same factory, but packaged for private-label customers.)

On their first trip to the market together under their new plan, Brian brought a calculator. He was the designated pricing detective. It was his job to determine the better buy by comparing the weights and unit prices between the brands. They discovered that some boxes that look the same and are priced the same are in fact entirely different weights. Ergo one is a much better buy than the other as long as the quality is comparable.

A quick comparison between a ten-ounce box in bulk of hot cereal and the same brand of five ounces in individual packages revealed that the unit price of the bulk package was significantly lower than that of the single-serving package. This was true of just about every other food that was offered in bulk versus premeasured.

PLAYING THE NUMBERS

Buying in large quantities is a good way to save, generally, but not always. Do not assume that the larger package is a better buy than the smaller. That's where the calculator comes in handy. Next to your list, it is the most critical item for shopping trips. The calculator will tell you in seconds the unit price. The lower the unit price, the better the buy.

Shopping clubs such as BJ's, Pace Membership Warehouse, and Costco offer institutional-size packages usually at lower unit cost than in supermarkets, often at just pennies over wholesale. The trick when shopping at these clubs is knowing the supermarket cost of the items you intend to purchase, to determine if and how much you are saving. Another caveat is not to be swept up by the enormous selection and the "bargains." A bargain is not a bargain if you don't need it. Stick to your list and use your calculator.

Shopping clubs cost around $25.00 a year for the first person to join. Three or four others can be added to that membership for an additional charge of around $15.00 each. This would bring the average cost to $17.50 each if a group of four join together, a worthwhile investment given the potential savings on purchases. You can also arrange with this same group to divvy up the giant packages such as the thirty-six-roll toilet paper pack or the twelve-box tissue pack, to take advantage of the greatest savings without having to lay out large amounts in one shopping trip or to find a place to store these monster packages.

Coupons are a plus, if used wisely. Some stores even deduct double the face value, but make sure you are not paying more in the end for the extra discount. Some markets that offer this come-on raise prices considerably to cover the cost. Also, compare what a name brand costs minus the value of the coupon to the regular price of the generic brand. More often than not, the generic brand is still cheaper.

HELP IS WHERE YOU FIND IT, AND YOU CAN

One of the best cooperative food programs in operation today is SHARE (Self Help And Resource Exchange) U.S.A. A self-sustaining private group, SHARE offers $30 to $35 worth of food for $13. Its motto is, "If you eat, you qualify."

The food is first quality, purchased in bulk from the same vendors from whom the supermarkets buy. Distribution centers are set up once a month in churches, schools, and civic organization offices. Volunteers pick up the supplies from area warehouses and separate family-sized portions into cartons. In New England alone there are over 200 distribution centers.

Contents of the carton vary from week to week but always include fresh fruit and vegetables, frozen meat and/or chicken, and some staples. For example, one carton contained around 3 pounds of chicken, 16 breaded fish patties, a package of chicken franks, 4 pork chops, broccoli, carrots, 2 pounds of onions, 3 pounds of red potatoes, 3 pounds of apples, 4 pears, 4 oranges, 1 pound of pinto beans, 1 pound of rice, a package of Velveeta cheese, and a box of Lipton Cup-A-Soup. SHARE customers must advise distribution centers in advance of their intent to purchase. There is no limit on the number of cartons they can buy, but they must give two hours of community service for every carton purchased. "Community service" had initially been loosely defined, but SHARE now requires participation in more structured projects, generally determined by the organization that sponsors the distribution centers.

SHARE's structured projects vary from volunteering at a hospital to leading a Girl Scout troop. Some SHARE centers accept neighbor-to-neighbor community service. For instance, you might drive someone without transportation to the doctor, baby-sit for someone who works but cannot afford child care, or clean house for someone who is ill. In all SHARE programs, a "community service receipt" is signed by the person who gets the service, then returned to SHARE for credit.

SHARE operates twenty-one area offices, with some satellites in sparsely populated locales. The main office is in San Diego, California. Michelle Medugno, SHARE U.S.A. Communications Specialist, reports that 3,168,444 cartons were distributed in 1991 and demand is rapidly increasing, particularly in the more upscale suburban areas.

Contact SHARE area offices, listed under "SHARE" in the telephone book, or call the San Diego office at 619-525-2200 for information on your nearest distribution center.

Because today's underemployment, budget cuts, and high food prices compromise a household's nutritional status, a network of federal, state, and local food and nutrition programs have been established to increase access to food. These programs go under a variety of names—Open Pantry, First Call, Project Bread, Hunger Coalition, or similar euphemisms.

In Michigan, numerous organizations stock emergency food pantries for the homeless and others who can document need. One example is Detroit's Mayor's Emergency Hot Line (313-267-6679), which directs needy people to appropriate resources. There are even some food pantries that provide kosher food, such as Yad Ezra (313-548-3663). Contact the local office of the Combined Jewish Philanthropies (CJP) for information on where to find kosher pantries in your area. Information on food pantry programs can be accessed through your local public health department, department of welfare, or unemployment office. Newspapers and radio and TV stations also disseminate information on these programs with public-service announcements.

Churches and civic organizations are responding to the ever-increasing demand for assistance in an effort to close the gap left by government programs. In Burlington, Massachusetts, several churches banded together to form People Helping People (PHP). In addition to operating a food pantry, PHP's covenant is to ensure basic needs are met and to provide help with any emergency that threatens survival. This includes anything from burst water heaters to prescriptions for the elderly.

Some of PHP's clients may be waiting to get on federally or state-funded programs or for unemployment benefits to kick in. PHP also helps to guide clients through the system— where and how to apply for government programs, which they may qualify for, and so on. Recipients must document immediate need.

Check your local religious and civic organizations for similar programs. Also, make inquiries at your city's veteran's agent or schools, which can often provide a list of privately funded agencies.

A federal program called Special Supplemental Food Program for Women, Infants, and Children (WIC) provides nutritious foods such as milk, formula, cereal, and fruit juices to low- and moderate-income pregnant or breast-feeding women and to children under 5 who are at nutritional risk.

The Expanded Food and Nutrition Education Program, regarded as the nutrition education component of food stamps, provides individuals and small groups with education on food budgeting, menu planning, and food preparation.

Another excellent source for nutrition information is the Department of Nutrition Services of the University of Alabama. Funded by the National Institutes of Health, the university's Nutrition Information Service (NIS) furnishes a wide spectrum of nutritional information, including budgeting, how to make the most of food, and suggested diet changes to cut cancer risks. A toll-free line (1-800-231-DIET) is staffed by registered dieticians and a dietetic technician to answer specific questions, fulfill requests for educational materials, make referrals, and assist in program planning. Also contact the American Dietetic Association for similar materials (1-800-366-1655).

Geri Henchy, senior policy analyst for the Food Research and Action Center in Washington, D.C., strongly advises the unemployed: "Take advantage of food programs right away. Don't 'spend down' before you ask for assistance. You don't know how long you will be unemployed. Even with all available government supports, you still need a cash reserve each month to see you through."

Henchy points out, "Food programs are a safety net, there for people who need it, paid for by taxes. People can think of it as money in the bank. They made deposits, and now they need to make a withdrawal. This is a land of plenty, and they deserve to be able to feed their children."

"It's not unusual to need help," she adds. "One out of ten people in our country use the services of food programs. Almost 26 million are on food stamps alone. In fact, food stamps are a better indication of the economy than unemployment." Henchy recommends contacting the local department of health for information about locally available food programs, especially the Women, Infants, and Children program (WIC). Additional benefits to check when you contact the department of health are free immunizations and well-child care. Check your state or local government listings in the phone book under "Health" or "Public Health."

Meals on Wheels, also known as Congregate Meals or the like, provides nutritious meals to any senior 60 years or older regardless of income. This program is generally administered by the state department of elder affairs.

The state department of agriculture under the umbrella title of "Farmers' Markets" provides information on how and where one can access low-cost fresh fruits and vegetables by buying directly from farmers at farmers' markets. These markets have gained in popularity and are held at least once a week, regardless of weather, across the country, offering other homemade items such as bread, honey, and preserves along with produce.

Many farmers allow customers to pick produce from their fields at substantial savings. A directory of these farms can be obtained from your local department of agriculture's county extension office. Plan menus using fruits and vegetables that are in season, when they are least expensive. Your county extension office can advise you on the seasonal availability of produce in your area.

Free or low-cost school lunch and breakfast programs are available for schoolchildren and can be accessed through the student's school principal's office. (See chapter 7, "School Maze.")

Food stamps are administered through your local welfare office. This program is available for low-income families with limited property and savings. In an emergency, applications can be processed in five days or less. Expedited service is granted when a family has less than $150 income in one month and less than $100 in resources, or if the combined income and resources are less than combined monthly rent or mortgage and utility expenses. The homeless also qualify for this expedited service.

Households (defined as individuals or groups who buy, prepare, and eat food together) can qualify for food stamps even if receiving income from such sources as a job, child-support payments, unemployment benefits, or a pension. The amount of income depends on the number of people in the household and the gross household monthly income before deductions. For example, as of the fall of 1991, a household of four could have a maximum of $1,376 in gross income per month and still qualify for food stamps.

Assets considered for qualification are cash on hand, savings and checking accounts, and the cash value of some cars. Those not counted are your home, your personal belongings, and the cash value of your life insurance policy. The total value of your counted property, called resources or assets, cannot exceed $2,000 unless the household includes at least one person 60 years old or over. The limit is then raised to $3,000.

Food-stamp applications may be obtained at your local welfare office. If you cannot get there, you may designate an authorized representative, someone you trust, to apply for you. For the housebound, a food-stamp worker can make a house call.

When applying, bring with you:

- Identification—a birth certificate, driver's license, school or work ID, voter registration card, a sworn statement from a person who knows you stating your full name and complete address, or a temporary identification form from general relief. If you have no permanent address, be prepared to say where you are staying. If you are not a U.S. citizen, bring proof of legal alien status.
- Social Security numbers for all household members.
- Income statements—last four pay stubs, pay envelopes, letter from employer on letterhead that states your income received for the last thirty days or five weeks, W-2 form, wage tax receipt, state or federal tax return, or self-employment bookkeeping records. For unearned money from benefits, bring Social Security letter, copy of benefit check before cashing, unemployment compensation letter or check stubs, pension letter, VA notice, or income tax records.
- Bank book or current bank statements and proof of any other resources.
- Utility and rent bills.
- Receipts of child care or other dependent care.
- Medical bills if over 60 or disabled.

In some cases, as with students, strikers, or aliens, additional information may be required. Inquire in advance if you suspect you may fall within a unique category, to save yourself an extra trip. And don't panic if you can't provide all of the material required. Your food-stamp worker can contact your employer, landlord, neighbor, or social-service agency to provide the collateral information necessary for qualification.

Emergency food programs are also available and are geared toward those who have no income or benefits to purchase food and need to be referred to emergency food pantries or meal sites.

Most of these programs are conducted under the umbrella of your state's welfare office, which may offer separate hot lines for the specific programs. These numbers are listed in your telephone book under your state welfare office heading.

Tony and Susan establish a gardening exchange with friends and neighbors to provide a variety of fresh fruits and vegetables throughout the growing season, with enough left over for freezing and canning. They extend the invitation to apartment dwellers as well, since their community, like many others, offers patches in communal gardens on a first-come-first-get basis. Susan creates a flyer announcing the initial meeting of the gardening exchange. Tony posts copies on community bulletin boards and sends one to the local paper for announcement in the community calendar section.

At the meeting, each member is assigned different crops. For example, Tony and Susan plant tomatoes, beans, and squash. Another member of the exchange grows lettuce, radishes, peas, and potatoes, and another grows cucumbers and cantaloupe. When gardens begin to produce, everyone involved meets once a week, alternating backyards, to exchange their surplus.

Laura's 16-year-old son Matthew looks for a part-time job to help out with household expenses. He focuses his search on restaurants and caterers where he may be allowed to eat some meals free while he's on the job and to take leftovers home.

CLEANING UP AND OUT

At least one-third of every dollar spent in the supermarket is for nonfood items. This is the category where the greatest savings can be achieved. For example, virtually every heavy-duty cleaning agent we buy for floors, tile, bathtubs, and walls can be replaced with simple vinegar (½ cup), clear ammonia (1 cup), and baking soda (¼ cup), mixed with 1 gallon of warm water; much less expensive and more convenient than maintaining an arsenal of specialized cleansers, and even more efficient. (When using this formula, work in a well-ventilated area and wear rubber gloves.) For light cleaning, ½ cup of ammonia in a gallon of water will do the trick at a cost of less than two cents per gallon. Additionally, these compounds are ecologically friendly.

Overuse of paper products, too, is not only costly but a blight on our environment. Think of all the trees that could be saved if we all gave up our paper napkins by using cloth. The names of each member of the family could be stamped on a cloth napkin to be reused by them during the week and then washed for the next. The convenience of paper plates should be reserved only for outings away from home where use of china is impractical. Held only a few yards or so away from the kitchen sink, backyard barbecues do not qualify for disposable products. When plastic utensils are used, wash them out and use them again. Plastic bags, too, may be rinsed out for reuse.

Disposable hard goods such as cigarette lighters, flashlights, razors, and now even cameras can put a dent in the marketing budget as well as in our environment. Whenever possible use permanent products, preferably rechargeable to eliminate the need for batteries. (A good rechargeable flashlight costs less than $10, lasts almost forever, and is ever ready.)

New parents should weigh the cost (and ecological advantages) of cloth versus disposable diapers. Modern washers and dryers do a good, thorough job of washing cloth diapers clean (particularly when baking soda is added to the wash cycle), taking just a little over an hour for a fresh batch. Consider the cost of the power (electricity or gas) used for each load and the availability (or scarcity) of water in your area when deciding which to use. You may find alternating cloth and disposable is the best way to go.

Economy and ecology are symbiotic. Your thrift saves more

than money. Reuse and reduced consumption in any form contributes to the earth's well-being for generations to come.

GREAT-GRANDMA HAD THE RIGHT IDEA

Equipped only with a heavy pot and a dime-store strainer, Great-grandma cooked and pureed her baby's food. Only then could she be sure of the ingredients and their quality. Today, with the help of sophisticated food processors and blenders, baby food can be prepared with very little effort and at half the cost of store-bought food. Breast-feeding until the child is ready to be weaned to a cup is also advisable, both in benefit to the child and as a cost-saving measure.

Great-grandma also preserved and canned a long time before the advent of supermarkets. This is a great way to take advantage of low in-season prices or garden surplus. Flea markets and garage sales are the best places to buy canning jars really cheap. Most general cookbooks have a chapter with instructions for canning.

Admittedly, canning is still almost as time-consuming as it was in Great-grandma's day, but we have another option that she didn't—freezing. With a freezer and a few containers or freezer bags, a sizable amount of food can be processed and preserved in an afternoon.

One of the reasons Great-grandma canned and preserved was to store away a larder for lean times. This, too, is not such a bad idea. An emergency larder could help to reduce some of the stress and worry at the end of a pay period or when benefits run out. Squirreling away a supply of soups, pastas, and sauces or any filling and nutritious foods that have a long shelf life guarantees food on the table even when there's no money in the wallet.

Given Great-grandma's limited mobility (few women had their own "wheels" in those days), much of her social life was centered on her family, her neighbors, and her church. Of course, eating was the main form of entertainment. She could count on at least one potluck dinner or church supper a week, an excellent way to feed the family for very little cost. Take a page from Great-grandma's datebook. Look around for the church suppers where membership is not a prerequisite for attending. Arrange with family, friends, and/or neighbors to hold a once-weekly, round-robin potluck supper with each participant taking turns contributing the part of the menu that may cost the most. If you gather six families, your investment could be minimal for five out of six weeks. What may be even more advantageous is that you would have a party and a nice break in routine to look forward to every week.

During the Depression, homemakers had many tricks that served their families well. One cook, now in her seventies, remembers her mother's adage: "Stretch what you cook by using carbohydrates, avoid any waste, and shop wisely." This golden rule still applies.

This still-thrifty woman saves every tablespoon of vegetables, for instance, to use in omelets; uses the water from cooking vegetables as soup stock along with meat or chicken bones; and skims the fat off soup to use for frying (who knew about cholesterol in the thirties). Beans are prevalent in her recipes, including chick-peas, kidney beans, navy beans, pinto beans, and black-eyed peas. Beans are a great stretcher for a recession-proof diet: low in fat, high in fiber and nutrition, and cheap.

One-dish meals of stir-fries, casseroles, stews, and soups can help the budget and are used the world over in Chinese, French, Italian, and Spanish cuisines. Most ethnic cooking is created by using only morsels of meat or fish with lots of vegetables, all bound together with starch. For other cost-saving tips, consult Depression-era cookbooks or women's magazines at your local library.

Now that Richard was home with the baby while Anne was at work, he had a lot of time on his hands. He began to apply his basic creative talents to baking. His cakes and pies, particularly his cheesecake, became legend among their friends and family. When one cousin joked he should be selling the stuff, not giving it away, it occurred to him that his culinary prowess could pay off. He canvassed restaurants and gourmet shops and was soon getting more orders than he could handle, making a profit of anywhere from $5 to $15 on each item ordered.

FOOD FOR THOUGHT

Writer-reporter Calvin Trillin once noted, "The most remarkable thing about my mother is that for thirty years she served the family nothing but leftovers. The original meal has never been found." With ingenuity and determination you can create original meals and leftovers that are both satisfying and healthy for the family.

CLOTHES ENCOUNTERS OF THE PRACTICAL KIND:
Clothing the Family

Beau Brummell, an English gentleman who became a legend in his own time (1778–1840) for his pacesetting fashion, was living proof that clothes make the man. But old Beau had to spend every shilling he had to maintain his image. You don't!

I HAVEN'T GOT A THING TO WEAR

That usually means "I hate everything I own and wish I could afford to dump everything and start all over." Bulging closets and drawers do not a well-dressed person make. Some of the best-dressed people have just a few outfits and a lot of imagination. The first rule of saving on clothing costs is to take a new look at what you own with an unjaundiced eye.

COMING OUT OF THE CLOSET

Take an inventory of everything you own. Dig out the stuff you never wear but loved when you bought. Include the pile you have been meaning to have altered or repaired. Are they worth having fixed? If so, a quick trip to the tailor or the shoemaker will perk up your wardrobe. If not, get rid of them; sell them at a garage sale or give them to someone who can use them.

When you have all wearable items put together, count up how many you have in each category. If you have enough to take you through one full week for all phases of your lifestyle, even if it takes mixing and matching to do it, you probably have enough to keep you going for a while.

Take a new view of your wardrobe. You picked everything out, so you must have liked them when you did. Take the items you have been avoiding wearing and try them with a new scarf, tie, shirt, sweater, belt, suspenders, or any one of the array of inexpensive accessories that can entirely change the original look. Check the fashion magazines for tips. You probably already own many accessories similar to those shown, but you just haven't been making the best use of them.

BACK TO BASICS

Reheel and resole shoes. A good shoemaker can make shoes and boots look like new for less than replacing them. A good jacket or coat may require only a new lining, new buttons, or leather patches on the sleeves to give you several more years of good service.

Trim jacket lapels and remove cuffs from trousers rather than discarding them when styles change. When pants wear out at the knees, cut them down for shorts. When long-sleeve shirts or blouses sprout holes in the elbows, convert them to short sleeves.

Rotate your clothes and your footwear. When something has lost its luster, don't be so quick to discard it. Move it from the "best" category to the "not-so-terrific" to be worn for shopping and hanging out. *The Tightwad Gazette* suggests the three-year plan for sneakers, jeans, and the like. The oldest is reserved for chores such as gardening or housecleaning, the middle for less messy jobs, saving the newest for informal gatherings, shopping, or any casual outings.

Think twice before throwing anything away. Fashion is cyclical. You may be able to resurrect that garment in three or four years and once again be in the height of fashion.

Try not to gain weight. Aesthetics and health aside, practicality is motive enough for maintenance. More weight means a larger size and very possibly a new wardrobe. If you lose weight, you can size your clothes down, but rarely can you let out enough to accommodate increased girth. If you do lose weight, don't get rid of those clothes. Chances are you may need them again.

Don't be so quick to refuse an offer of a dress, suit, or coat from a friend, particularly an affluent one. From the generosity of that gift horse may come an attractive, expensive garment that has hardly been worn. Hand-me-downs for children make the most sense. Kids grow so fast, four or five could take turns using the same garment before wear and tear even begin to show.

Nick is in the thick of a growth spurt. He outgrows his clothes faster than Susan can buy them. Though she buys only in discount stores or on sale, the cost of keeping up with Nick's clothing needs is more than the family can afford now that Tony is unemployed. She asks the director at Nick's day-care center if she may be permitted to establish a Mutual Assistance Program for trading up clothes. Aware that so many families are in the same tight spot, the director gives Susan the green light.

Susan sends a notice to all the parents at Nick's school notifying them that a clothing "goodie" box is set up at the front door for deposit of clean used clothing. Parents can pick out what they need but are exhorted to wash and return outfits when the children outgrow them.

BYE BYE BLOOMIES

A total refurbishing of your wardrobe as well as that of the rest of your family may not eliminate entirely the need to supplement, particularly if you have growing children. In that case, implant one word firmly in your mind—"Bargain!"

Even the affluent are openly flocking to bargain stores. Once upon a time, the service and ambience of upscale department stores were the trade-offs for their higher prices. With the drastic reductions in sales staffs and only cashiers left to ring up your purchases (if you're lucky), these stores have lost their edge. Service is no better than in the discount stores, where the selection is just as varied and the prices are much gentler on your pocket.

The stigma of scrounging through the mark-down tables is gone. Getting the best bargain has become the new status symbol. Tours are offered to factory outlet malls, and the buses are almost always filled by an equal mix of shoppers with large disposable incomes and those with limited budgets. For some, the hunt is the thrill; for others the thrill is outfitting the family at affordable prices.

Sometimes priority must be given to investing in the unemployed person's image to increase chances for landing a job. The job seeker must have at least one outfit that is contemporary in style and in good condition.

While clothes make the man, or woman, so do updated eyeglasses, a stylish haircut, even hair coloring or a facial. In our society, so infatuated with youth, older workers, men as well as women, are even resorting to plastic surgery.

A new outfit may not erase wrinkles, but it will go a long way toward making you feel better about yourself as well as making you more attractive to a potential employer. Price does not dictate quality, however. Just because something costs more doesn't mean it's better. You could be subsidizing heavy advertising campaigns and paying dearly to display someone else's name prominently on your breast or rear end. Learn what to look for—reinforcement at stress points, heavy seams, natural versus synthetic fabrics, or hand-stitched hems rather than machine-stitched ones that unravel with one pull.

Cut down on cleaning and laundry bills by buying washable garments whenever possible. Look for wash-and-wear garments to save on ironing or those that require only light pressing for crisping.

WHEN THE GOING GETS TOUGH, THE TOUGH MUST KNOW HOW TO SHOP

Off-price merchandise is not damaged or any different from what you would find in department stores or boutiques. It means exactly what it says—merchandise discounted up to 60 percent (even more) off the original price for various reasons such as manufacturer's surplus or canceled orders. The concept has been available to consumers for decades, but the outlets were few and far between. Shoppers looking for quality merchandise at reduced prices had to wait until Saturday mornings when factories would open to the public for three hours, or drive long distances to the scattered locations where the very few off-price pioneers such as Loehmann's and Marshall's were offering more for less.

In the last ten years, traditional retailers have been quaking over the proliferation of factory outlet stores, indeed whole malls. There, even the likes of Anne Klein, Liz Claiborne, Ralph Lauren, and Perry Ellis offer their overruns at well below original prices. And that's not all! The smorgasbord includes books, bedding, baby clothes, dishes, kitchen utensils, toys, etc., etc., etc. If they are manufactured, they are discounted.

Some of these stores do offer "seconds," prominently marked and priced accordingly. The damage may be major or minor, but since the prices are outrageously low, it's worth the time to look for something passable. Invest $5 in magnifying spectacles, available at most pharmacies, to wear when scanning garments. As good as your eyesight may be, you may miss something without a sight enhancer.

Not everything in these outlets is a raging bargain; it may well sell for close to the price you would pay in a department store. Do some scouting at regular malls to price the items you need. Become familiar with labels. That helps in comparison shopping.

Be sure to check return policies before buying. Up until recently, if you bought something in Loehmann's, you owned it forever as far as the store was concerned. Most stores will accept returns, but many give only merchandise credit. You cannot get your money back or a credit posted to your charge account. Once you've forked over your money or signed a charge slip, you are trapped until you find something else in that store to which you can apply your credit.

If you are not a resident of the state in which you are shopping, you may not have to pay applicable sales taxes if you send the merchandise home. You will, however, incur a shipping charge, so calculate the difference between paying the tax and the shipping to determine which gives you the greater savings.

SALE-ING, SALE-ING

Faced with the competition from outlet and discount stores, traditional retailers are slashing their prices before Christmas, after Christmas, all year long. While January and August used to be the months to get the best price on coats, major sales now begin in November and continue throughout the prime selling season.

Despite all the come-ons offered throughout the year, buying out of season still presents the best opportunities for savings. An air conditioner, lawn furniture, or a gas grill costs less in September, when the demand is less, than in June, when sales are brisk. Prices on woodburning stoves and firewood are generally lower in the spring.

Dealing with traditional retailers still has some advantages.

They're conveniently located, they stand behind everything they sell (generally even six months or more after a purchase is made), and they give cash refunds even on sale items. Some will sell major items for less than the ticket price if you document that you can buy it somewhere else for less.

Surprisingly, the ticket price is not set in stone the way it used to be. You can make deals, particularly in smaller stores where the owner is almost always there. If you are making a large purchase, or several small ones that add up, the owner may be amenable to a 10, 15, or even 20 percent discount just to make the sale. If you don't ask, you don't get. Even giving a 20 percent discount, a merchant still is making a tidy profit while getting a loyal customer who will recommend that store to others.

Sensitive to the current economy, many major chains have initiated new policies to cater to families in economic distress. For example, Athlete's Foot has advised its salespeople to fit children in shoes that will accommodate growth—large enough to use for a longer period of time, but not so large as to jeopardize growing feet. They also urge the purchase of generic styles (usually made by branded companies) and those that are more durable.

Athlete's Foot also offers a frequent-buyer program. Anyone who buys twelve pairs of footwear can apply the averaged price of the twelve purchased to the thirteenth. Look for the bargain tables in these stores. Display, "blemished" (not damaged), and discontinued models are sometimes marked down 50 percent. Check other chain stores for similar programs.

With their first baby on the way, Richard and Anne had hoped they could borrow a crib, carriage, and other necessities but can't find anyone within their families or circle of friends who isn't still using these items or who hasn't already loaned them out. Though money is tight with Richard out of work, they have no choice but to buy what they need.

They spend their weekends shopping flea markets and

garage sales. Anne and Richard discover that the best places to find good, serviceable, inexpensive baby furniture are at garage sales in "second home" neighborhoods—those where families have upgraded to larger homes, do not anticipate having any more children, and are eager to sell these items as soon as their youngest child outgrows them.

Unwilling to buy used clothing for their firstborn, however, Richard and Anne find new garments and diapers at flea markets and store sales for at least 50 percent (sometimes more) off regular retail prices. An accomplished seamstress, Anne whips out a few items on her trusty Singer. She makes several variations of the same pattern, using remnants she found at discount fabric shops.

Unadorned baby clothes, generally less expensive than the lavishly trimmed, can be perked up with appliques cut from fabric scraps or old clothing. Trains, animals, flowers, and the like can be added to plain bibs and outfits to make them special. Old clothes can be recycled into a play quilt by cutting them into squares and connecting. The variety of patterns and fabrics gives the still-immobile baby exciting vistas to explore.

A PENNY EARNED IS A PENNY SAVED

Consignment shops offer two-pronged opportunities. You can convert your unused clothing to cash and replenish your wardrobe to accommodate your new lifestyle for minimal cost. Many of these shops also take toys, bric-a-brac, sporting goods, even furniture.

While the long, long road through the recession is littered with victims, consignment shop owners have emerged victorious. More than 15,000 shops across the country are doing brisk business catering to both men and women. Although secondhand, the selection is generally good quality, high style, and always clean and in good repair. Prices run between 60 and 75 percent below retail.

Most of the stock comes from people who are tired of some of their clothes, or from their children who have outgrown outfits, often expensive gifts from doting grandparents. Some items have never been worn, possibly gifts not to their taste or the wrong size. The split is usually 60/40, the larger percentage for you. You get paid when the item is sold. The policy of some shops is to donate merchandise not sold within a specified period (generally four to six weeks) to charity. Check on that before making your deal if you want your unsold merchandise returned to you.

Kids' resale shops in particular are booming. One retailer, Children's Orchard, has 41 franchises from California to Massachusetts and expects to have as many as 300 to 500 units in the next five years. It was started by one enterprising woman who found a hole in the marketplace and filled it.

Merchandise is accepted only in season. Don't try to unload your summer clothes at the beginning of the winter. Items must be in style (that's where classic wins out again), clean, and in good condition. Bring everything in on hangers in plastic dry-cleaning bags for better presentation. Shop owners almost automatically reject merchandise crammed into shopping bags.

Before you start schlepping your clothes around, visit the shops in your area to see what they specialize in or if they are buying at that particular time. Get the criteria for acceptance in each and find out about payment arrangements. While you're there, check the racks. You may find that perfect interview suit you've been looking for at a surprisingly gentle price.

A good source for buying and selling used sporting equipment is Play It Again Sports, a national chain with 300 stores (they also sell new products). Equipment for virtually every sports activity can be purchased used, at half the cost of new. Those who want to sell can opt for a consignment deal—60 percent for the owner, 40 percent for the store, a trade-in for other equipment, or a total buyout. The price paid by the store depends on condition, age, and season. The only exceptions are guns and knives, neither of which is bought or sold. Look under "Sporting Goods" in your Yellow Pages for the nearest location.

Thrift shops, too, can be a treasure trove of bargains if you don't mind doing a lot of sifting through the bad (lots of it) to get to the good (not as much). These shops raise money for charities or "good works" and are run by hospitals, schools, religious groups, or such organizations as the Salvation Army, Goodwill Industries, and Morgan Memorial. All merchandise is donated. Donations are tax-deductible, so get a receipt for the estimated worth.

If you have a marriageable-age daughter, your jobless status will probably have little influence on her love life. If she meets and wants to marry Mr. Right while you are still out of work, you can get her attired for her big day for as little as $100. Haunt consignment and thrift shops for wedding gowns. Most wedding gowns, after all, have been worn only once, but the cost is a fraction of what you would have to pay in a bridal shop. Check ads in local papers and shopping publications (found on most newsstands). Often women whose marriages ended in bitter divorces offer their wedding ensembles (dress, veil, and undergarments) at ridiculously low prices just to rid themselves of something that conjures up bad memories.

With a little initiative, the groom could find a tuxedo for less than the cost of renting. Many rental shops sell off tuxes after a certain number of months' use at greatly reduced prices. Consignment shops are another place to look, and don't forget the thrift shops. If you're lucky and patient, you may find one for $5 or $10, complete with suspenders.

Consult your Yellow Pages for resale shops in your area. Look under "Consignment Shops (or Services)," "Clothing Bought and Sold," "Resale," "Secondhand," "Thrift Shops," and "Used Clothing." Also check with your church, synagogue, local schools, and hospitals. Since these shops are operated primarily by volunteers, hours and days may vary from week to week. Look for organization-operated stores under individual headings, e.g., "Salvation Army."

ONE-NIGHT STANDS

Another business spawned by the recession is rental shops. You can rent anything from a leather briefcase to a wedding gown. These shops cater to those who have special occasions that need something spectacular, but don't have the money or the inclination to make an investment in something that may be used too infrequently to justify the cost.

For about $100 you can rent a formal dress for an evening or a designer suit. If you have an interview coming up in which you feel expensive trappings may make an impression, you can rent a Filofax, a $500 briefcase, maybe even a Mont Blanc pen. Wedding gowns are available from $200 up, plus alterations; headpieces and veils for around $75. Look under the "Rental" listing in your Yellow Pages for locations in your area.

TO MARKET, TO MARKET

An amazing variety of clothing, both new and used, can be found at flea markets, along with toiletries and makeup. Flea markets operate all year round, inside in the cold weather, outside in the warm. Mostly you will find such merchandise as socks, underwear, men's shirts, work clothes, jeans, and sweaters, but some dealers offer leather and suede coats and jackets and designer (so they say) purses and wallets. The prices are good and can get better if you are a good horse trader. The key word here is *negotiate*.

Street vendors operating out of kiosks or wagons offer some very attractive merchandise at very reasonable prices. Most of these vendors concentrate on such merchandise as scarves, leather goods, costume jewelry, T-shirts, and sweatshirts. Others are artisans who offer their own creations. Some are flexible on price, others aren't. You have to test the waters before buying.

Some really beautiful, stylish clothes may be found at garage and yard sales, particularly those held in affluent areas. Sellers are often more concerned about getting someone else to cart away their unwanted items than about the price they get for them. Find the right yard sale and you could outfit yourself for a year for under $100 ($5 for dresses, $10 for suits, $1 or $2 for a pair of shoes, $2 to $5 for blouses and sweaters).

Flea markets and yard and garage sales are listed in the classified sections of local newspapers. On a nice day, particularly in the spring and fall, which are popular moving seasons and when most people choose to clean up, pick a good location and take a ride. You'll undoubtedly find signs for at least a half-dozen sales, probably more.

OILING UP YOUR SINGER

The ability to make your own clothes is not an innate talent; it's an acquired skill. If you're not inclined to start from scratch, sewing skills are useful for doing your own repairs.

Creating a new garment is not always inexpensive. You can get carried away with the cost of the raw materials. (On a small scale, it's analogous to constructing a new home—"As long as I'm building, I might as well add . . .") Stick to your budget. Buy your fabrics in discount stores, at rummage sales, or flea markets. Look for end-of-the-bolt bargains or specials for discontinued patterns. Pull a Scarlett O'Hara. Make a dress out of unused drapes. The good parts of your old linens could make a cute summer short set for your little girl.

An accomplished seamstress, Anne offers to size down some dresses for her friend Carol, who has lost thirty pounds. In exchange, Carol agrees to help produce résumés and job inquiry letters on her computer and laser printer for Anne's husband, Richard, who is having no success finding a new job since he was laid off from the printing company.

CUT FROM DIFFERENT CLOTH

There's an old saying that goes "I cried because I had no shoes until I met a man who had no feet." As bad off as we think we are, there are so many more out there who would happily trade their problems for ours. Relinquish that old coat, jacket, and sweat suit you never wear but can't bear to part with. Take them to a homeless shelter. Even in hard times, those of us with the feet should share with those without.

A TICKET TO RIDE:
Transportation

We are a highly mobile society. Many Americans think nothing of traveling a hundred miles or more in a day to work, shop, visit friends or family, or just to enjoy the scenery. The trick is to find less expensive and more energy-efficient ways to get around.

UNDER COVER

If you own a car—and judging from our clogged highways, almost everyone does—insuring your vehicle is one of your major annual expenses. Since few of us are willing to give up our wheels (Americans have had a love affair with cars since Henry Ford began making automobiles "affordable for the common man"), insurance is a fact of life. However, there are several ways a car owner can keep costs for coverage to a minimum and still be reasonably protected.

Requesting higher deductibles (the portion of the repair bill for which you are responsible) on your collision and comprehensive (fire and theft) coverage can lower your costs substantially. For example, increasing your deductible from $200 to $500 could reduce your premium by 15 to 30 percent.

If you own a car worth less than $1,000, it probably is not cost-effective for you to carry collision or comprehensive coverage. The cost for coverage added to your deductible would probably exceed any reimbursement to which you would be entitled.

Medical payments coverage (for injuries to the driver and/or passengers in your car regardless of liability and for the policy-holder and family members injured in someone else's car) might duplicate or overlap your health insurance. Therefore, $5,000 to $10,000 coverage may be sufficient. By eliminating this coverage entirely, you could lower the cost for personal injury protection as much as 40 percent in some states.

If your health and collision coverage already covers you, or if you live in a strong no-fault state, you may also be able to eliminate uninsured/underinsured motorist coverage that provides for injuries sustained by you or your passengers caused by uninsured, underinsured, or hit-and-run drivers. If your state requires this coverage, you may want to consider, at least until you are back to work again, $15,000/$30,000 coverage that pays up to $15,000 for one injured person and a maximum of $30,000 for each accident.

Make sure you are getting all discounts to which you may be entitled. For example, some companies offer discounts to drivers who log fewer than a predetermined number of miles each year, usually around 10,000. Other opportunities for discounts may be for automatic seat belts and/or air bags; for safe driving records (no accidents or moving violations for a specified number of years, usually three); for drivers over 50; for a second car; for antitheft devices such as alarms, special locks, or LoJack (a device that emits a homing signal to assist police in tracking a stolen car); for antilock brakes; for drivers who have completed driver training courses, or for those who have two forms of insurance with the same company. If you no longer have students driving your car, make sure the extra charge has been deducted.

For advice on the best methods to lower your insurance costs, contact the Insurance Information Institute at 1-800-942-4242.

SHOP AND SAVE

Review your insurance once a year to make sure that your policy reflects your current status. Most important, comparison shop. Prices for the same coverage can vary by hundreds of dollars.

Check consumer guides, ask your friends, and call your state insurance office for help in steering you in the right direction. Call several insurance agents and companies direct to give you an idea of price range. It's up to you to prod them for methods to lower your costs without being underinsured.

Don't shop for price alone. Excellent service and convenience are important too. Also, check the financial ratings of the companies you are favoring. When you've narrowed the field and find that each offers the same good service, price should then determine your ultimate decision.

AN APPLE A DAY FOR YOUR CAR

Properly attended to, your car will give you good gas mileage and will live a longer repair-free life. You also have the very real satisfaction of helping to save the planet in the process.

Preventive health care for your car is pretty basic, even cost free. For example, rotating your tires every six months reduces wear and tear. Maintaining proper inflation pressure on your tires also promotes longer life as well as better fuel economy. Most gas stations offer free use of an air gauge and pump.

According to Texaco, an estimated 4.2 million gallons of gasoline could be saved in the United States per year if every car ran on properly inflated tires. You can measure your own savings by determining the number of pounds of tire pressure below recommended level on which you have been operating your car. Experts say that gas mileage decreases 1 percent for every pound below the recommended level.

Failure to replace relatively inexpensive air and fuel filters at least annually (more often if you drive on dusty gravel roads) can lead to higher gas consumption, increased emissions, and premature engine wear. Change your oil and check fluid levels every 3,000 miles or four months, whichever comes first. Professionally done, the cost is between $10 and $25, a small price to pay to keep your engine humming.

If you change your oil yourself (and why not; it's relatively easy to do), safely dispose of used oil. Most dealers, service stations, and quick-change shops are selling used oil to contractors who collect it for recycling. To find out where you can bring your used oil for recycling, call your local EPA office or write to Used Oil Coordinator, Mail Code OS 301, U.S. EPA, 401 M St., S.W., Washington, DC 20460, for the toll-free number of your nearest used-oil coordinator.

Don't overfill your gas tank or let the attendant do it to squeeze in the extra few drops to round out to the nearest whole number. The gas that invariably sloshes out may not look like very much, but it adds up. On hot days, don't fill your tank to the brim. When heated, gasoline expands much more than water and could overflow. Don't use a higher octane level than your car calls for. Why pay extra for something you don't need?

Insist on rebuilt replacement parts. They are much less expensive than new and carry similar guarantees. Don't let your repair shop talk you out of it. Their motive is purely profit. Rebuilt parts have a lower profit margin than new ones. (The one exception to using reconditioned products may be recycled automotive antifreeze, not yet widely accepted by car dealers.) Try to find an environmentally responsible repair shop that willingly recycles, offers rebuilt or used parts without being asked, and has the equipment and expertise to make a sound diagnosis.

Becoming familiar with what makes your car tick would

give you a definite edge when it begins to "tock." In the face of your apparent knowledge, your mechanic may be less likely to embellish your car's woes and pile on extras you don't need. You may find that you have a propensity for completing some of the less complicated tasks yourself, such as changing filters and spark plugs, saving a considerable amount on labor charges. The knack is as close as your public library, where you will find shelves of do-it-yourself books.

Keeping your car clean helps to prevent it from rusting and pitting. Washing your car often is particularly important if you live in an area that uses sand and salt to melt the snow. Residents in these areas jokingly allude to their cars as "Margarita mobiles" (rimmed in salt), but only the buyers and the car dealers are still laughing when the time comes to trade or sell the car.

The most basic rule of all is to avoid using your car for isolated errands. Wait until you have two or more things to do in an area before going. Even better, leave your car in the driveway and walk whenever possible. You can do your errands and get your exercise in the same trip.

Consider biking when the distance is not unrealistic for you and you can fit whatever you need in your basket. If you don't own a bike, search out church or school sales as well as flea markets for the best deals. Keep a sharp eye out for a bike that has been discarded and set out curbside for the trash. Many of these require only minor repairs for many more years of service.

THE EXORCISM

That which is possessed can be repossessed. If you have financed your car and you miss payments, your creditor has the right to take back your car without going to court or, in many states, without giving you advance warning. If you see the tread marks on your driveway (a similar danger signal to the handwriting on your wall), inform your creditor of your temporary financial constraints. Stress "temporary"!

Exude confidence that with some time (for you) and patience (by your creditor), you will be able to resume full (if you are requesting reduction) or deferred payments (if you are seeking a moratorium).

If your creditor agrees to accept late or reduced payments, the terms of your original contract may no longer apply and could save your car from repossession, at least for a while. Be sure to get the new agreement in writing so that it cannot be ignored later.

Even without a new arrangement, you are not without some rights. The creditor's right to repossess is subject to limitations on how the vehicle may be repossessed or resold to reduce or eliminate the debt. Violation of these rights could result in the creditor's having to pay you.

Although the laws of most states permit your creditor, once you are in default, to repossess your car at any hour without prior notice and to come onto your property to do so, your creditor cannot commit a "breach of peace." Using physical force or threats of force, taking your car over your protest, or removing it from a closed garage without your permission all may constitute a breach of peace depending on the laws of your state.

In the event of a breach of peace, the creditor may be required to pay a penalty to compensate you for any harm done to you or your property. The creditor may also lose the right to collect a deficiency judgment (the difference between what you owe and the price realized when reselling your car).

Don't depend on your creditor's breaching the peace to protect you from repossession, however. Most will proceed in an orderly fashion, merely trying again when your car is not locked away in your garage or when you are not around to object. Each attempt by the creditor adds to the expenses, for which you are responsible.

If you are unable to come to a new agreement with your creditor or if your mercy period runs out, you may want to consider a "voluntary repossession" to avoid additional financial obligation. Unfortunately, you are still subject to any deficiency on your loan and a notation of repossession on your credit report that could prevent you from financing the purchase of another car for a long time.

Once possessed, your car may be kept by your creditor as full compensation for your debt or be sold in a private or public sale. Either way, you must be informed. If your car is worth more than the debt you owe, you have the right to demand the sale of the car and the return of the excess funds to you.

You are even entitled to redeem or buy back the vehicle by paying the full amount owed plus the expenses connected with its repossession, such as storage and preparation for sale. Some states, including California and New York, allow you to reinstate your loan. You can reclaim your car by paying only the amount you are behind plus the creditor's repossession expenses.

For advice on how to deal with automobile creditors, contact the Federal Trade Commission at 202-326-2222.

Tony and Susan have two cars, one of which is two years old with two more years left on the loan, the other four years old, all paid off. Fearing they would lose their newer model car through inability to meet their loan payments, they decide to sell the older one to pay off (or nearly so) the newer one. They pledge to stick to a priority schedule for using the single family car and not to argue over who gets it when.

Laura's friend Janet is in a similar financial bind—no job and nearing the end of her unemployment benefits. Neither can afford to maintain their cars alone. They make an agreement that Janet sell her car to pay off Laura's loan, making them partners in the one car and sharing in all expenses such as insurance and maintenance. A mileage check each time one uses the car determines the cost of gasoline for each. They make a schedule for use that best suits each of them, allowing for flexibility should one need the car for a job interview or a medical/

dental appointment. Living in such close proximity as they do makes this arrangement even more feasible for them. To pay for her share of expenses, Laura uses some of her car time providing a transport service for people in her community at $35 per trip to and from the airport.

Regulations covering transport services vary from city to city and airport to airport and should be checked before using a private car for commercial purposes. Some cities do not require licensing for vehicles that do not pick up at specific locations such as a hotel. The airport that services that city, however, may require a ground transport permit that calls for up to $750,000 in auto liability insurance and a minimum monthly charge of $25. Others will allow a drop-off at designated areas, usually a distance from the terminals. Solicitation for passengers at the airport is generally not allowed. Anyone crossing state lines must consult with the Interstate Commerce Commission.

TO OWN OR NOT TO OWN

In the last decade, automobile leasing by consumers (as opposed to corporations) has increased enormously. Some say for very good reason: it's less costly and more maintenance free. Just the amount your new car depreciates in the first year can cover a large chunk of your rental costs for that same time period. Add to that the down payment for your new car, taxes, your monthly loan payment (interest for which is no longer tax-deductible), insurance, registration, and plates. Your monthly payment for leasing including maintenance, repairs, loaner cars when needed, and insurance may be the same or even less, but you will always be driving a fairly new car.

No equity for monthly outlay is the most common argument against leasing set forth by diehard owners. But few of us ever really own our cars. We pay off our loans monthly for at least three years (or more). At that time we merely use the car as a down payment for a new one, taking on the responsibility for a new car loan. Or we keep driving the paid-off car, which is bound to cost us big bucks for repairs and will be worth next to nothing when we ultimately get rid of it, a no-gain situation at best.

Some people, particularly those who live and work in congested cities, have given up their cars in favor of using public transportation or taxis for short local rides and leasing a car for longer trips. At the end of the year the cost of transportation, fares, and hiring a car only when needed is considerably less than owning.

If you decide to go the leasing route, choose your leasing company wisely. Independent companies tend to offer a wider range of services and types of cars than dealer-affiliated offices. Many companies offer discounts on rentals if you take additional services such as repairs and insurance. As with anything else, shop around until you get the best deal from a reputable company that will stand behind its claims.

NOT OWN A CAR? NOT IN THIS LIFETIME!

For some, not owning a car is analogous to paralysis. However, buying a new car today is a major investment, second only to buying a house. According to the National Association of Automobile Dealers, a new car now costs nearly one-half the annual earnings for a median-income family as opposed to seventeen weeks' earnings in 1973, and the price is still rising.

Used cars, therefore, are becoming a more affordable option; and given the growing demand, the industry is becoming more scrupulous about repairing and servicing older cars before offering them for sale. More high-quality cars are showing up on used-car lots. Nearly new cars sold by car rental companies are a particularly good buy. With only 15,000 to 25,000 miles on the odometer, these cars are selling for 25 to 35 percent less than new cars. Some banks and credit unions are forming associations with car rental agencies to offer a package deal of a discounted car and a loan that will be processed in twenty-four to forty-eight hours.

Applying the principle of caveat emptor (let the buyer beware) is still critical when buying a used car, but there are more legal protections today than ever. The Federal Trade Commission's Used Car Rule requires that dealers post a buyer's guide on each car disclosing any known information about the car's condition and any guarantees offered, and the rule is being enforced. Don't buy from any dealer that doesn't post a buyer's guide, and report violators to the FTC, Public Reference Branch, 6th and Pennsylvania Ave., N.W., Washington, DC 20580.

Rolling back the odometer to raise the value of the car is a crime but is still widely done. In all states except California, Ohio, and Nevada, the law requires that odometer readings be written on the title when the car changes hands. More and more states are requiring dealers to disclose whether a car has been rebuilt after extensive damage resulting from an accident. Even so, this information is not always forthcoming from the dealer.

"As is" sales are still allowed in most states, but you may nevertheless have some protection if the car doesn't run. Some states have used-car "lemon laws" that cover this. At least eleven states limit or prohibit "as is" sales. Contact your local consumer protection office for information on the limits of your protection under the law in your state.

GOING PUBLIC

Add the P-word to your vocabulary of methods for getting around. Public transportation offers a low-cost alternative to using your car and helps the environment in the process. Most buses and commuter trains offer reduced-cost monthly passes for frequent users. Also check with your employment office for the availability of free transport or vouchers for job interviews; with medical facilities for a like service; with shopping malls for free shopping shuttles.

Community centers and senior centers often offer free transport to and from the activities they are sponsoring. Check with your police and fire departments for the availability of transportation in case of emergency. This information is particularly critical if you have no access to a car at all. Forewarned is forearmed!

In most cities and towns senior citizens and the physically impaired are given special discounts on local and intercity transportation, including some cab companies. The age at which you qualify as a senior citizen could differ from service to service—as young as 55 or not until 65. City agencies and privately funded groups also offer free transportation to those in need for medical appointments and shopping.

Check with your local and intercity carriers for all discount programs offered. If you are a frequent user of a toll road, bridge, or tunnel, call your state highway authority for the availability of frequent-user rates, generally in the form of a monthly coupon book or an annual sticker. Senior citizens should check with their local council on aging (be ready to provide documentation of age and, in some cases, residency), while the handicapped should call their city's special needs office (a form signed by a physician verifying condition will probably be required).

EVERYONE INTO THE POOL

If a car is the only way you can get to where you have to go, look into ride sharing. Canvass your neighborhood, friends, and family to determine who goes where, when. Pin up notices on community bulletin boards usually found in supermarkets, shopping malls, schools, churches, and synagogues. You may find that someone down the street is driving her son or daughter daily to the same Little League practice or music lesson, or that another neighbor does food shopping and errands on the same day you do at the same places. Dividing the driving responsibilities between the two families (or more when possible) saves both money and time, wear and tear on both you and the car and, of course, the atmosphere.

Carpooling information is generally available through your community's commuter information services. Most offer a "matching network" and ride sources for cost-effective transportation options in your area. The information provided by these services will include names and telephone numbers of other commuters with whom you can set up your own car pool or start a van pool. Van pools consist of twelve to fifteen commuters sharing the same trip. In some areas you can drive the van and commute free. Contact your state's department of public works or transportation, highway division, for information on available services in your area.

Anne has returned to work and requires the use of the family's only car every workday because she was unable to set up a car pool. None of her coworkers live close enough to her to make a car pool cost-effective or feasible. That leaves Richard without a car to get to job interviews or to do the myriad errands required in his role as "Mr. Mom." He makes an arrangement with a woman in his neighborhood who owns a car but is afraid to drive because of failing eyesight. He chauffeurs her anywhere she wants to go on Thursdays in exchange for the use of her car on Tuesdays, another good example of a MAP (mutual assistance program).

I'LL FLY TOMORROW

Being unemployed may have temporarily clipped your wings, but at times you or members of your family may need to get to a distant city or state quickly. Last-minute airline fares, however, are exorbitant.

In emergency situations such as a death in the family or

serious illness, some airlines will give discounts if you provide documentation such as a copy of the death certificate or a letter from the attending physician. You will need to call each of the airlines that service the area to which you will have to go. You will discover that one will be generous, while another will be totally indifferent to your plight. If you can afford the extra travel time, check train services or car delivery services that pay for your ticket home and other expenses for driving the car to its destination. See "Car Transport Services" in your Yellow Pages.

With the advent of nonrefundable tickets came a new listing in newspaper classified sections. This column lists an array of destinations that ticket holders whose plans have changed are offering at reduced cost in an attempt to recoup some of their losses. Airlines will reimburse or change reservations for these nonrefundables only in cases of documented serious illness or death, and refunds can be delayed for a month or two pending application and review by the home office.

Private airports may present opportunities for low-cost or even free rides with private pilots who may take you on just for the company in transit. You may also be able to barter services for transport. Look deep into your talents and expertise to determine what you can offer in exchange. Also check air courier services (see chapter 16, "Is the Party Over?").

THAT'S THE TICKET

You may have been feeling that your ticket to ride has been punched and invalidated. Now (hopefully) you know that all you need is a new ticket that comes almost automatically with a new attitude and approach.

SCHOOL MAZE:
Covering School Expenses

Even during hard times, parents must recognize that school
activities and day-care programs are very important and
need not fall victim to reduced income. Structured activities
build self-esteem and develop social skills. Keeping children
in the same routine also helps to minimize stress within the
family.

Parents should consider the consequences of removing
their children from after-school and day-care programs—
hours in front of the television, talking on the phone, nap-
ping, and playing Nintendo. Finding a way to continue to
provide what may seem a luxury is, in fact, a necessity.

> Now that neither Susan nor Tony is working, they can
> no longer afford tuition for the preschool that their older
> child, Nick (4½), has been attending for the past year. Yet
> they are very concerned about the effect withdrawing him
> from the program will have on him.
> - Since the birth of Nick's sister, Natalie (2½), who suffers
> from severe epileptic seizures, Susan has been forced to
> divert more than a fair share of her attention from Nick.
> Tony's preoccupation with finding a new job has also
> deprived Nick of much of the togetherness he has come
> to expect from his father. The school, therefore, filled in

some of the gaps and gave Nick companionship and an outlet for his energies. Susan, too, welcomed the time to concentrate on Natalie without feeling guilty.

As difficult as it is for them to ask for help, Susan and Tony decide that Nick's welfare is much more important than their pride. They speak frankly with the director of the preschool, who informs Susan and Tony that there are subsidies and sliding-scale tuitions available to those in financial distress. It will still be a stretch, but Nick can stay in school for now, hopefully until he enters public school in eight months.

DAY-CARE AND PRESCHOOL PROGRAMS

Private day-care and preschool centers often have access to government funds for parents undergoing financial hardship. As Susan discovered, other centers have a sliding-fee tuition based on ability to pay. Conversations with the program director should be followed by a letter. School or daycare administrators may need written notification to secure funds from government sources, or they may simply wish to retain records for their files. A letter should contain:

- Explanation of change in income
- Significance of maintaining the service for your child
- Request for alternative arrangements for payment
- Inquiry about documentation required for assistance

See the sample letter on page 81.

When day care was provided by the employer, unemployment can strike the family doubly hard. The answer here may be to barter child-care time with other people from the company who also lost their jobs. This allows the children to continue to see one another during this period of readjustment, while giving the parents time to attend to their job search.

Some families may have no alternative but to withdraw the

LETTER TO DAY CARE OR PRESCHOOL

(Date)

(Name of contact person)
(Title)
(Name of school or Day care)
(Street address)
(City, state, ZIP code)

Dear (contact person):

• describe
situation

My son, Nick, is currently enrolled in your preschool program. My husband has lost his job, however, and the income loss leaves us unable to continue paying current tuition rates at this time.

• outline
significance
of keeping
service

The structured activities and social interaction provided by your daily program are vital to Nick. Because of the constant supervision required by our daughter, who has severe epilepsy, Nick does not receive the attention he deserves. Therefore, you can understand that withdrawing him from the preschool would have a devastating effect on him.

• request
payment
alternatives

My husband and I are hoping that we can discuss with you a more affordable method of meeting our payments. We would be grateful if you will meet with us to examine alternatives.

• inquire about
necessary
documentation

I will call you on Monday to set up a convenient time for our meeting and to inquire what documentation you will need from us to expedite a solution.

Sincerely,

(Your name)
(Your address)
(Your city, state, ZIP code)
(Your telephone number)

child from day-care programs. There are, however, other low-cost options. Many churches sponsor "mother's day out" programs. Check with libraries, community recreation centers, and Y's for children's activities and play groups. Or create your own program. Contact other people in the neigh-

borhood who have children near the age of your own. Plan
structured activities similar to those in preschool programs.
At the library, parents can find enough inexpensive craft,
music, game, and snack ideas to keep kids happy and busy
until they are ready to enter public school.

READING, 'RITING, AND 'RESTLING THE BUDGET

Unfortunately, public school is not necessarily synonymous
with no cost. There are still expenses for lunches, some student supplies not provided by the school, and extracurricular
activities such as music lessons, band and cheerleader uni-
forms, sports, plays, and excursions. All of these activities
are as critical to a child's education as the classroom work
and should not be curtailed because of the parent's inability
to pay.

Most schools have provisions, commonly known as booster
funds, to assist needy students. First contact the office of your
superintendent of schools to check on what programs are
available on a districtwide basis. The principal's office or the
office of human resources in your child's school should have
information on individual funds set up through PTO efforts
or other fund-raising activities by the music and athletic departments. See the sample letter on page 83.

PUTTING ON THE FEDERAL FEED

An astounding number of people are turning to the federal
government to make sure their kids get a proper lunch. Gov-
ernment-subsidized lunches are not a new concept, however.
Many students in large cities have been taking advantage of
this program for years. For example, in San Francisco 90
percent of the meals served are either free or sold at reduced
prices.

The rise in the number of unemployed has now resulted
in a massive jump in applications in affluent suburban com-

LETTER TO SCHOOL

(Date)

(Name of contact person)
(Title)
(Name of school)
(Street address)
(City, state, ZIP code)

Dear (contact person):

- describe situation

My son, Matthew, is a sophomore at your school. Recently my business folded, leaving my family without a reliable source of income.

- request notification of any new problems at school

I am aware that the circumstances in our household may have an effect on Matthew at school. I would be grateful, therefore, if you would keep me apprised of any signals from Matthew that may require my special attention.

- outline child's school activities and request assistance if needed

Matthew participates in athletics and the music program. These activities have provided him with outlets for his energy and creative talents and are even more critical to him now. Fees for extracurricular activities and field trips present a financial hardship at this time. Does the school have provisions to waive fees or defer payments until I am reemployed?

- inquire about necessary documentation

I will call you on Monday for an appointment to discuss the situation, options for assistance, and required documentation.

Sincerely,

(Your name)
(Your address)
(Your city, state, ZIP code)
(Your telephone number)

munities. In Santa Clara, California, there has been a 21 percent increase; in Fairfax County, Virginia, a 35 percent jump; and in Evanston, Illinois, a 16 percent rise. Nationwide in 1991, the number getting free or subsidized lunches was up by 12 percent.

Only one-third of the schools that qualify are taking advantage of federally subsidized breakfast programs because of "administrative hassles" and reluctance to rearrange school bus and morning monitor schedules. Only parent pressure may get them to change policy.

The U.S. Department of Agriculture oversees the school lunch program. For information on who qualifies for free or reduced-cost meals (some schools do serve breakfast as well as lunch), contact the Bureau of Nutrition, listed in the telephone book under "Federal Government."

Joseph's youngest child, Timothy, is in his first year of college. The college fund that Joseph and his wife, Barbara, began amassing some twenty years prior has been depleted by the education of their three older children. Too late they realized that the money they set aside so scrupulously over two decades could not begin to cover the enormous rise in tuitions by the time their children were ready for college. Yet as long as Joseph was working, they managed to augment the fund from current earnings and see their kids through graduation. They never even considered seeking loans or grants, believing that as an upper middle–income couple, they would not qualify.

Without a job or a college fund, Joseph is filled with fear and guilt that he can't do the same for Timothy as he did for his other children. Although Timothy's first semester was paid for before Joseph became unemployed, the payment for the second will be due in three months. Determined to keep Timothy in school, Joseph and Barbara plunge into an investigation into how and where to obtain financial assistance.

DOLLARS FOR SCHOLARS

Every year thousands of college students are funded through scholarships, grants, and other aid from private sources. Though a scholarship search takes an enormous amount of time and effort, it's worthwhile since this type of financing is the best—there is no obligation for repayment as with loans. Give yourself as much time as possible and use every reference source available to you:

1. Ask your family and friends. They may be able to tell you about employers, community groups, unions, local businesses, alumni organizations, and churches that offer scholarships.
2. Check with high school guidance counselors, your state department of education, the federal Department of Education (Inspector General's office: 1-800-MIS-USED). Request a free booklet titled *The Student Guide* from the Federal Student Aid Information Center (1-800-4-FED-AID). Updated each year, the guide lists available student loans and other funds from the federal government. Check college financial aid offices or other educational agencies such as educational opportunity centers or higher education information centers, often part of the local library system. Be sure to ask about National Honor Society and National Merit scholarships.

    Note: When contacting your state agency, ask about the Robert C. Byrd Honors Scholarship Program (for students who have demonstrated outstanding academic achievement) or about the Paul Douglas Teacher Scholarship Program (for students interested in pursuing a teaching career and willing to make a commitment to teach two years for each year of scholarship assistance received). When contacting the Federal Student Aid Information Center (P.O. Box 84, Washington, DC 20044), get information on the Pell Grant program and the Supplemental Educational Opportunity Grant (SEOG). Undergraduates with exceptional need may qualify for both (Pell Grant recipients are given priority for SEOG), which could add up to around $6,500 a year.
3. Contact your community organizations and civic groups such as the chamber of commerce, the American Legion,

the YMCA, 4-H Clubs, Kiwanis, Jaycees, and the Girl Scouts and Boy Scouts.

4. Check with private organizations such as veterans', women's, and minority groups; religious organizations; and the fraternity or sorority of which you were a member. These fraternal organizations often have scholarship funds for "legacies," children of former members.

5. Investigate organizations connected with the student's field of interest such as the American Medical Association or the American Bar Association.

6. Enlist the aid of a reference librarian to help search out the obscure scholarships for which few apply because few know about them. Some were established years ago for specific careers. In Boston a fund has been established to assist all children of taxi drivers. Throughout the country, funds have been established to assist students majoring in specific fields, for athletes, for sons and daughters of club or union members, or for those from certain geographic areas or states. Other little-known scholarships are available for lineal descendants of Confederate soldiers or signers of the Declaration of Independence, for students with surnames of Gatlin or Gatling, for Yale-bound students with the surnames of Defores or Leavenworth. If drama is your chosen field of study and you will be attending a college in San Diego County, you may qualify for the Laurel and Hardy Sons of the Desert Scholarship Fund.

7. Computerized scholarship searches are available for a fee. Scholarship information can be accumulated without cost, but the task is very labor intensive. Be sure to note the deadlines (May 1 for a Pell Grant, with no extension) and requirements for each scholarship. Requests for additional information should be clear, concise, and neat.

One very good, very reasonably priced scholarship search service is College Resource Materials of San Antonio, Texas

(1-800-545-8616 or 512-614-5919). Owner Cynthia Ruiz McKee developed her business out of a need to find tuition money for her son, who ultimately went to Yale on full scholarship. A generic package with forms, calendars, sample letter applications, and an overall list of available scholarships can be purchased for $29.95. For $99.95 you can get a more comprehensive package tailored to the student's specific area of study. Students also get tips on how to fill out forms and applications, receive updates on new scholarships as they become available, and can continue to confer with the service until their education is completed.

According to McKee, older students have almost as much opportunity for scholarship assistance as those out of high school. Also, students from middle-income families can qualify nearly as often as those with low income.

Ideally, advises McKee, begin your search as early as seventh grade. The money is out there waiting to be found. For example, one determined Washington, D.C., high school senior applied for fifty to fifty-five scholarships and got seven totaling $29,000, more than enough to pay her first year's tuition at Princeton (around $22,000 for 1991–1992). Another young lady from Pennsylvania had to come up with only $433.50 toward her first year at Lafayette College as a resident student (total cost: $20,375 for the year 1991–1992) thanks to almost $20,000 in scholarship grants.

Students who have not achieved high academic records should not be discouraged from searching out scholarships and grants. Many are awarded for a particular talent, ethnicity, religious affiliation, or even place of residence. *Dollars for Scholars: Barron's Complete College Financing Guide*, by Marguerite Dennis (Barron's, 1989), is an excellent sourcebook.

FREE THINKERS

If your prospective college student meets the entrance requirements to Cooper Union in Manhattan, you won't have to worry about tuition—Cooper Union is tuition free. It is also among the most selective institutions in the country.

Berea College and Alice Lloyd College (both in Kentucky) charge minimal fees for Kentucky residents. Tuition and fees are only $177 at Berea and $270 at Alice Lloyd. Also, students must work at least fifteen hours a week, starting with jobs such as raking leaves or running the power plant. Upperclassmen get the more cushy jobs of working for the school newspaper or assisting in the academic departments. Contact the admissions office of each school for more information on entrance requirements.

HI HO, HI HO

Many students attend college through cooperative or work-study programs. The College Work-Study Program, administered through the U.S. Department of Education, provides jobs for undergraduate and graduate students to help pay educational expenses. The job usually involves work that is in the public interest. Employers are generally private or public nonprofit organizations or a local state or federal agency. Some schools, however, provide on-campus jobs or make agreements with private-sector employers as well. The school the student attends arranges the job and assigns the work hours on the basis of the student's class schedule, health, and academic progress.

A cooperative education program allows the student to alternate work assignments with college studies over the course of the collegiate program. In better economic times a cooperative program not only helped to pay the bills but also gave the student the additional benefit of testing career interests in jobs related to a chosen field of study. Now most cooperative students will take any job they can find during the classroom hiatus. Cooperative school job coordinators are having a much more difficult time signing up employers to participate, but many organizations such as AT&T, Digital, Eastman Kodak, Ford, GTE, and Automatic Data Processing

(ADP) are still committed to the program. Thus a cooperative school is still a viable alternative for funding a college education while getting on-the-job training.

ROMANCING THE LOAN

Financial aid is also available in the form of low-interest loans. These generally need not be repaid until after graduation, on the theory that the student will then have a job and will be able to afford to make the payments. The federal government administers the Perkins Loan Program (formerly the National Direct Student Loan Program), which allots up to $9,000 per student in bachelor degree programs (greater amounts for juniors and seniors) and up to $18,000 for graduate or professional study, at 5 percent interest.

Students may be allowed up to ten years to repay. Monthly payments on $4,500, for example, will be $47.73 for 120 months; the total repaid will be $5,727.60. In specified circumstances repayment of a Perkins loan is canceled, such as in the case of death, permanent disability, or if the borrower volunteers for Head Start, VISTA, or the Peace Corps.

A Stafford Loan is for a student attending school at least half time. The interest rate on this loan is generally 8 percent for the first four years of repayment and 10 percent after that. Undergraduates may qualify for up to $4,000 a year, graduate students for up to $7,500 a year.

Other education loans available are:

- Supplemental Loan for Students—for independent undergraduate or graduate students or dependent undergraduates whose parents are ineligible
- PLUS Loan—for parents of dependent undergraduate or graduate students
- TERI Supplemental Loan and Professional Education Plan (PEP) for students or parents
- Family Education Loan/Graduate Education Loan—bor-

rower can be parent, legal guardian, or spouse with student as cosigner
- Security Education Loan—borrower can be student, parent, or anyone willing to make a savings deposit to be held until loan is repaid
- SHARE and GradSHARE—borrower can be undergraduate or graduate student, parent, spouse, or other responsible person
- EXCEL—borrower can be undergraduate or graduate student, parent, spouse, or other responsible person

Information on these loans may be obtained through your state's higher education information center or through the department of education (state and/or federal), any or all of which provide, free of charge, printed booklets and brochures outlining requirements, qualifications, and how to apply.

In a decade when the cost for one year's education has as many digits as a long-distance telephone number, private colleges and universities are beginning to show some initiative to help families ease the burden caused by astronomical tuitions and depleting incomes. The University of Pennsylvania, an Ivy League school, is now exhorting students not to be put off by its annual cost (some $22,000 for tuition, room, and board). The university is offering $25 million a year in a variety of programs, including lines of credit and guaranteed four-year tuition, to be repaid in monthly installments after the student graduates. The University of California set aside 20 percent of its 40 percent increase in fees to assist needy students.

YOU'VE GOT THE POWER

With all the options and alternatives available, students bent on higher education but with limited or no funds can realize their goals if they are willing to roll up their sleeves and not take no for an answer.

WHEN AN APPLE A DAY ISN'T ENOUGH:
Meeting Medical Expenses

I f your health insurance went the way of your job, the first option for continued coverage that you should investigate is the Consolidated Omnibus Budget Reconciliation Act of 1985 (COBRA). If you qualify, this could buy you a minimum of eighteen months' coverage under your former employer's plan while allowing you sufficient time to shop around for a new one. Finding a new plan that fills your needs without making you sick over the premiums may take longer than finding a new job.

PUTTING THE BITE
BACK INTO YOUR COVERAGE

COBRA entitles you and your dependents to continued coverage for at least eighteen months under your former employer's plan (including a self-insurance plan) *if* you worked for a business with twenty or more employees, were not employed by a church organization, are not covered by Medicare or another medical insurance plan, or did not work for a federal agency. (A recently enacted law provides a similar contingency for federal employees. Contact the personnel officer of the federal agency or department where you were employed or the Office of Personnel Management, 1900 E St., N.W., Washington, DC 20415, tel. 202-606-0500.) You get an additional eleven months of coverage (a total of twenty-nine) if you are disabled and were eligible for Social Security disability when your employment was ended. COBRA also provides for coverage of up to thirty-six months if you were insured through your spouse's plan at work and he/she dies or becomes eligible for Medicare, or if you become separated or divorced.

Although COBRA is probably one of the least expensive ways for you to be protected, it's still not cheap. You are required to pay 102 percent of your group insurance premium. That is the portion that your employer had been paying that you must now assume, the portion you were already contributing, plus 2 percent for administrative costs. Loss of coverage through COBRA results if you don't pay the premiums, if you become eligible for Medicare, or if your former employer discontinues the health insurance plan.

Joining another plan could also exclude you from COBRA. The exception is if you have an existing medical condition for which your new plan imposes a waiting period. In that case you may keep your COBRA benefits until they run out. Hopefully, by that time your coverage on the new plan will kick in.

Since COBRA is considered an administrative hassle by some employers, they have been known to offer departing employees a "simple" alternative. *Simple* is the key word here: the insurance covers only injuries suffered in an accident. The lure of a greatly reduced rate—a few hundred dollars a year as compared to a few thousand for COBRA—is hard to resist. This is a classic case of "carrot dangling" for the "scared rabbit," however, and is not recommended unless you are very young and more likely to be a victim of accident than an extended illness.

If you do not qualify for COBRA, you may have an option for extending your coverage under state regulations. More than two-thirds of the states have comprehensive continuation laws that provide for extension of your coverage—as little as three months in some states, as much as eighteen in others. Many of those that don't are examining the possibility, given the spiraling unemployment rate, and may well be initiating some assistance as we write. If you were in a self-insured plan, you may be out of luck no matter what state you live in. Unlike COBRA, states usually exempt those who were in a self-insured plan.

Although COBRA is a convenient way to keep coverage while you shop for another policy, some insurance professionals warn you not to become too complacent with it. They advise getting into a new plan as soon as possible, pointing out that any serious illness that develops during COBRA coverage could jeopardize your chances for qualifying for a new plan.

IF COBRA RECOILS

If you are not eligible for COBRA or if it runs out, a conversion policy is an option, especially for those who have an existing medical condition. Around forty states have a law that requires employers who normally offer conversion policies to departing employees to extend that option to former employees whose COBRA benefits have run out. In most states you are allowed only thirty-one days to sign up for a conversion policy once your COBRA benefits run out.

The drawback to conversion coverage is that it is almost always inferior to your group plan and often more expensive. Where you once had major medical coverage, you may qualify only for hospital-surgical benefits that may not cover the cost of a tonsillectomy.

A conversion from your former company's group plan to your own is just about the only arrangement whereby you can't be rejected if you have health problems. Insurers must make these policies available to anyone regardless of their health.

In some states (around two-thirds) insurers are required to offer conversion options to people losing coverage as a result of termination of the group plan by the insurance company. Several states, however, do not require these options for members whose HMO has gone out of business. It is up to you to make the inquiries, but knowing what you are looking for and what questions to ask will make the task a little easier.

If only one member of your family suffers from a chronic medical condition, consider taking the conversion policy for that member and shopping around for less expensive, more comprehensive coverage for you and/or the rest of the family. Or look into a high-risk pool for the family member with the problem. High-risk pools are for those whom insurers have rejected. Originated in the 1970s as the industry answer to national health insurance, high-risk pools are available in fewer than half the states. Rules vary from state to state as well. In some, you can't get pool coverage if you are eligible for a conversion policy upon leaving a group plan.

Premiums for pool policies are high, of course, since the nature of the coverage is indicative of the certainty that almost every policyholder will file claims, probably more than once. Furthermore, this type of coverage is available to only a small percentage of those who really need it.

The research and development company that Joseph worked for employed fewer than twenty people; thus he does not qualify for COBRA. Neither does the state in which he lives provide for a conversion policy. Too young for Medicare but at an age when they can expect the unexpected, Joseph (55) and Barbara (52) believe the lack of any coverage is too much of a gamble. Yet they need time to shop around for a way to get in on a plan that will give them adequate protection at a cost they can manage. Joseph knows all too well that advancing age is a definite deterrent to obtaining any insurance, let alone an affordable policy.

Aware of their dilemma, a friend informs Joseph and Barbara that some insurers offer short-term policies for people between jobs, particularly to those with no existing serious medical problems. He suggests the Milwaukee-based Time Insurance Company (414-271-3011, ext. 8335), which offers a ninety-day policy for around $100, as well as Metropolitan Life, through its associated firm Celtic Life (212-578-2211), which also offers short-term policies.

YOUR STATE OF HEALTH

Some states offer health security plans that provide medical security for families receiving unemployment benefits whose income falls below certain limits. Those limits vary from state to state. For example, in Massachusetts, if you qualify for the state continuation plan, you can maintain the individual or nongroup plan you had while employed and receive partial reimbursement for the premiums that you pay.

Reimbursement is based on your family's size and income during the twelve months prior to application. To be reimbursed for any calendar month, you must have received unemployment benefits for at least two weeks of that month and provide proof of premium payment. Your total family income for the fifty-two weeks prior to the date you file your claim for unemployment benefits must not have exceeded $19,860 for one, $26,640 for two, and going up in increments of $6,780 for each additional member of the family.

Massachusetts' Direct Coverage Plan is designed for those who have no current health plan or who choose not to continue their previous coverage. It ensures medical care only while one is collecting unemployment. There are no monthly premiums. Copayments and deductibles depend on the type of care received. Patients may choose their own physicians and medical facilities. There are no restrictions on preexisting conditions.

Check with your unemployment office for the availability

of similar plans in your state. Once again, if you don't ask, you may not get.

THE GOLDEN YEARS

Medicare is available for people over 65. A federally administered health insurance program for the elderly, Medicare is divided into two parts—Part A (hospital insurance) and Part B (medical insurance for physician and surgeon charges in and out of the hospital). If you have sufficient credits for work under Social Security, you are eligible for Medicare Part A when you reach 65, whether or not you are retired.

Medicare Part B is optional medical insurance for which a monthly premium must be paid. Like Part A, enrollment in Part B is automatic for persons receiving Social Security or Railroad Retirement checks. Unless you inform your Social Security Office that you do not wish to purchase Part B coverage, you will automatically be enrolled upon reaching age 65. The monthly premium for Part B will be deducted from your Social Security check. It is to your advantage to sign up for Part B coverage, since much of the cost is financed by the federal government.

Medicare supplement (Medigap) insurance policies pay for a higher proportion of services and expenses that are not completely covered by Medicare. A Medigap policy may be purchased on an individual basis or through group plans such as those available through a religious, aging, or fraternal organization.

Examine any policies carefully to be sure that the features most important to you are included. Also, make sure you are not overinsured. Beware of duplicating or overlapping coverage. Contact the American Association of Retired Persons, at 1-800-523-5800, or your state's commission on insurance or aging for free assistance in analyzing appropriate coverage. Write to Consumer Information Center, P. O. Box 100, Pueblo, CO 81002, to request the current pamphlet by the Health Care Financing Administration on Medicare coverage for more information.

LET YOUR FINGERS DO THE WALKING

Shopping for a new health plan can be a nightmare. Begin by becoming an informed consumer as recommended in chapter 10, "Obscene Phone Calls." The difference here is that you do not exercise the same power. Health insurance carriers have the last word, and that could well be "No" if you or anyone in your family has a preexisting health condition. Start with "A" in the Yellow Pages and keep calling until you find an insurer that will accept you with a policy that is acceptable to you; in short, a policy that provides you with the coverage you seek at the lowest cost available.

As you shop, knowing what you are up against will help. Become acquainted with the three basic kinds of health insurance coverage:

- Major medical—the most comprehensive, covers physician services in and out of the hospital and stays in the hospital.
- Hospital-surgical policies—covers surgical procedures and hospital services only.
- Hospital-indemnity and dread-disease policies—offers very limited benefits and is rated by *Consumer Reports* to be the worst buy in health insurance.

Two pamphlets particularly helpful when shopping for a new health plan are: *Buyer's Guide to Insurance*, published by the National Insurance Consumers Organization (NICO), 121 Payne St., Alexandria, VA 22314, tel. 703-549-8050; send $3 plus a stamped, self-addressed envelope, and *A Consumer Guide to Health Maintenance Organizations*, from National Consumers League, 815 15th St., N.W., Suite 928, Washington,

DC 20005, tel. 202-639-8140; send $2 (members) or $4 (non-members).

A software program is also available for evaluating health insurance: MedSure v1.12 ($90) from Time Solutions, 203-459-0303 or 1-800-552-3302. System requirements: 512K IBM compatible, one drive, mouse optional, DOS 2.1.

Another good idea is to check ratings provided by Standard & Poor's Corp., 212-208-8000; National Association of Insurance Commissioners, 816-842-3600; A.M. Best Co., 908-439-2200; and Moody's Investment Service, 212-553-0300. Your local library should have these listings. Also contact your state's insurance commission for more information.

Check out policies offered by professional/artisan associations of which you may already be a member or are qualified to join. There's a group for almost every profession and trade. The membership fee, though outwardly steep, may more than justify the savings you will realize from qualification for a group plan. Contact Group Health Association of America, a trade group for HMOs, at 1129 20th St., N.W., Suite 600, Washington, DC 20036, tel. 202-778-3200. Religious and fraternal organizations may also offer group plans.

Be wary of trade associations that market to the self-employed. (If you are consulting in any way, from auditing a company's books to baking pies in your kitchen to sell, you qualify for this designation.) The National Insurance Consumers Organization (NICO) advises being careful of these groups, which may offer inferior products and may represent unstable insurance companies.

You may find buying through an insurance agent who represents more than one company much less of a hassle and a time-saver. He or she is intimately acquainted with all the possibilities available to you and can spot flaws in policies that you may miss. Be sure to investigate the reputation of the agent you ultimately use, to satisfy yourself that he or she will not recommend a policy on the basis of the highest commission earned. To be absolutely certain, you may want to deal with a fee-only broker who charges you a set fee rather than rolling your costs into a commission.

LET THE BUYER BEWARE

Many families who are fairly young and all healthy are opting for high deductibles to save on premiums and are investing the difference in hopes of covering the unexpected. By opting for a $10,000 deductible instead of $1,000 you can cut your premium by up to $2,000 or more per year. Invested in a mutual fund that could yield around 8 percent to 10 percent in the current market, the savings would probably achieve a break-even figure in three years if catastrophe doesn't strike. The cost for the higher premium could be justified only if the family experiences around $4,000 a year in medical expenses. Many who are young and healthy feel this route is an acceptable risk.

A relatively young and healthy family without special allegiance to a particular doctor may also be the ideal candidate for a health maintenance organization (HMO). HMOs focus on preventive medical care covered in full (or with a $3 to $10 copayment), such as regular checkups, which are not covered by the "Blues," Blue Cross/Blue Shield. Enrollment costs may be as high as other insurance plans, but you would be fully covered for everything from the flu to catastrophic illness.

Of course, as in almost every aspect of our lives, Murphy's Law has a way of rearing its ugly head. Advantages are almost always accompanied by drawbacks. You may be trading savings for impersonal, inferior care; long waits in clinics or for appointments; or no guarantee of seeing the physician of your choice.

If you decide to go with an HMO, inquire of friends, family, and colleagues about their experiences with their plans. Visit HMO clinics in your area and sit in the waiting room to get a sense of how they operate. Rate the cleanliness, efficiency, and level of caring. Find out how many of the staff physicians are board certified for their specialties by an American Medical Association-approved medical specialty board. Make sure that the HMO you ultimately choose on the basis of your investigation accepts members from your geographic area and offers hours commensurate with your schedule.

GOING IT ALONE

When pressed, insurance professionals will concede there are some situations where health insurance is not worth the investment. The NICO *Buyer's Guide to Insurance* advises: "If you can't afford good health insurance, you may be better off not buying any policy and putting the money in the bank." This situation occurs when you have preexisting conditions that disqualify you from a good plan, and if all you can afford is a bare-bones policy that covers hardly anything.

Some schools of thought hold that if you are young, not a property owner, and money is tight, health insurance should not take precedence over putting food on the table or keeping a roof over your head. After all, if you have very little to lose except your credit record, and that is already tottering on the brink of disaster, a massive tab resulting from a long hospital stay could be wiped out by declaring bankruptcy.

SELF-HELP

Free pamphlets that can be of assistance when shopping for a health care plan are *Consumer's Guide to Health Insurance, Consumer's Guide to Disability Insurance*, and *Consumer's Guide to Long-Term Care Insurance*. Write to Health Association of America, P.O. Box 41455, Washington, DC 20018, or call 202-223-7780.

To check the rating of an insurance company before you buy a policy, consult the *Best's Agents Guides*, published by A. M. Best Company, usually available in the reference section of your local library. *Moody's Financial Guide*, also in the reference section, reports on the current financial standing of the company. Further information on insurance agents or companies, such as licensing and present standing, is available through your state insurance commissioner's office. Check the state listings in your phone directory under "Insurance."

BIG BROTHER, CAN YOU SPARE A HAND?

The federal and state governments provide various health programs for the indigent. Medicaid provides comprehensive health benefits for individuals and families, including pregnant women and young children, who meet certain income, age, and/or disability requirements.

Most states offer prenatal services to pregnant women within certain income categories. Information and referral services to assist pregnant women in finding affordable prenatal care are available to anyone.

Help is generally available as well for disabled working adults and disabled children meeting SSI disability requirements. Premiums for coverage depend on family income.

Many states also offer neighborhood health centers that provide primary and preventive health care services. Fees depend on family income, and arrangements for partial, deferred payments may be made.

Free hospital care may be obtained through the federal Hill-Burton program. In exchange for money for construction and modernization from the federal government, hospitals and health facilities agree to provide a reasonable volume of services to persons unable to pay and make their services available to all persons residing in the facilities area. The Department of Health and Human Services (HHS) is responsible for the administration of this program.

Hill-Burton facilities may apply different eligibility standards. At some, you may need to fall within the poverty income guidelines published annually by the HHS. At others you may be allowed free service with income up to double the poverty income guidelines. Each facility can choose which types of services to provide free or at reduced cost. Each must provide a specific amount of free care each year and may cease free service once the agreed amount has been fulfilled.

You can determine if a facility is part of the Hill-Burton program by the sign that must be prominently displayed in the admissions office, business office, and emergency room.

For more information, call your regional department of
health and human services office or the national hot line at
1-800-638-0742. (Maryland residents, call 1-800-492-0359.)

Your state's department of health may provide free immu-
nization shots for preschool children as well as flu shots for
adults or base the fees on a sliding scale. Other services that
may be available are well-baby clinics for physical checkups
and screenings for cholesterol, lead poisoning, and blood
pressure.

Public health nurses may make free visits to the homebound; also check with your visiting nurses association. Most
charge a minimal fee of $10 to $15 for home visits and may
provide other services free. Check under your state's or city's
listing for the phone numbers of the department of health
and the visiting nurses association.

Many private physicians have sliding-fee scales for immuni-
zation and flu shots, charging only for the cost of the vaccina-
tion and not for the office visit. The doctor, however, does
not generally advertise this reduced cost, so you must make
inquiries in advance. Your state's medical association can usually provide you with a list of physicians for your area.

The four-legged members of your family may also qualify
for free or low-cost preventive health care. Many communities
sponsor twice-yearly clinics for administering rabies shots and
other inoculations. Check with your local animal officer for
places and dates.

Free or low-cost dental care is more difficult to find. Some
Hill-Burton facilities also offer this service. Neither free nor
cheap, dental schools are still much less expensive than private dentists. Preventive medicine is the best course for anyone, rich or poor. Brush often, floss, massage gums, and avoid
foods that yank out fillings and cause cavities.

Older people may avoid or delay entering a long-term care
facility by using free or low-cost community-based services. A
variety of agencies provide assistance for maintaining independence. Help is also available for families trying to cope
with the emotional and financial stress often associated with
caring for an aging parent.

Now that Joseph has had to accept early retirement, his ability to provide financial support for his aging mother has greatly diminished. She lives alone and refuses to move in with him for fear of losing her independence, nor will she agree to live in a nursing home. Her failing eyesight and a range of other medical problems, however, require that she have daily assistance.

Joseph contacts his area agency on aging for information and referral on access to services for his mother at minimal or no cost. He is referred to the appropriate agencies that provide:

- *Adult day care*—supervised care provided in a group setting for frail older persons needing health care and social stimulation. Services include nursing, counseling, physical therapy, and recreational activities.
- *Nutrition services*—hot meals delivered to homebound older persons, or served in an adult day-care center or senior citizen center.
- *Home health services*—nursing and personal hygiene assistance.
- *Homemaker and chore services*—household tasks and home repairs for older people living independently.
- *Transportation and escort services*—travel and escort to doctor and other appointments as well as shopping and banking.

Since his mother has no income other than her Social Security and meets other eligibility requirements, she qualifies for most of the services she needs free or at minimal cost. (Most of the agencies Joseph investigated are subsidized by the federal government or some other funding agency.)

Area agencies on aging are listed in local phone directories, or you can write the National Association of Area Agencies on Aging at 1112 16th St., N.W., Suite 100, Washington, DC 20036, or call 202-296-8130. Other organizations that offer volunteer services are the American Red Cross; church, civic, and service organizations; and the departments of social services, human services, public assistance, or welfare. All numbers are listed in your phone book.

WHAT'S IN A NAME?

More often than not, generic drugs are as effective as brand names but are a great deal less expensive. A free brochure titled *Myths and Facts on Generic Drugs* is available from the U.S. Department of Health and Human Services by writing to Food and Drug Administration, Office of Consumer Inquiries (HFE-88), 5600 Fishers Lane, Rockville, MD 20857.

If your budget runs short one week and you need a prescription filled, request your pharmacist to provide a day's or week's worth of medication. Leave the balance of the prescription to be filled when you can better afford it.

PHYSICIAN, WAIT THYSELF

If you say "pretty, pretty please" and throw yourself at the feet of your doctor's or dentist's bookkeeper, who would choose a root canal over letting you leave the office without paying, you may be allowed to make monthly payments for services or defer your payments for a period of time. You should also ask for a reduced fee, but that should be done before the services are rendered.

Be honest! Tell your medical practitioners about your temporary financial constraints and why you are in this position. It's probably a good idea to inform them by letter prior to needing their services, making new arrangements then (if they let you) so that you won't be gun-shy about going in when you have to.

THE MAKING OF A REFORMATION

The health care reform debate rages nationally. Some states are proposing single-payer plans—a government-run system wherein taxes replace insurance premiums. Many Americans would prefer that we enact a national health system analogous to that offered by England or Canada. Final legislation on health care reform bills could take months, years, even a decade—little consolation for those who need help now. However, lots of little voices whispering into the ears of our legislators could result in the mighty roar that would get them moving more quickly.

KEEP THE HOME FIRES BURNING:
Housing and Utilities Payments

What we are talking here are the real basics of life—a roof over our heads, heat, hot water, and lights. These run a pretty close second to life, liberty, and the pursuit of happiness in the must-have department: can't live without them! don't want to! So how do we go about protecting these basics during hard times?

SEEING THE LIGHT

"Waste not, want not" may conjure up unpleasant memories of childhood, but now that you are paying the bills, these should be words to live by. A good place to start, if you haven't already, is with your heating and utilities costs.

Start with simple measures such as turning down the temperature on your hot water heater, installing water savers on showers and faucets, using thick quilts instead of electric blankets, making sure there is nothing blocking your heating registers, fastening plastic over windows, and using bath/shower/wash water for irrigation.

More ambitious measures are suggested by utility companies, most of which offer free energy surveys. They are the "ghostbusters" of the conservation set, ferreting out the invisible, but certainly felt, energy-robbing apparitions that haunt your home. You will receive a concise report of all of your problem areas. Some utility companies will even wrap your water heater and install water savers at little or no cost.

Other suggestions include caulking and weatherstripping doors and windows; insulating attics and basements, heating pipes and ducts, and hot water pipes; replacing inefficient heating/cooling systems; installing storm windows and doors; and use of passive solar and wind systems. A list of state-approved contractors is also provided for the work you can't complete yourself.

For more information, contact your state's department of public utilities (DPU), consumer division (listed in your phone book under "State Government") or contact your regional light and power company directly.

PAYING THE PIPER

Utility companies are not the impersonal, bureaucratic organizations they appear to be on the surface. They care; they care. They even understand that more and more customers are having trouble paying their bills. When that happens, they urge people to contact them to develop a payment plan that is mutually acceptable. The plan will address the amount in arrears as well as current and future use. See the sample letter on page 108.

It may be a good idea to make new arrangements before payment problems begin. For example, you could change to a continuous budget-billing plan that divides your estimated yearly bill into twelve equal payments. If, at the end of the year, your estimated payments exceed actual usage, the excess is applied to your next bill. The few extra dollars you may have paid each month may not have been missed, but having to pay only a small fraction of your next bill is a much-welcomed respite.

LETTER TO UTILITY COMPANIES

(Date)

(Name of contact person)
(Title)
(Name of utility company)
(Street address)
(City, state, ZIP code)

RE: Account # (your number)

Dear (contact person):

- describe situation

Recently I lost my job and find I am temporarily experiencing some difficulty in making my monthly payment.

- request payment alternatives

Please inform me of any company policies for partial or deferred payments. In addition, I would appreciate information on Energy Assistance Programs for which I may qualify.

- inquire about necessary documentation

I will call you on (day) morning to discuss payment alternatives. Please let me know then what documentation you require to expedite a new arrangement.

- reiterate intention to cooperate

With my expertise and experience, I am confident I will find employment soon, when I can resume full payments. In the meantime, thank you for your understanding and cooperation.

Sincerely,

(Your name)
(Your address)
(Your city, state, ZIP code)
(Your telephone number)

BABY, IT'S COLD OUTSIDE

Some utility companies have initiated energy funds to help qualified low-income customers. Sometimes the money comes from contributions by other customers, with matching funds from the company. A private charitable organization, such as the Salvation Army, generally administers the fund. You should also inquire about reduced rates. Your state DPU may require that utility companies offer reduced rates for low-income customers.

Some nonprofit agencies offer no-interest loans. Unlike other fuel-assistance programs that serve only low-income families, these agencies will provide loans for middle-income families that are experiencing temporary difficulties. While funds for these programs are drying up, some are still operational, particularly for replacement of inefficient heating systems. The savings realized by the more energy-efficient system usually cover the average $50-a-month payback.

State programs, too, are coping with federal cutbacks on low-income home-heating assistance. Only about one-fourth of those eligible for aid get it, but don't let the statistics scare you away from applying if you think you qualify. Basic requirements are generally those households that earn within 150 percent of the federal poverty level; a family of four, for example, must earn less than $20,100 to receive aid.

Without any unemployment benefits to buffer her and with the drastic decrease in interest payments on her investments, Laura's family income falls within the limits set for her state's fuel assistance program. She checks with her department of welfare for the appropriate documentation and is informed that she must provide a written explanation of her situation, proof of income, and copies of her fuel bills. Fortunately for Laura, she is among the one-quarter of the needy to receive assistance. Although she is reimbursed for only about one-third of her yearly heating costs, it helps.

For information on all available programs, contact the consumer division of your department of public utilities, the state agency regulating privately owned utilities that provide gas, electric, water, and telephone service to retail customers; or apply to your department of public welfare, listed in your phone book under "State Government."

OFF AGAIN, ON AGAIN

If you certify a financial hardship, each state utility regulatory agency provides special protections to ensure that you continue to receive service under certain circumstances. For instance, most guarantee that you cannot be deprived of gas or electric service between November 15 and March 15 if either of these directly or indirectly supplies heat to your home. You also qualify for this protection if a member of your household has a serious illness or if a child under 12 months resides in your household.

In many states your utility services cannot be shut off, regardless of whether you are experiencing financial hardship, without the written consent of your DPU if you and all members of your household are 65 or older.

Unless you have one of the above protections, your residential service can be shut off if your bill remains unpaid for forty-five days after the billing date and the company has sent a written notice that indicates the shutoff date. Service may not be shut off on a Friday, Saturday, Sunday, holiday, or the day before a holiday, and may be terminated only between 8 A.M. and 4 P.M.

If your service has been shut off, call the credit department of your utility company immediately and try to negotiate a plan to pay over a period of time. You may have to pay more dearly, however, for your procrastination in dealing with your problem. The company may require a substantial down payment to restore service.

KEEPER OF THE KEYS

Now that you are primed on how to keep home and hearth warm and lit, you need some tips on how to keep home and hearth. If you are a renter, only your landlord can determine if you stay or go, so it's time to stroke the landlord.

Even the Simon Legrees of the landlord world can be convinced to wait awhile for the rent, knowing full well that

LETTER TO LANDLORD

(Date)

(Name of landlord)
(Name of company, if applicable)
(Street address)
(City, state, ZIP code)

Dear (landlord):

- describe situation

As you are aware, my family and I have been good tenants for (number) years and have always made prompt payments. Recently I lost my job, however, and find that I am temporarily experiencing some difficulty in meeting my regular rent.

- request payment alternatives

Can we make a temporary rent arrangement that would work in the best interests of both of us? Would you be willing to accept partial payment, with the balance payable at a later date? Or perhaps you would consider a trade in painting or repairs in lieu of full rent.

- state intention to cooperate

My family and I enjoy living here and intend to remain responsible tenants. I am confident that I can resume my normal payments plus pay a reasonable sum monthly toward the amount I am in arrears until it is paid in full. In the meantime, I appreciate your cooperation and understanding.

Sincerely,

(Your name)
(Your address)
(Your city, state, ZIP code)
(Your telephone number)

ejecting a tenant is unpleasant at best and costly in time and money at worst. Share your plight with your landlord. That may not pay her/his taxes and mortgage, the response you will surely get when asking for some leniency in rent payments, but it may buy you some time. See the sample letter above.

Rebut with the argument that waiting for full payment

from a tenant with good intentions is better than the risk of having no paying tenant at all during eviction proceedings and for a long time after. Drop a hint (don't threaten) that should you be forced to move, you would be much too busy packing to allow the showing of your apartment to potential renters. This could delay new occupation for at least a month, maybe two or three more. The time frame for completing the eviction process depends on the laws of your city and whether they are slanted toward landlords or tenants. Your landlord could be looking at six months with no rent coming in, and she/he knows it.

Evictions can often be delayed by such stalling tactics as filing housing code violations, asking for a stay pending examination of premises by the board of health, or requesting a jury trial. If your property is rent controlled or covered by Section 8, investigate any applicable codes within these programs that may prevent or delay eviction.

Stalling tactics could backfire, however. Some landlords can be more vindictive than greedy. Don't ignore the notice of eviction when served on you. The ostrich approach does not work here. You must answer the complaint and "file for discovery" (give the facts) to put the matter off as long as possible.

Certain restrictions apply to a landlord even when he is holding a writ to evict you. He cannot change your locks, put your furniture on the street, or disturb your peace in your home. Under some cities' ordinances, tenants living in a rent-controlled building who are elderly, handicapped, low income, or (sometimes) moderate income may be entitled to relocation costs depending on the reason for eviction.

Some unsavory landlords may try to convince tenants to waive their rights under summary process (action for eviction). This is illegal and cannot be enforced. Tenancy laws, however, vary from city to city. Once again, knowing your rights is your best protection. Consult an attorney who specializes in tenancy laws if possible, or contact your Legal Aid office for advice and direction. (See chapter 11, "Equal Justice.")

Don't ever minimize the effects of eviction. Once accomplished, the stigma can follow you like a shadow for a long time to come. You will be required to explain away that notice on your credit record each time you apply for a job, a credit card, or another house or apartment rental. You may also find that your bank account has been attached, or your paycheck when you get another job. Moving out of state may be the only escape from retribution, but that may not discourage a former landlord with a long memory and a short temper.

Rather than go through the hassle of a court-ordered eviction, some landlords will pay tenants to leave without a fight. They may offer you the return of your security deposit despite minor damage and/or offer to pay for moving expenses. This "friendly eviction" may be the best compromise for you both in the face of the inevitable.

OUT BUT NOT DOWN

If your current apartment is too expensive and/or you have a totally unsympathetic landlord, investigate temporary low-cost housing through companies that provide management for properties on the market that are vacant and therefore not as attractive to the unimaginative potential buyer. These companies serve families that have had to relocate without being able to sell their homes.

Families with attractive furnishings are sought by these companies to occupy vacant homes at bargain prices. Renters get a nice home at a fraction of the cost, while owners are assured that their property is well cared for and will show well to prospective buyers. Renters must maintain the property and must cope with a continuous train of prospective buyers. When the house is sold, the renters must be ready to move as soon as the papers are passed, but the management company will probably offer them another vacant house. Moving expenses are the responsibility of the renters.

A property managed by these types of companies sells

about 30 percent faster and at about 12 percent higher than a comparable house that is vacant. Yet given the sluggish real estate market, you may still get six months or more before you have to move again. Owners receive no rent but save on utilities (paid by renters) and insurance, which is one-eighth the cost for a home that is occupied as compared to one that is vacant. Renters are also responsible for mowing the lawn and for shoveling the snow, other cost-savers for the owner.

The Atlanta-based Showhomes of America and Denver-based Caretakers of America are two companies serving owners and selected renters. If you are looking for temporary homes in Oklahoma City, Dallas, or Orange County, California, contact the Federal Deposit Insurance Corporation, which is placing temporary renters in foreclosed homes in these areas.

MODERN PIONEERS

The Urban Homesteading Program provides for the transfer of federally owned one- to four-family residences to communities with homesteading plans approved by the Department of Housing and Urban Development (HUD). These properties are transferred for a nominal fee to qualified people who can document need for housing as well as financial or physical ability to accomplish the necessary repairs. Special priority is given to applicants whose income is at or below 80 percent of the median for the area. Current owners of residential property are excluded.

The homesteader must agree to repair, maintain, and occupy the property for a minimum of five consecutive years. The property must meet health and safety standards within one year and must be brought up to local standards for decent, safe, and sanitary housing within three years. When all requirements are satisfied, the homesteader receives full and clear title to the property.

For more information, or to determine if your city has a

homesteading program, contact your HUD city or field office, listed under "Federal Government" in your phone book.

MEANWHILE, BACK AT THE RANCH

For most of us, a home is the single greatest investment we make in our lifetime. Protecting it is almost a primordial instinct. Paying the mortgage, therefore, becomes the highest priority among all other bills. When resources don't match this preeminent goal, it's time to act.

As soon as you see the handwriting on your wall, contact the institution to which you are making your mortgage payments. It may be, but more than likely is not, your original lender. Request a "workout" plan that reduces your payments now, to be made up later; see the sample letter on page 116.

With growing numbers of people having trouble meeting their mortgage payments, lenders are becoming more willing to accept partial payments. Even a lender who has sold your mortgage to investors may be convinced to make a new arrangement. In this case the lender pays the investor on schedule, ultimately collecting from you or the company that has insured your loan, if you carry insurance.

This new arrangement, however, is fairly temporary. If your lender decides that you will never be able to catch up with your payments, you will be forced to sell or go through foreclosure.

Other payment arrangements to investigate are changing from an adjustable-rate to a fixed-rate mortgage, or extending the length of your loan to lower the monthly payments. If your mortgage is through the Federal Housing Administration (part of HUD), you should inquire whether you qualify to switch to a mortgage that reduces your payments, such as the Graduated Payment Mortgage (GPM). With a GPM, initial monthly payments are low, gradually rising for a set period of years, then leveling off for the balance of the mortgage.

LETTER TO MORTGAGE COMPANY

(Date)

(Name of contact person)
(Title)
(Name of mortgage company)
(Street address)
(City, state, ZIP code)

RE: Account # (your number)

Dear (contact person):

- describe
situation

(Number) years ago, (company name) financed the purchase of my home. I am presently out of work, though I am confident that with my expertise and experience I will soon find new employment.

- request
payment
alternatives

In the meantime, I have some difficulties meeting prior financial obligations. Would you please advise me of alternatives for interim payments until I can restore my income?

- inquire about
necessary
documentation

May I have an appointment with you to discuss possible options? I will call you on (day) morning to arrange a convenient meeting time. Please let me know then what documentation you will require to expedite a new arrangement.

- reiterate
intention to
cooperate

My family and I have made an enormous investment in our home, both financially and emotionally. We will make every effort within our control to meet our obligations and retain our home. Thank you for your understanding and cooperation.

Sincerely,

(Your name)
(Your address)
(Your city, state, ZIP code)
(Your telephone number)

Although lower interest rates make refinancing your home sound like the answer to your prayers, keep in mind that you would probably need a mini-miracle to qualify. Lenders have this quirk about requiring their mortgagees to be gainfully employed at an income level commensurate with their ability to pay their debt service. Also, if you bought your house in the roaring eighties, it may not appraise out now at its original purchase price and thus not qualify for the amount of the mortgage you need to carry.

Refinancing can be costly as well. Most lenders charge from 1 percent to 3 percent (known as points). That's a minimum of $1,000 for a $100,000 mortgage, not to mention the fee for the bank's attorney, which could be several hundred, and the fee for your lawyer (should you feel more secure having one), another few hundred dollars. Then there are the fees for having the house appraised, tracing the title, and filing the documents; tack on another few hundred dollars.

Before making any moves in this direction, add up all your costs, including the loss of any tax deductions, and compare them with your savings. The money you save on monthly mortgage payments should equal your closing costs within two years. For those who have the up-front cash and intend to stay in their homes long enough to realize the savings, refinancing could be a wise move. This is not the solution, however, for those who are looking for more immediate relief.

THIS LAND IS MINE

In case of fire or natural disaster, the land your house sits on and the surrounding property will still be there pretty much intact even if your house is destroyed. Therefore you should be carrying insurance only for the existing structure, not for the land. To trim your premiums even more, you may also want to take a higher deductible. The savings would probably justify the risk of having to cover a greater portion of minor repairs. Your main concern now is to cover the cost of replacing your house should it be totally destroyed.

Reexamine the coverage on your personal property. Protect only those items that you would replace if lost or damaged. If you own valuable jewelry or a silver service, put it in a safety deposit box at a cost of $20 to $90 a year, depending on the size of the box. Safety deposit insurance is around one-sixth the premium you pay for protecting those valuables when kept at home. You can use them when you want them and be covered when you do. You just need to inform your insurance agent in advance (and probably in writing) when you intend to take something out of your safety deposit box and when you expect to return it. If you keep it out any longer than the date you specified, you won't be covered.

THE MORE, THE MERRIER

Now that you have trimmed your housing costs and made new arrangements for payments, you probably still need some quick cash to meet your remaining expenses. Consider a housemate or a boarder. If you live alone in a three-bedroom house, consider two housemates. Increasing numbers of unrelated people with similar lifestyles and financial concerns are opting for a nineties version of communal living. The concept is alive and well and even found on television (in syndication) in the form of "The Golden Girls," three middle-aged divorced or widowed women (and the mother of one) who share a single-family home that one of them owns.

Money, of course, is the main reason for taking in housemates, but there are other advantages—companionship, security, and help with the chores. The flip side is loss of privacy and the possibility of having undesirable tenants who may not pay the rent on time, monopolize the telephone, are sloppy beyond redemption, or who use your home as a social center/rest stop for a succession of friends.

Even if your walls are already bulging with family, you may still find room for a boarder who could produce immediate revenue for you. Look for someone who would fit in with your family situation, such as a student attending a local college or an elderly person who is healthy enough to maintain independent living but does not want to live alone. Your arrangement could be for just the room, or for board as well. (As long as you're cooking, what's one more place at the table?) With a little luck, your boarder could become a surrogate big sister/brother or grandmother/father, adding a new dimension to your family's dynamics. For the most part, with planning and preparation, the advantages to shared housing far outweigh the disadvantages.

Your library should have a whole shelf of books to guide you on how to choose your housemates and how to manage your household. One book to look for is *Living with Tenants: How to Happily Share Your House with Renters for Profit and Security*, by Doreen Bierbrier (McGraw-Hill, 1986).

Richard and Anne bought a five-room "starter" house shortly after they married three years ago. Since they both had good jobs that appeared secure at the time, they believed they could manage the mortgage payments and ancillary costs without too much difficulty.

Now, two-and-a-half years into the mortgage, Richard has lost his job, can't find another, and Anne has just given birth. Although Anne will return to work as soon as possible, her salary coupled with Richard's unemployment benefits is not enough to keep up with the mortgage payments, particularly now that the family has grown to three.

They decide to rent their house and move in with Anne's parents until Richard finds another job. While they are living rent-free with Anne's parents, they can apply all of the money they get from their tenant to the mortgage payment, thus holding out until they can afford to move back in again.

The decision to move in with Anne's parents was not made lightly. They discussed all the pros and cons with each other and with Anne's parents who, fortunately for the young couple, are eager and willing hosts. The older couple is happy to help in any way they can and are delighted to have their new grandchild in such close proximity.

MULTIPLE CHOICE

Pride of home ownership should not preclude a multifamily dwelling. Where a single-family home was once the American dream, it has become a nightmare to sustain in the austere nineties. Trading your one-family home for one that gives you a nice place to live as well as an income to help pay the mortgage may get you out of the bind you're in while providing the potential for future growth.

In a perverse way the recession offers us opportunities that may have been out of the realm of possibility in the expensive eighties. Properties of all types are available at rock-bottom prices, sometimes by merely assuming the existing mortgage. Granted, this means that the property you currently own may be worth less than you anticipated, but it still may provide you with enough equity to reinvest in another that you could afford to maintain by virtue of a second (maybe even a third) apartment.

A well-maintained, attractive apartment should not be difficult to rent. According to *Money Dynamics for the 1990s*, by Venita Van Caspel (Simon and Schuster, 1988) multifamily housing, properly managed, is one of the most profitable investments that you can make in this decade. The potential for making excellent future profits and solving current mortgage payment problems presents a most convincing argument for considering a multifamily dwelling.

REVERSAL OF FORTUNE

Losing one's home may be the greatest fear experienced by the unemployed, and it's certainly not an irrational one.

Though it's a worst-case scenario, you may have to face up to this possibility. When foreclosure is looming over your head like Damocles' sword, you may want to do some sidestepping to avoid a direct hit.

Foreclosure creates a seven-year blot on your credit record and could also result in the loss of most or all of the equity in your property. You could even end up owing your lender if the forced sale price does not satisfy your debt.

Abandoning your mortgage and mailing back the key to your lender will not absolve you. Neither will a "friendly foreclosure" whereby you willingly deed your house back to the bank. In the latter case, of course, you will save on the costs of foreclosure proceedings, for which you are responsible.

If you don't repay the remainder of your debt, your lender may go after any assets you have now or in the future, including your car, your bank accounts, or your salary when you get a new job. Even if you get away (by some miracle) without paying the shortfall, the IRS may well step in to tax you on your "forgiveness of debt," considered a payment from the lender to you and thereby taxable.

Selling your house before the bank closes in and while you are still in some position of strength may be your best escape. Your dedication to getting the maximum amount possible for your property, unlike the bank, may preserve some of your equity or at least save you from a deficit.

GOING, GOING, GONE!

Selling by orthodox methods in a soft market is no picnic. You may want to consider auctioning the house off. Auctions are realizing 90 to 105 percent of assessed value. While buyers going through traditional channels tend to "low-ball" their offers and walk away when they are not accepted, bidders get caught up in the competitive spirit of the auction and come closer to or even go beyond the fair price.

The cost for an auctioneer is about the same as for a broker.

Additionally, an auction generally assures a sale in about two months from the date you sign the contract to put your house on the block.

There are two forms of auctions you may choose. One allows the withdrawal of the property from the sale if you feel the last bid received wasn't high enough. The other calls for absolute bidding, requiring that you accept the final, best offer. You may, however, set a minimum at which bidding must begin. The second form of sale usually draws a larger crowd.

Before putting your house up for sale, attend some auctions to become acquainted with the dynamics. Make sure you deal with a reputable auctioneer with a good track record.

Look in the real estate section of your newspaper for auctioneers' ads. Select those who appear suitable for your purposes and request additional information. You may find that some auction houses will not list individual homes of single sellers but pick up properties in blocks from developers instead.

YES, I CAN!

New real estate services are giving do-it-yourself sellers better odds for success. Some real estate firms now allow you to choose the level of services you require. For example, New Visions–Prestige Real Estate (619-236-1186), based in San Diego, will give you a sign, a lock box, and some real estate forms as well as get your house into multiple listings for around $500. This requires an up-front fee, however, whether or not the house is sold. According to New Visions' co-owner Tom Krause, franchises are operating in Southern California and in Colorado.

Help-You-Sell, real estate brokers with nationwide franchises, assigns clients some of the responsibilities for selling their property to reduce the size of the fee. With Help-You-Sell, you and the broker share the responsibilities of selling your property, thereby reducing the size of the fee. While policy and cost vary somewhat from franchise to franchise, generally Help-You-Sell charges a flat fee that equals a little more than half the traditional commission of 6 percent. The fee is paid only if the house is sold. Contact the company at 1-800-526-2625 for a local referral.

Also available through some realtors is a computer printout of selling prices on comparable homes in your area with general information on the condition of the home when sold. This information helps you to set a realistic price for your house. Sale prices are a matter of public record on file in your local registry of deeds, but you have to do the digging (very labor intensive), and the records contain no notations on the state of the property.

MAYBE I CAN'T

Once again, it's time to take out the mental scale to weigh the advantages and disadvantages of self-sale versus broker handled. According to Iverson Moore at the National Association of Realtors in Washington, D.C., "Most people who try to sell a house themselves end up listing with a broker in thirty to ninety days. They would actually save more money by listing with a broker from the beginning." Self-help services and newspaper advertising costs begin to add up, and your time is valuable too. You may be able to make a deal with a realtor that won't cost much more than what you must invest to sell your house yourself. "Brokers generally charge between 6 to 8 percent of the selling price," says Moore, "but most will negotiate fees."

Barry Nystedt, of Re/Max (1-800-821-5270), a national real estate firm, believes that "The issue of savings at this point may be an illusion, since the seller's optimum desire is to sell for the highest possible money in the shortest amount of time." To achieve these results, he suggests that the seller consider enlisting the aid of the most professional service skills available. Interpreting the market and comparative sales are keys to a quick sale or rental. "Market averages are not great indicators at all," he adds. "The numbers need to be relative to the type of property being sold and the neighborhood location. Plus the property should be available to be shown at all times. This may be difficult for those who are job seeking or assuming other responsibilities at the same time they are trying to sell."

Another possibility for a seller to save money is to contact a buyer-broker, a realtor who has been hired by a prospective buyer. If a client through this type of agency purchases your property, you are responsible for only half the broker fee. The other half is paid by the buyer.

A BIRD IN THE HAND

To prepare for the sale, scrub your house from top to bottom, giving particular attention to bathrooms and kitchen, often the clinchers for a sale. Windows, too, should be sparkling, and landscaping neat and manicured. Get rid of as much of the clutter as you can (it makes the house look smaller), but don't toss it into closets. Neat closets that appear more spacious are also a selling point.

Be flexible during negotiations after someone has made an offer. Remember that for the same reason you are out of a job and can't get a new one—the recession—your house has lost value, maybe more than you are willing to accept. Naturally you want to realize a return close to the selling price (if it was realistic to begin with), but taking a bit less can give you the cash in hand now, when you need it to carry you until you get back on your feet again. You could wait a long time before another bidder comes along.

HOME SWEET HOME

The famous madam Polly Adler called her book *A House Is Not a Home*. If you take a different interpretation than she perhaps intended, her observation has much greater depth. Your physical surroundings don't make a home; you do. Whatever arrangements you are forced to make to accommodate these difficult times, your home goes where you go. Corny as it sounds, home *is* where the heart is, so take heart.

OBSCENE PHONE CALLS:
When Creditors Become a Problem

T he wolves are at your door or at least baying on your telephone. How does one keep them from attacking? Throw them a bone!

THE PETER/PAUL PRINCIPLE

With so many people in financial trouble today, creditors are a bit more sympathetic and cooperative, particularly with those who demonstrate good faith. Partial payment or even a plea for patience generally separates the good customers with a temporary problem from the deadbeats who ignore their financial woes.

Debt management is more than borrowing from Peter to pay Paul, a favorite form of creative bookkeeping. Reestablishing payment terms that everyone can live with is the real talent. *Then* you can borrow from Peter to make Paul happy, and vice versa.

CALLING ALL CREDITORS

Try to fend off obscene calls from creditors by calling them first or, whenever possible, making a personal visit to the credit office. Insist on speaking to a supervisor, someone with some clout and autonomy. Your "customer service representative" is generally not empowered to do any more than reiterate to you what you already know—that you are in arrears. These front-line people can do little more than read your record off their computer screens and (if you're lucky) make a request for someone to get back to you on your problem (which they rarely do).

When appropriate contact is made, first point out the duration of your relationship with this creditor (the longer, the better) and your prior record of payment (the better, the better). Be honest about your predicament and your unemployment status. Ask how (not if) a new arrangement for reduced payments can be initiated without further blemishing your credit record or adding unreasonable interest charges.

Always get the name, title, and telephone number of the person to whom you are speaking, whether on the phone or in person. Then, if one hand of the company doesn't know or care what the other is doing and calls you to demand payment "or else," refer the caller (whose name and number you have taken) to your contact at the company and hang up. If he or she doesn't call back, don't assume the two hands joined. Let your contact know that someone else has called you from the company. If you-know-who calls back, you may have to start all over again. This time, however, you'll have a name to ask for, saving you from having to beg your "customer service representative" to refer you to a supervisor.

"You-know-who" may have called the first time because no notation of your arrangement had been inserted in your file. Be sure to request of your creditor the addition of this information to your records immediately, preferably as you wait.

Also request an immediate report to the credit bureau that your account is current.

TALLY HO!

You have made initial contact, but the hounds need repeated reminders before they delay chasing after the fox. Follow up your call or visit with a letter noting your new arrangement, and request written verification from your creditor as well. Send a copy of the agreement to any recording credit bureaus. (See chapter 18, "Are We There Yet?" for credit bureau addresses.) The best way to verify whether your creditor has erased the negative notation on your credit report as agreed is by requesting a copy of the report. You have a right to know which consumer reporting agency your creditor reports to. If there are negative notations on your report, you are entitled to receive a copy.

Your rights under the Fair Credit Reporting Act are outlined in a booklet that may be obtained from the Office of Consumer Affairs, Federal Deposit Insurance Corporation, 550 17th Street, N.W., Washington, DC 20429 or from regional offices (eight throughout the country). Call 1-800-424-5488 for the location of the office serving you. Consumer reporting agencies are supervised by the Federal Trade Commission. Questions or complaints should be directed to the FTC, Division of Credit Practices, Washington, DC 20580.

You may reach a point where you need to go higher up in the company. In dealing with bureaucratic organizations, you may have to do a little digging to determine the appropriate corporate consumer contact. Try the reference section of your local library for copies of *Standard & Poor's Register of Corporations, Directors, and Executives, Standard Directory of Advertisers, Thomas Register of American Manufacturers,* or *Trade Names Directory*. Each of these volumes is published annually.

Before making any long-distance calls, check on toll-free 800 numbers. Call AT&T's "800" directory assistance for this information at 1-800-555-1212.

You may find yourself going back to the same well over and over again, but dedication and patience will bring their own rewards. You may get through these hard times with an unblemished credit record and without the daily go-round of unpleasant callers chasing you for payments.

SOMEONE TO WATCH OVER ME

If contacting all of your creditors for special payment arrangements is too overwhelming for you, professional financial or consumer credit counselors are available to help you. Some universities, local courts, military bases, credit unions, and banks operate credit counseling programs and charge little, if anything, for their services.

You may also obtain this service through your local Consumer Credit Counseling Service, a nonprofit financial counseling agency with offices in all 50 states. Contact the National Foundation for Consumer Credit, Inc., at 8701 Georgia Ave., Suite 507, Silver Spring, MD 20910, or call 301-589-5600 for the location of the office in your area.

A financial counseling program sets up repayment plans. You pay the program a certain amount each month. The program then distributes the money among your creditors. Creditors often provide support for financial counseling services, preferring this kind of plan to bankruptcy, which yields only a small percentage of the debt. Some creditors will even waive interest charges and delinquency fees under a financial counseling program.

For a complete explanation of your rights under the Consumer Protection Act of 1968, request a copy of the *Consumer Handbook to Credit Protection Laws*, published by the Board of Governors of the Federal Reserve System. Copies may be obtained by writing to the Publications Services, Division of Support Services, Board of Governors of the Federal Reserve System, Washington, DC 20551.

The Consumer Information Catalogue lists more than 200 free or low-cost federal booklets that address consumer complaints and problems; it may be ordered by sending your name and address to: Consumer Information Center, Pueblo, CO 81009. You may also want to consult *Conquer Your Debt: How to Solve Your Credit Problems*, by William Kent Brunett (Prentice Hall, 1990). Check your library for a copy.

AN EQUITABLE APPROACH TO DEBT CONSOLIDATION

If you are approved for a home equity loan, you may want to access it to consolidate your debts. The interest on a home equity loan is generally considerably lower than on unsecured debts such as credit cards. Monthly payments on $5,000 worth of credit card debts (interest around 19.5 percent) could be reduced by some $80 when converted to a home equity loan (interest around 11.5 percent). An additional savings is realized through the allowed tax deduction for interest paid on a home equity loan.

Securing a home equity loan while you are unemployed may be quite a coup. Not absolutely impossible, however, if you have sufficient equity in your home to justify the loan and/or if you have a gainfully employed cosigner. A home equity loan is a line of credit up to an established amount secured by the equity in your home after other liens (first mortgage, etc.). If you don't draw on the funds, you pay no interest. You pay interest only on the amount drawn and not on the entire amount.

SHUFFLING THE CARDS

If you have enough cards to play one-handed poker (or more), all waiting for you to ante up with around a 17 percent vigorish (interest), you may want to look into a plastic consolidation plan now offered by many banks. The lure is a reduced interest rate of around 12 percent on the balance transferred.

Some are even offering no annual fee for the first year on the new card. New purchases, however, revert to existing interest rates that vary from 16.5 percent to 19.8 percent. Watch your local newspaper for ads on the banks in your area that offer this program.

OWING MUST EQUAL KNOWING

Despite all your efforts, your creditor(s) may turn over your account to a debt collector or a debt collection agency. In that event, you should become familiar with a federal law known as the Fair Debt Collection Practices Act (FDCPA), which protects a debtor from any abusive, deceptive, or unfair debt collection practices.

The FDCPA defines a debt collector as someone other than a lender who regularly collects debts for others. Although lenders are not addressed by the FDCPA, they are governed by similar state laws covering collection practices.

Gone are the days when a debt collector could park himself on your doorstep daily, call you at midnight to harass you, or even threaten you and your family with bodily harm. A debt collector is also precluded by law from threatening your property or reputation, using obscene language or profanity, making repeated calls, making calls or sending telegrams collect, advertising your debt, or divulging details of your credit history to a second person, even one who is part of your household.

A debt collector's statements are also regulated by the FDCPA. You cannot be told that you will be arrested or that your property will be attached unless one or both is legally possible and under serious consideration if debt is not paid within a specified term. Neither can a debt collector misrepresent the amount of the debt nor give the impression in any way that he or she is an attorney.

Contact by creditors may be made by mail, in person, by telephone, or by telegram during convenient daytime hours, but not at a place of employment if the boss objects. Such contact may be made only between the hours of 8 A.M. and 9 P.M. unless the debtor agrees otherwise.

Within five days of initial contact, the debt collector must inform the debtor in writing of the name of the lender to whom the money is owed, the amount owed, and the proposed course of action. If the debt collector does not hear from the debtor within thirty days, he/she has the right to assume the creditor's claim is valid.

After initial notice, a debtor may discontinue all contact from the debt collector, except for notices of legal or other action, by notifying the debt collector in writing. Notification by the debtor that the debt is in dispute also precludes the debt collector from further contact until proof of the debt, such as a copy of the bill, is produced. Then the debt collector may resume collection activities.

Despite legal guidelines, some creditors become more aggressive in a bad economy. Contact your attorney general's office if you believe your creditor has crossed the line into illegal debt collection practices.

ON THE ROAD AGAIN—OR NOT

Until the last payment on your vehicle is made, it doesn't really belong to you. Your creditor retains significant rights in your vehicle, established by the contract you signed and by the laws of your state. In many states your creditor has the right to repossess your car without going to court or without warning you in advance. Therefore, the call to the creditor who holds the paper on your car should be one of the first you should make to try for a new arrangement for payment. Many creditors are willing to accept delayed payments if they believe you will be able to pay later. (See chapter 6, "A Ticket to Ride.")

CHIPPING YOUR PIECE OF THE ROCK

If you fall within the national average, you spend 12 percent of your annual income for insurance. Before your piece of the rock begins to crumble, you should examine your health, property, life, and automobile insurance policies to determine where you can reduce costs without sacrificing protection. The typical family should be able to save around $500 a year merely by eliminating duplications in coverage and taking greater control over costs, by increasing copayments, or by shopping around for lower priced yet equally protective policies. You may even find that there is gold in them thar life insurance policies that can yield enough cash to cover premiums at least until you get back to work.

Whole life policies generally have borrowing provisions. If you have sufficient equity, you may be able to borrow against the cash value of your insurance policy. You will, of course, be charged interest at current rates. Should you die while the loan is outstanding, the unpaid amount will be deducted from the benefits. Conversely, those who leave their cash value intact could realize a greater return on their money if their insurance company offers "direct recognition." Under this practice, insurance companies pay higher dividends to those who do not borrow against their policies.

You may be able to use the cash value in your current "traditional" whole life policy to buy a single-premium whole life policy that, as the name implies, requires a one-time lump-sum payment when the policy is taken out. The cash value of the policy will grow as interest accrues. Death benefits on this type of policy, however, are far less than those paid on other forms of life insurance that build up higher face-value protection through premiums paid over an extended period.

Insurance advisers do not recommend single-premium policies for people who need a great deal of life insurance to protect their dependents. According to the National Insurance Consumer Organization (NICO), your policy should yield, in the event of your death, seven times your normal income if you have two or more children. But tough times sometimes call for extreme measures. Conversion to a single-premium policy is an option for those with a temporarily limited cash flow. Before converting, inquire about the possibilities and ramifications of reconverting to term insurance when you are back to work again.

Most insurance advisers recommend term insurance as the most affordable for adequate coverage. Ask your insurance company or agent whether and how you can use the cash value of your whole life policy to purchase a term insurance policy. Don't be put off by arguments against this by your insurance agent, who has his or her own axe to grind. Agents make more commission on whole life policies than on term. Insurance companies don't push term insurance either, since profits are lower. For an impartial evaluation consult NICO, 121 N. Payne St., Alexandria, VA 22314, tel. 703-549-8050.

Term insurance provides coverage for a specific time. Make sure your company will guarantee in advance that it will renew the policy for another term without the need for you to prove you are still insurable.

If you participated in a group life plan offered by your company, find out how long you have after your termination to convert your policy and if you can avoid additional charges for this conversion. Some companies have charged up to $1,000 when a terminated employee converts to whole life without a medical exam. The human resources office in your former company can answer these questions or direct you to someone who can.

Look into other group life insurance opportunities through other associations where you may have a connection, such as credit or charge card companies (American Express, Visa), American Association of Retired Persons (AARP), American Automobile Association (AAA), or fraternal organizations such as the Masons or the Elks.

If you are on your own without dependents, life insurance is unnecessary. Without dependents, there would be no economic consequences of your premature death.

Reevaluate your auto and homeowner's insurance as well. Take higher deductibles on your auto and homeowner's policies. With new deadbolts on your doors and a pledge of very safe driving from everyone who drives the family car, you can minimize risk while lowering your premiums.

Don't take the towing rider on your auto insurance coverage if you belong to an auto club that offers that service as part of the membership fee. Make sure you are getting all discounts due you. For example, you may be eligible for a reduced rate for your under-25 drivers if they are students making good grades. If all of your under-25 drivers have left the nest, make sure you're not still paying extra for them. (See chapter 6, "A Ticket to Ride.")

Given the astronomical cost of medical care, health insurance is vital, but there might be some ways to pare costs. Consider doing without major medical or raising your deductible (copayment) if you and your family are young, in good health, with no existing conditions or injuries that could flare up at any time.

If you lost your health coverage along with your job, check into COBRA to extend your coverage for 18 months after termination. (See chapter 8, "When an Apple a Day Isn't Enough.") Try to maintain some protection. No coverage at all could be a classic case of "penny wise and dollar foolish." One major illness or an injury not covered by other insurance could wipe you out. Your life savings, even the equity in your home, could fall prey to hospitals and doctors seeking payments for extended care.

If you have disability insurance, you may want to keep it intact even though you don't have an income to protect. That's only temporary. Dropping coverage now and renewing later could be more costly in the long run. Also, if you decide to become your own boss and work at home, disability insurance is hard to get.

Unfortunately, disability insurance can be even more expensive than health insurance. You can keep your premiums down somewhat if you are in your 30s and 40s with an annually renewable disability policy that starts off with lower premiums and rises as you get older. At 50 or over, you are better off with a fixed premium policy. Once again, your number of dependents should be reflected in the amount of your coverage.

An informed consumer can save impressive amounts of money even when shopping for or reevaluating existing insurance policies. Before making any decisions, do your homework.

- Consult your state insurance department (listed in your phone book under your state's heading).
- Visit your library for its free sources such as *Consumer Reports* and *Best's Insurance Reports*, which is published annually. Other highly informative books explaining types of insurance available and how to save include *Winning the Insurance Game*, by Ralph Nader and Wesley J. Smith (Knightsbridge Publishing, 1990).
- Contact NICO for advice and printed materials.
- Contact the Insurance Information Institute, 1-800-221-4954 for advice on property/casualty insurance.
- Request information from the American Council of Life Insurance, 1-800-423-8000.
- Shop around to determine what each company is offering and compare prices and the range of policies and services.
- Target the kind of coverage you need and learn as much about it as you can so that you can't be talked into something simply because you don't understand the concept.

ENDING ONE CHAPTER TO START ANOTHER

You may reach a point when all of your efforts to ward off your creditors just aren't enough. This may be the time to consider some form of bankruptcy as the only realistic alternative. Filing bankruptcy in any form, however, should be a last resort, since the memo remains in your credit file for as long as ten years. In today's economic system, such a blot on your credit record could continue to haunt you long after you get on your feet again.

The most common forms of bankruptcy proceedings fall under Chapter 7 (straight bankruptcy), Chapter 13 (for a wage earner with a steady income), or Chapter 11 (generally not for consumers but for businesses that are restructuring while continuing operations).

About one-fifth of nonbusiness filings under the bankruptcy code are under Chapter 13. It is available to borrowers who have less than $100,000 in unsecured debts, such as credit cards, and less than $350,000 in secured debts, such as mortgages and car loans.

Unlike Chapter 7, which forbids you from filing more than once every six years, Chapter 13 allows you to file repeatedly. Chapter 13 also generally sits better with potential credit grantors, who have more tendency to extend credit to those who attempted to pay back the bulk of their former debts. The fly in the ointment is that the filer must also have a steady income to arrange for the required payment plan.

Straight bankruptcy under Chapter 7 allows you to discharge most debts. As of the date you file your petition, your assets are under the protection of the court, and most collection efforts against you must cease. All of your nonexempt assets must be turned over to the trustee of the bankruptcy court. This generally includes all your real property (real estate, etc.) and all of your personal property such as household goods, clothing, cash, retirement funds, and accrued net wages.

Generally exempted property includes some equity in your home, some personal items and clothing, the tools of your trade, and household furnishings of nominal value. You may also petition the court to allow you to keep other possessions. Approval by the court is based on your promise to pay any debts attached to these possessions and whether the creditor approves of the arrangement.

Although Chapter 7 will free you of many of your debts, it

does not discharge some tax claims, child support, and most student loans. You will also still be responsible for existing punitive damages for "malicious or wanton" acts such as drunk driving.

Before embarking on this last-ditch attempt to solve your economic troubles, consult a financial expert and/or an attorney. A lawyer or other professional who specializes in bankruptcy can help you decide what is best for you. (See chapter 11, "Equal Justice.")

THE OSTRICH APPROACH

You could, of course, make like an ostrich that sticks its head in the sand to avoid its enemies, and thwart obscene phone calls by disconnecting your telephone. Unfortunately, the outcome would be similar—a very painful bite on the backside when you least expect it.

11

EQUAL JUSTICE:
Legal Services

Life goes on even when you are unemployed. Therefore you may find yourself embroiled in disputes over, for example, unsatisfactory services rendered to you, money owed to you, or contract disagreements. Lack of funds should not preclude getting the right advice and direction from the appropriate sources.

Three months after accepting early retirement at age 55, Joseph P. discovered that he was replaced by a younger, lower-priced colleague. When confronted about this, his former employer maintained that Joseph had "willingly" accepted a "generous severance package." Joseph asserted that he was given little choice. Termination appeared to be his only option to accepting retirement, though he conceded that this was never really verbalized by his boss.

Joseph began to believe that he may have been the victim of wrongful discharge. He contacted his local office of the federal Equal Employment Opportunity Commission (EEOC) for more information on workplace discrimination. Several booklets on law and the workplace were available to him free of charge.

The booklets outlined the examples of wrongful discharge, among them discrimination against race, religion, sex, age, or handicap. Joseph was appalled to discover that women have been let go shortly after announcing pregnancy or that other workers were given pink slips for reporting safety violations or other illegal acts to the proper authorities; for exercising free speech; for refusing to commit an illegal act or to violate their morals; for exercising a legal right, e.g., filing a workers' compensation claim; for performing a legal duty, e.g., serving on a jury; or for exercising rights spelled out in company policy, e.g., putting in for commissions owed.

Joseph now knew that employees discharged for any of these reasons can not only sue for damages resulting from the job loss but for any mental anguish they suffer, and in some states for reinstatement as well.

Joseph's study of the material further revealed to him that damages are generally decided on the basis of wages lost during a reasonable period between discharge and obtaining a new job. If his claim got that far, a jury would decide on the length of a reasonable period based on his professional skills and his efforts in seeking a new position.

Joseph decided to consult an attorney for advice on the wisdom of initiating suit for wrongful discharge under his state's statutes (laws differ from state to state), and for an educated opinion on his chances for prevailing.

Joseph hoped the attorney would be willing to take his case on a contingency basis, to be paid (generally one-third of the judgment) only if he won his case. He feared that the attorney would require a fee up front, as most do.

Fortunately for Joseph, the attorney agreed to work on a contingency basis because she believed that Joseph's case was a blatant example of age discrimination under that state's statutes.

Joseph's case was not, however, a quick fix for unemployment. Although he ultimately settled out of court for six figures, final resolution of his case didn't come until five years after suit was filed on his behalf.

The national office of the Equal Employment Opportunity Commission is located at 2401 E St., N.W., Washington, DC 20507, tel. 202-663-4000.

JOB EQUITY

Up to now, the United States has been the only industrial democracy without a definitive law requiring employers to justify a worker's dismissal. A doctrine that has governed the American workplace since the mid-1800s held that employers can discharge an employee without giving notice or any explanation. Exceptions to this doctrine began with the passage of the Civil Rights Act of 1964, which bars employment discrimination on the basis of race, color, religion, sex, or national origin, as well as other laws to protect "whistle-blowers," those who report illegal or immoral practices. This prohibits discriminatory firings but not the discharging of employees for other arbitrary reasons.

During the mid-1980s, many state courts also began to recognize "implied contracts" as exceptions to the long-accepted doctrine. This held that oral assurances or statements in employee manuals could protect an employee from being fired except for good cause.

The Employment Termination Act, expected to be adopted by up to twenty-five legislatures by 1995, would prohibit companies from firing workers except for "good cause," such as chronic absenteeism or substandard performance. (See chapter 3, "Bridge over Troubled Water," for more extensive explanation of "good cause.") Known as the "wrongful discharge" law, it calls for speedy settlement of disputes through arbitration, in contrast to the time-consuming procedure required to pursue a discrimination complaint.

The proposed law, which would not apply to union members, part-time or temporary employees, or contract workers, is designed primarily to protect employees from arbitrary dismissal but also recognizes the employer's right not to be saddled with incompetent, uncooperative workers.

Another aspect of discharge that should be clarified is whether the termination is temporary or permanent. Though viewed as temporary, a layoff can effectively end the working relationship as finally as a dismissal but sometimes affords more severance benefits. Since your benefits may be your only source of income for some time, you must investigate carefully to ensure you are getting all that is due you. Check with your company's human resources or personnel office for further clarification of your situation.

Also make sure you weren't fired to prevent your benefits from vesting. Once vested, an employee's benefits cannot be denied. However, workers lose full benefits, having access only to their own contributions, if fired before the pension vests. For more information on your pension rights, contact the Pension Rights Center, Suite 704, 918 16th St., N.W., Washington, DC 20006, tel. 202-296-3776.

HERE COMES THE JUDGE!

Sometimes disputes can be settled in small claims court (also called magistrate, justice of the peace, or pro se courts), where you can represent yourself whether you are the plaintiff (the one who sues) or the defendant (the one who is being sued). The amount that can be sought in these courts differs from state to state, ranging from a few hundred to a few thousand dollars. You act on your own behalf (no legal fees to worry about) and need no specialized training, but you should be well prepared to tell your story to the judge by doing all pertinent research and gathering all of the documents you need to back you up. Also, bring any witnesses who could substantiate your claim.

In a case where it is the plaintiff's word against the defendant's with no documents or witnesses to back either up, the judge will consider the case on the basis of credibility of both parties. If the credibility of one is doubtable, the other will most likely prevail. If both are equally believable, the judge will generally find for the defendant since the burden of proof is on the plaintiff. No proof, no victory.

Laura's younger son Brian, 11, took on a paper route to help out until his mother finds a job. One morning while delivering his papers, he was attacked by a dog owned by one of his customers. The dog knocked Brian off his bicycle onto the asphalt driveway. Brian's ankle was broken, for which he required medical treatment that cost $275 at an emergency clinic. In addition Brian lost around $100 in wages and tips from his paper route, since he couldn't maneuver his bicycle with a broken ankle.

Laura sought restitution against the dog owner in small claims court for the medical expenses and lost wages. The filing fee in her state is $14, for which she was entitled to a hearing before the judge.

The dog owner (the defendant) claimed that her dog is gentle and placid and that Brian had provoked the attack by teasing and kicking the dog each time he delivered the paper. Brian countered that he never did anything more than toss the paper onto the front steps and leave quickly, because the dog was always out on the lawn, unleashed and growling at him. Brian brought three friends with him to testify that the dog "is mean" and that they were all afraid of it. The defendant offered nothing more than protestations and accusations. The judge found for the plaintiffs (Laura and Brian) in the sum of $375 plus court costs.

Although the losing parties must follow the court's decision, they often do not. Up to 30 percent of small-claims-court judgments go uncollected. Some states allow the winner to subpoena the loser back to court. Even then many losers remain uncooperative, especially if they have no money or assets. Judgments, however, are good for several years, so keep track of the debtor's future financial status.

When there are assets, show your determination to get paid by availing yourself of all avenues the court allows. Threatened with the attachment of assets to satisfy the judgment, the debtor is more willing to pay up to avoid further action. Some courts are empowered to force the sale of property to satisfy the judgment or to attach the paycheck or bank accounts of the losing party. However, most judges reserve these decrees until they are convinced that losing parties are thumbing their noses at the courts.

If you are a defendant, the same caveat applies—be prepared. Some states consider unemployment and inability to pay as grounds for dismissal of the suit. A Petition of Poverty granted by the court could prevent the initiation of any suit by a creditor for the period designated in the petition.

THERE GOES THE JUDGE!

For a quick, inexpensive, and less stressful alternative to the courtroom, nearly all states have established dispute centers (also called neighborhood justice centers, citizens' dispute settlement programs, or night prosecutors' programs). These centers specialize in helping consumers, landlords and tenants, neighbors with boundary line disputes, and family members with such problems as divorce (who gets what) or child custody.

Often the cases handled by a dispute center have been diverted from small claims court when both parties involved in a suit agree to appear before a mediator. Trained in the art of resolving problems, the mediator helps to identify, define, and discuss the elements about which the parties disagree. Generally the parties still have the option to go before a judge should they not agree with the decision of a mediator.

While her husband Tony was still a bank vice president, Susan bought a sequined cocktail dress for the bank's annual banquet. She didn't wear the dress again until Tony's sister's wedding a year later. After the wedding Susan sent the dress to the cleaners. When the dress was returned, half of the sequins were either missing or hanging by threads.

The cleaner maintained that it was not his fault, that the dress was defective and should be returned to the store where she bought it. The proprietor of the store, in turn, blamed the cleaner. She further pointed out that the dress was more than a year old and that she was not responsible, in any case, after all that time.

Determined to get some satisfaction, Susan asked the cleaner and the proprietor if they would allow a mediator to resolve the problem. Informed that she would sue if they didn't, both assented. After listening to everyone's claims, the mediator suggested a compromise that all parties begrudgingly accepted, finding it preferable to spending another day or more in small claims court. Susan agreed to reduce her claim by one-third (since she wore the dress twice), and the cleaner and proprietor split the difference.

Disagreements can also be resolved through arbitration, a more formal process. Both sides present evidence and witnesses to a presiding arbitrator (sometimes two or three). Usually arbitration is binding. The disputing parties must agree in advance to accept the arbitrator's decision as final. Sometimes the results can be appealed to a higher court. Many organizations offer arbitration services, including the American Arbitration Association, 140 W. 51st St., New York, NY 10019, tel. 212-484-4000.

PARENT TRAP

Another area where you may need legal counsel is in child support. If you are a noncustodial parent, you may ask the court to reduce the amount of child support you have been paying. A change in circumstances in the needs or resources of the parent charged with child support payments may convince the court to reduce those payments, at least temporarily. This may also be possible in the case of alimony payments.

If you are the custodial parent, you may petition for an increase in support because of higher expenses in caring for the child(ren). If you are receiving no support at all, there is no better time than now, during your term of unemployment, to seek what is due you. The extra money, should you (1) find the nonsupportive parent; (2) convince the court that he/she is capable of contributing; and (3) actually collect the payment monthly, could help tide you over until you get a job.

Unfortunately for the custodial parent, the record of collecting child support payments is a national disgrace. Recently, however, more stringent legal efforts have been initiated to locate and force offenders to pay. One method is to attach the wages and/or assets of parents delinquent in child support payments. Another is to withhold federal or state tax refunds due the offender. Some states will make automatic deductions from unemployment checks.

Laura had been divorced for two years. Her two sons live with her. Neither Laura nor her former husband, Tom, contested the divorce. Both reached an amicable agreement that included monthly child support payments by Tom, who was earning considerably more than Laura.

Six months after the divorce, Tom moved out of state and stopped making his child support payments. Laura didn't know where he had gone. His only contact with the children was by telephone, never revealing through these calls where he was. Fearing that legal pursuit of the payments would prove expensive and fruitless, Laura never attempted to find Tom. As long as her advertising business was prosperous, she felt she could manage without the child support. When her agency failed and she couldn't find a job, the payments became critical to her children's welfare.

Laura learned about her state's Child Support Enforcement (CSE) program and went for help. During the time it took to force Tom legally to meet his child support obligations, Laura qualified for Aid to Families with Dependent Children (AFDC). The agency would ultimately be reimbursed in part or full if and when Tom made his back payments. The AFDC payments would cease once Laura was receiving regular child support payments from Tom.

The CSE office asked the State Parent Locator Service (SPLS) to conduct a search for Tom. Using his social security number, the SPLS checked the records of other state agencies such as motor vehicle registration, unemployment insurance, and income tax. Information was also sent to the Federal Parent Locator Service (FPLS), which can search for a current address in the records of the IRS, the Department of Defense, the National Personnel Records Center, the Social Security Administration, and the Veterans Administration.

Convinced that Laura would never have the resources to initiate a search for him, Tom did little to cover his tracks and was found working in a neighboring state. It isn't always this easy, but thanks to a reciprocal agreement between the states, Laura was awarded a judgment against Tom for back and future payments.

Tom continued to ignore the court order, thinking there was little anyone could do to force him to pay. He was wrong. His wages were attached, and when his boss found out why, Tom was eliminated from consideration for a promotion.

Additionally, the state in which Tom resided permitted property to be attached or seized and sold to pay the debt. His new condo was attached.

Tom finally realized that this judgment had teeth and was clamping down on him. He made the back payments and sent his monthly checks. He even reestablished visits with his children.

Any parent or person with custody of a child who needs help to establish child or medical support obligation or to collect support payments from the noncustodial parent can apply for assistance through the local Child Support Enforcement office. The number can be found in the local telephone directory under the state/county social services agency. There may be an initial fee of around $25, but some states absorb all or part of the fee or collect payment from the noncustodial parent. Costs for the legal work done by agency attorneys and for locating an absent parent may be deducted from the child support payments collected or charged to the noncustodial parent.

Medical support is now included in any petition for child support when health care coverage is available to the noncustodial parent at a reasonable cost. Court orders can also be modified to include health care coverage if they were written before this law took effect or if coverage became available to the noncustodial parent after the court order was established. The noncustodial parent is now required by law to carry dependent minor children on his/her insurance.

When the parent obligated to pay child support lives in another state, collection is much more difficult but not impossible. All states are required to pursue child support enforcement as vigorously for children who live outside their borders as for those under their own jurisdiction. The primary legal tool for interstate enforcement is the Uniform Reciprocal Enforcement of Support Act (URESA), whose basic mechanism is the two-state lawsuit in which the enforcement agency (or private lawyer) files a petition with the enforcement agency or court in another state.

Your CSE office can also assist you in enforcing child support judgments when the noncustodial parent lives in another country. Many foreign countries recognize and help enforce these judgments. For information on how to enforce a support order in a country where there is no reciprocal agreement, contact the Department of State, Office of Citizens Consular Services, Washington, DC 20520.

For a free handbook on child support enforcement, write to the Consumer Information Center, Pueblo, CO 81009.

The federal Office of Child Support Enforcement is under the aegis of the United States Department of Health and Human Services, Family Support Administration, Washington, DC 20447. Information on child support issues may also be obtained by writing to the National Support Enforcement Reference Center, Office of Child Support Enforcement, 370 L'Enfant Promenade, Washington, DC 20447.

BAILING OUT

When all rights have been exhausted and there is still no job, a form of bankruptcy may be the only realistic option available to you. Bankruptcy could be a mixed blessing, however, since you could be sacrificing your credit rating for up to ten years in exchange for an almost clean slate. Filing does not wipe out your existing debt to Uncle Sam, for example. (See chapter 10, "Obscene Phone Calls.") Seek the advice of a lawyer who has a good reputation and is familiar with bankruptcy laws and procedure.

Your local bar association is generally a good resource for referral. Organizations for people with special needs such as the elderly and handicapped often provide referral services. Perhaps the best resource is the recommendation from a friend, family member, or associate who had a good experience with an attorney with the special expertise you need.

Remember to discuss the fees in advance so that you know exactly how much the procedure will cost you. Get it in writing. Under certain circumstances, the lawyer can be paid from the assets of your estate administered by the court in the bankruptcy procedure.

The Federal Trade Commission (Public Reference, 6th St. and Pennsylvania Ave., N.W., Washington, DC 20580) publishes any number of consumer publications (many in Spanish) that are available just for the asking. Among them are *Fix Your Own Credit Problems*, *Solving Credit Problems*, and *Refinancing Your Home*.

JUSTICE IS NOT JUST FOR THE RICH

There are more than 1,000 Legal Aid offices across the country (listed in the phone book under state services) that help people who cannot afford to hire private lawyers or that can refer you to other local, state, or national organizations that offer advice or help. Legal Aid offices generally offer legal assistance with such problems as landlord-tenant relations, credit, utilities, family issues, Social Security, welfare, unemployment, workmen's compensation, and criminal charges. The catch is one must be just about destitute to qualify for legal aid assistance.

If you do not qualify for any of the free legal services offered, the Lawyer Referral Service of your state, city, or county bar association (listed in the phone book under "[name of state/county] Bar Association") will advise where you can obtain a low-cost consultation or representation on a sliding scale, a fee based on a client's ability to pay.

Some states have initiated a "Dial-a-Lawyer" program under the aegis of the bar association. Attorneys volunteer to be available at a given time on a given day to answer questions free of charge. Many law firms now offer this free service as well. Finding them may require calling around or watching for ads or commercials, now that attorneys are permitted to advertise. Some law schools offer clinics dealing with consumer problems.

Some "retired" attorneys are establishing free storefront family law centers for those who don't qualify for assistance anywhere but can't pay for private attorneys. Unfortunately, these centers aren't as widespread as the need dictates. Your local bar association should be able to tell you if one is available in your area.

A low-priced alternative is hiring a paralegal, who is trained in some aspects of the law but not a member of the bar and is thus prohibited from any activity that could be construed as practicing law. Paralegals typically prepare uncontested divorce papers, child support agreements, wills, routine contracts, name changes, and partnership agreements, and may also provide services in matters of bankruptcy and immigration. While a lawyer may charge several hundred dollars for preparing papers in an uncontested divorce, a paralegal may charge as little as $25.

Attorneys warn against using the services of a paralegal who is not monitored by a member of the bar. They point out that what may seem like a simple matter may turn out not to be so simple and may require the services of an attorney who could ward off a problem before one begins. The price structure for paralegals, however, continues to increase demands for their services. For example, a paralegal charges from $50 to $150 for a will and from $20 to $75 for contracts, considerably less than attorney's fees. Over 6,000 paralegals were operating in 1992, and the number steadily increases. To find one in your area, consult the Yellow Pages under such headings as "Divorce Assistants," "Paralegals," "Legal Forms," or "Legal Clinics," or call the National Paralegal Association at 215-297-8333 (Pennsylvania).

Other sources for referrals to lawyers are: National Resource Center for Consumers of Legal Service, 1444 I St., N.W., Washington, DC 20005; AARP Worker Equity Department, Advocacy Programs Section, 601 E St., N.W., Washington, DC 20049; and National Employment Lawyers Association (for lawyers who specialize in employment law), 535 Pacific Ave., San Francisco, CA 94133. NELA publishes a directory of its members for a $10 fee.

BALANCING THE SCALES

Jimmy Buffett wrote a song titled "If the Phone Doesn't Ring, It's Me." You, on the other hand, must make the phone ring anywhere there may be a chance for assistance. Justice is blind, not deaf. If you speak loud enough, someone will hear and help.

I WORK, THEREFORE I AM:
Maintaining a Sense of Self

AND WHAT DO YOU DO?

In our work-oriented society, a large percentage of conversations center on our jobs. Introduce yourself at a party, and someone is likely to ask what you do for a living. "What do you do?" really means "Who are you?" In the past you might have answered "I am an engineer." As an unemployed person you might feel you should respond "I am a nobody." Wrong! You are still an engineer, albeit an unemployed one.

Men are more typically victims of this syndrome than women. From the beginning of time, the man was expected to slay the wild boar and drag the carcass home. The contemporary man has not completely shed the caveman instinct. His wild boar is a regular paycheck, his hunting ground his place of employment.

The man who rode the golden staircase to an exalted career suffers the most. He believed that success was due him because he worked hard. He never had any reason to doubt that. Such men never had to face themselves; they don't yet know what they are really made of.

SAME PERSON, DIFFERENT DAY

Unemployed workers lose their sense of self-worth when they lose their job. They measure their value by their paycheck, define their status in their community by their vocation. Feeling worthy hinges on achieving success in business. Feeling a failure, therefore, is a natural progression when the raison d'être, the job, has been taken away.

Orienting life around one goal is not only too narrow, it's passé. Allowing one objective to define life was a phenomenon of the extravagant eighties and is considered counterproductive in the more realistic nineties.

The person who loses a job is the same the day after notice of termination as the day before. His/her value is neither eradicated nor minimized. Only the direction in which to channel that value has been changed. Recognize that only your employment status is different, you aren't. Infinitely more tragic than unemployment is letting the best parts of yourself slip away with the job.

Take this time to balance key aspects of your life, to reassess and reclarify the real meaning of success. Spend time with your family, loosen up, start an exercise program. Schedule time away from the job hunt. Don't even think about it. R&R at any crossroads is advisable, but it's almost critical at this juncture and should be encouraged and supported by the entire family.

Keep moving. Stagnancy runs down your battery. Hope is the fuel that drives you forward; despair is the sinkhole that traps you. Cultivate hope by meeting people, renewing old contacts, and making new ones. Join a support group for constructive commiseration.

Loss of self-esteem may be based on your perception of how others see you. Too many believe they are judged by what they do, not by what they are. In truth, your perception of yourself is the most influential factor of how others view you. If you act like a winner, you are a winner, and everyone will have no choice but to agree with you.

Losing a job does not a failure make. Allowing it to affect what could be the rest of your life does. Remove labels. "I am . . ." should be followed by several sentences rather than just two words. Take a long look at the total person. See the many facets that make up the whole.

Since losing his job, Joe started getting up later each morning and watching television late into the night. He feels defeated and lost. He resents his wife, Barbara, for still having a job, for having a setting where she can be confident about her value. The tension has been building between them. Joe is convinced that Barbara blames him for losing his job. He even suspects her of withholding sex because she no longer respects him.

Joe chafes over his inability to reach into his once-deep pockets to help his kids when they need it. He doesn't want to see them because he is too embarrassed to face them. Joe is all too aware that he is sinking into a paralytic state, but he feels powerless to do anything about it.

The fear that your spouse and kids no longer respect you can be devastating. You wonder if they saw you only as a paycheck, and without it, they will see you as a failure. You shy away from friends, convinced they won't want anything to do with a "loser." The resentment builds, usually without any real basis in fact. The slide from pinnacle of pride to deep depression accelerates.

If your family reveled in the good times, that's only human, and you enjoyed it as well. Your family's comfort, after all, was a showcase of your capabilities as a breadwinner. Now stripped of what you have always considered to be your greatest contribution to the family, you question your place within the new structure.

In truth, you are probably the only one trying to figure out where you belong within the family framework. The "provider" was only one part of you, the rest is the same. Once again, it's your own perception of yourself as merely "a paycheck" that locks your family out. If you let them in, they can be your greatest source of comfort and support.

No one can deny that it's hard to cut back on things that you and your family took for granted before. On the television show "Northern Exposure," the disk-jockey-cum-pseudo-philosopher Chris Stevens commented, "Happiness doesn't come from having things, it comes from being part of things." Don't get hung up on things. Maintaining and enhancing family dynamics at this time is much more important.

Friends and extended family too can be your best allies if you reach out and show them you would welcome their support. Similarly, your religion or some sense of spirituality can provide strength and purpose. Don't get turned off by the few friends who avoid you, those who still have jobs and suffer from survival syndrome (fear that your unemployment will rub off on them). With a little encouragement, most friends will rally to your corner.

VIVE LA DIFFERENCE

No matter how enlightened we like to think ourselves, the man-as-breadwinner image is deeply imbedded in our psyche. Even if a man considers himself a sensitive new-age male, he probably grew up in a household where his father was the primary wage earner. The well-being of a family depended on Daddy's ability to bring home the bacon. Daddy's boys understood that someday it would be their responsibility to provide for their own families.

Men have traditionally defined themselves with a narrow focus, primarily by their career. Their vocation or profession may have influenced whom they could choose to marry, how they lived, their status in the community, and how they saw themselves. Seen from this viewpoint, a man's life is a house of cards built on his career. Rattle his career, and everything in his life collapses.

To a man who equates his masculinity with his achievements on the job, unemployment is particularly painful. He
has great difficulty accepting a role reversal with his wife and
doubts her ability to support the family.

Women grew up thinking they had a choice of home, career, or both. As dewy-eyed teens with rose-colored glasses,
they eschewed the possibility of divorce or single-parenthood
that has escalated the number of head-of-household moms.
Women in two-parent households still have more choices than
men. Generally the primary caretakers, women often have
the option of a full or part-time job, or not to work at all,
depending on the family finances. Some have been spurred
on to successful careers by mates who bask in the reflected
glory of their new-age trophy wives.

In the movement to have it all, women have defined themselves with a wider-range lens than men. They include all of
their attributes as mother, worker, homemaker, gardener,
fashion designer, artist, chauffeur, wife, and sex goddess.
However, as women assert themselves in a world formerly
dominated by men, they too begin to narrow their self-defini-
tion.

An unemployed woman finds that sympathy is not doled
out as generously for her as for the unemployed man. Studies
show our country traditionally favors the male breadwinner
during hard times. Although not as overt as in prior generations, discrimination against women is still fairly common.
Despite the rapid rise in the number of female heads of households today, a woman is nonetheless accused of taking a job
from a man who must support his family.

A woman looking for a job faces an extra set of problems
not encountered by men. A potential employer may harbor
the belief that hiring her would shortchange a man who
"really needs the job." She may also have to convince her
family that the job is important to her.

"A woman's place is in the home" is a credo many live by,
and that surprisingly large group may include your mate,
your children, your parents, and—shock, shock—your fe-

male friends. They may well believe that your job loss is a clear sign to stop working and concentrate on your family. Contrary to public opinion, this may not be the best time to start or add to your family.

Man or woman, you probably made many sacrifices in your personal life to accommodate your career. Now is the time to reevaluate your priorities. Taking one step back will help you move forward. Gather a new perspective and use your previous experiences as a measure. The choices you make now could influence your entire future.

THE LONG AND WINDING ROAD

During the early nineties, hardly a newspaper or magazine was published without some report on the recession. The stories centered mainly on the emotional and psychological impacts on the unemployed. The model generally presented for the emotional stages that one should anticipate was borrowed from studies made of people coping with grief, as in a death in the family. Since unemployment is often compared to a loss through death, the model seemed appropriate.

The pitfall in this comparison is that it falls short of defining persistent grief for a chronic situation. The unemployed indeed go through the same stages of grief, beginning with shock, then denial, then anger, and ultimately acceptance. Unlike someone coping with death, the unemployed go through the stages again and again with every job rejection, often increasing in intensity as the months go by with no new job in sight.

Those who are jobless for months on end begin to fear for their sanity because they are unable to put their grief behind them. Everything they have read tells them they should be long past these stages. "What's wrong with me?" they ask. "Am I going crazy?"

Studies of workers in the Great Depression of the 1930s showed that prolonged unemployment, regardless of psychic predisposition, caused a person's self-confidence to deteriorate. In her *Professionals Out of Work* (Free Press, 1981), one of the few comprehensive studies specifically of the unemployed, Paula Goldman Leventman says, "All of the unemployed ultimately became extremely distressed. Initial anger, rallying of resources and energetic job search, engulfing hopelessness coupled with continual failure, fear, acute anxiety, gradual retreat to apathy broken by episodes of rage or frenetic activity—these are the psychological effects of prolonged unemployment."

"The Great Depression" is a double entendre describing the economic as well as the psychological state of the era. "Depression occurs when we lose a job and our hopes are dashed," says psychologist Donald W. Steele in his self-published pamphlet *Coping with Unemployment* (available by sending $2.00 to Steele Publishing Co., P.O. Box 407, Mansfield, MA 02048; reduced rates for bulk orders).

"It is natural to feel discouraged, sad, or depressed. We may feel we have little control over our lives." He lists the signs of depression as:

• Subdued mood
• Low energy
• Inability to sleep well
• Poor appetite
• Difficulty getting up in the morning
• Crying easily
• Diminished sex drive
• Avoidance of others

Feelings of inadequacy interfere with looking for work. Depression feeds upon itself. To take steps to prevent the blues from getting out of hand, exercise, maintain a healthy diet, and develop a regular schedule. Seek out activities you enjoy, visit friends, and participate in community events. These and similar activities will help to give you a handle on who you are and where you're going.

Most of all, give yourself the credit you deserve. Coping the best you can in a bad situation is an achievement. Finding a job is certainly your goal but not the only measure of your value at this time.

For thirty-five years Joe's life was dictated by appointments and deadlines. He yearned for the day when he would have more free time. Forced into early retirement, he suddenly has all the time in the world. Yet he can't remember what he intended to do when he had time. He spends his afternoons eating potato chips and brownies, becoming more immobile with each day. Exercising just the right blend of patience and prodding, Barbara convinces Joe to volunteer to teach adult education courses. This single activity helps him begin to restructure his life.

Depression often goes unrecognized but can become a serious problem without treatment. Help is readily available. Lack of funds should not preclude seeking medical attention or professional counseling. In addition to ruling out serious illnesses as contributing to depression, your family physician can advise you of available counseling options in your community. Just about every major city in the country operates free mental health clinics. Check your local welfare or unemployment office for locations.

Concerns about where your next dollar will come from often triggers anxiety. Dr. Steele cites some common signs of anxiety:

- Shortness of breath
- Restless sleep
- Excess worry
- Preoccupation with troubles
- Difficulty concentrating
- Restlessness
- Lump in throat
- Short temper

Dr. Steele recommends adequate physical exercise to manage anxiety and release tension. He also advises focusing on the present and pursuing a relaxing activity.

The longer you're out of work, the more likely you'll experience an episode of panic, especially if you're older. Eighty percent of the jobless are over 40 and hear the clock ticking loud and fast. You can minimize panic by following suggestions to reduce anxiety and by avoiding situations that are apt to instill it. For instance, you may want to avoid "ain't it awful" stories about unemployment and foreclosure notices in the media. Staying away from friends who like to rattle on about the terrible economy is also a good idea.

Not having a clear target at which to direct anger may be the most frustrating aspect of unemployment. Should you be angry with the person who delivered the pink slip, even though he was merely following orders from a company president who had to make cutbacks for the survival of his business? Blame the economy? Whose fault is that? Whom do you punch out? (Figuratively speaking, of course.)

Are you angry with yourself for not finding work, or with your family for representing the financial burden you feel buried under? Misplaced anger can breed violent behavior. Take out your hostilities on a punching bag, a tennis racket, a baseball; then get on with your life.

MIRROR, MIRROR ON THE WALL

"First impression is significant," says Nancy Michaels of Impression Impact, a personal image and marketing firm. "Good or bad, that initial impression has lingering effects." Michaels cites the need for constant vigilance because "you never know when you'll be making that impression." You could be at the supermarket and meet someone who can give you a lead on a job. Or a prospective employer could be among the patients in the waiting room at your doctor's office.

Michaels urges, "Think of yourself as a product that needs to be marketed." Examine your product to determine your potential buyers. Investigate your marketing segment and its industry standards. This preparation not only helps your self-image but presents you in the best light during interviews.

The longer you are unemployed, the more tendency you have to overlook routine grooming. Why get dressed when you're just going to work on letters and make phone calls? Why bother fixing your hair if no one is going to see you? Why shave or put on makeup if you're not going out of the house? Before long, you end up looking like a derelict you warn your children against talking to.

Your state of "dis-dress" is bound to alarm your family and friends, even elicit pity for your deteriorated state, the last reaction you need right now. They don't understand why you don't pull yourself together. You don't understand why it takes monumental effort to dress yourself up now, when you never had a problem before.

By attending to personal grooming first thing in the morning, you take a major step in seizing control over yourself for the day. Not only will you bolster your self-image, you will be ready to act on any opportunity that arises. Even when you are running an errand, you may see friends or former coworkers who are tied into the network that could lead to your next job.

While personal grooming is important, it is only half of your image. Your facial expressions and body language make up the other half. Despair shows in your voice, your movements, and your expressions; so does anger. People around you react to your nonverbal messages. This includes not only your family but potential employers as well. Try acting *as if*.

Act *as if* you're cheerful, and people will react to you as if you are. Talk enthusiastically, walk briskly, and you will feel more positive. Acting *as if* sustains your family's confidence in you and pays off in job interviews.

INSIDE OUT

Nietzsche said, "That which does not kill me makes me stronger." Every experience in life is preparation for the next.

Each can bring out a new set of resources to add to your defense arsenal for coping with a new, unpleasant, or adverse event in your life.

> Since Laura's advertising agency failed, she has been overcome by terror, impeding her ability to find a new job. She puts on a great front for her sons, but in reality she is only an argument away from a breakdown. Any day she expects to find herself encased in a straitjacket and locked in a padded cell. She knows she is losing control over herself and her children, who have always relied on her strength and reassurance. Ever the survivor, Laura recognizes that she had better take hold of herself now or she will slip away entirely.
>
> Laura draws on her experience in weathering another bad time—her divorce. She did not fall apart then. She saw what had to be done and she did it. She was strong and resourceful before and can be again, she acknowledges. Reassured of her strength, Laura begins to face the world again.

BOUNCING BACK

In the eighties we saw the growth of the recovery movement, which examined codependent relationships and the permanent injury borne by "adult children" who grew up subject to abuse, incest, and alcoholism. In an article in *Psychology Today*, Dr. Steven Wolin, a psychiatrist, criticizes the recovery movement because it "glorifies frailty and lumps trivial disappointments with serious mental illness, completely bypassing the human capacity for strengths and resilience."

Dr. Wolin objects to "the modern-day voices of doom on both the professional and popular front" when addressing codependency and points to the "need to foster awareness of the human capacity for strengths and resilience."

"Resilience is the capacity to rise above adversity and forge lasting strengths in the struggle," writes Dr. Wolin, adding that it "develops out of the challenge to maintain self-esteem." He characterizes resiliency as "insight, independence, relationships (give-and-take), initiative, humor (finding the comic in the tragic), creativity, and morality (adhering to standards of decency)."

Dr. Wolin's observations relate well to a household where the primary provider is unemployed. An adverse situation challenges the family to experiment and to respond creatively. The nineties could well spawn a "rebound movement" that emphasizes the more positive aspects of interdependence as opposed to codependence.

As members of a family and of society, we are automatically interdependent. We must rely on each other to achieve the common goal that benefits the whole. Interdependency is give-and-take, an excellent premise to live by during the ups as well as the downs.

ONE HAND WASHES THE OTHER

It's hard to feel good when you're continually meeting with rejection. Blunt no-thank-you letters, declined interviews, and unreturned phone calls can wear you down. It's important to find a way to bolster your confidence to counteract the rejections you face on a daily basis. Build success into your life. Volunteer to do something you are good at, and help your community in the process.

Tony wants to start a worker assistance program. His wife, Susan, doesn't want him to "waste" the time or the resources on volunteer work that he should be applying to a job search. Having participated in a support group before, she worries that Tony might be engulfed in negative energy and have even more difficulty staying motivated to look for work. Tony thinks the group will help restore some sense of control over his life. In addition, he will have a chance to network with others who may share job leads not suitable for them. Most significant to Tony is that he wants to do something that makes him feel useful and less isolated.

Volunteers are no longer just homemakers looking for an outlet for their energies and creativity. Lawyers, engineers, bankers, and secretaries are using volunteerism to investigate career changes and network into new jobs.

One 45-year-old training manager is in demand running a job bank, giving speeches, teaching mandatory job-search techniques, and distributing information on support groups for the unemployed, all as a volunteer. He, too, is unemployed, but his volunteer work makes him feel good about himself while helping others like him to survive. Volunteers are growing and learning with their unpaid jobs and are often able to turn the opportunity into well-paying positions down the road. Even if a job doesn't evolve, volunteering bolsters self-esteem and gets people up and out the door.

You may want to start your own work support group. Working through churches, synagogues, libraries, and career centers will provide a place to hold meetings. For detailed information, sample forms describing various ways that support groups can develop and operate, and a list of existing groups, contact the Employment Support Center, 900 Massachusetts Ave., N.W., Suite 444, Washington, DC 20001 for a copy of *The Self-Help Bridge: How to Start, Maintain, and Expand Self-Help Support Groups for Job Seekers*, published in 1985. Also check with your local unemployment office for available literature on how to start a support group.

DOUBLE IMPACT

In a television interview, novelist Carolyn Chute, who writes about Maine's working class, told the story of a well-to-do neighbor who complained she wanted the Chutes to spruce up the appearance of their property. The woman explained she wanted the neighborhood to look nice because she and her husband had worked hard for what they had. "Well," said Chute, "Michael and I worked hard for what we *haven't*."

DAYS OF OUR LIVES:
Minimizing Stress Within the Family

Every family member feels the impact of unemployment. Hard times can cause an already troubled family to tear each other apart or to pull together toward a common goal. Family relationships change during unemployment like iron in the blacksmith's fire, emerging as tempered steel or as slag. How your family handles the initial news of job loss sets the tone.

> Susan is less surprised about Tony's layoff than he is, but considerably more anxious. How will they manage to take care of the kids? What will happen to Natalie's scheduled surgery? Setting her anxiety aside for now, Susan realizes that Tony desperately needs to talk. He is shocked and stunned. She arranges for a neighbor to watch the kids and makes reservations at their favorite restaurant.
>
> Over dinner at a quiet table, they discuss the recent events. She urges him not to blame himself, stressing he had no control over what happened. They discuss what actions they should take to secure their future. They share their concerns and set up strategies for the family's financial survival. Susan concedes her anxiety but reaffirms her

faith in Tony. She convinces herself that somehow they will manage this crisis together and lets Tony know by playfully raising her water glass and making a toast to a new adventure. This sets the stage for mutual faith and trust as well as for a positive outlook when dealing with the children.

WHERE DO WE GO FROM HERE?

Your reaction to your mate's unemployment may take you by surprise, swinging from resignation to fury. Your fears for your family's well-being and a feeling of utter helplessness could send you into a worse tailspin than the one who got the pink slip. You may even feel more betrayed, more panicked than your mate. Your initial response may be denial or the need to escape.

Your innate protectiveness toward a loved one can fill you with wrath and indignation. That anger may be directed at your mate's former company, vented on your partner, or both. Your incredible anxiety influences your ability to think clearly.

Tension over your sudden decline in income and doubt over when your mate will land another job are inevitable. Everything changes—routine, lifestyle, interaction with children, even your sex life.

STOP, LOOK, AND LISTEN!

Much of the tension can be alleviated at the outset by listening to your partner and examining your own feelings about the situation. Express your support and encouragement, but refrain from offering advice at this point unless asked. Urge your partner to verbalize how he or she is dealing with the job loss. Counteract feelings of worthlessness or self-blame with a reaffirmation of your mate's strengths. Try to put his or her self-perspective back on track.

If your own fears and doubts are getting in the way of helping your mate, you should consider professional counseling immediately. Whether you should go separately or together initially depends on the type of people you are and what makes you most comfortable. If you were not there emotionally for your partner at the beginning, apologize. Start over. Learn how to support each other now.

THE CHILDREN'S HOUR

Today's children are much more worldly than any other generation. Even the young ones are aware of economic hard times and the ramifications. Trying to protect them from news of your job loss will only backfire. They will sense something is wrong and may assume they are somehow responsible. Or they may find out anyway and harbor irrational fears.

Through the media, your children already know that your family is not in this alone. That's a good start. Be confident. You can count on children to take their lead from you, whether upbeat or gloomy. Be honest. This is a family situation. Let them know how they can help.

Even preschoolers have a right to know, but keep your explanation simple. Answer any questions they may have in uncomplicated terms. Don't overexplain. Tell them you no longer work for your company. If they sense that you are sad and ask why, explain that you will miss working with your friends at your old job. Reassure them that you will find another job soon where you will make new friends.

At 4½ Nicholas is old enough to understand and react to his father's sudden layoff from his job at the bank. Calmly, Tony and Susan explain that "the company had to cut down on the number of workers and didn't have enough money to pay Daddy anymore." They assure him that Daddy will get another job, but until then the family will have to change some things they have been doing.

They encourage Nicholas to ask any questions he may have, and answer as simply and as honestly as they can. Yes, he can still watch videos. Yes, he can still go to school. No, they don't have to move. Yes, Daddy will be home sometimes during the day, and Nicholas will need to be quiet when Daddy is on the phone. His curiosity satisfied, Nicholas goes outside to play on the swing, convinced his life as he knows it will remain intact.

"Children can be very sensitive to change and may react with anger," according to Joan Y. Reede, M.P.H., pediatrician and child psychiatrist at Boston Children's Hospital/Harvard University. "Do not feel guilty. Your children will adjust to the situation. In difficult situations, look for outside assistance and counseling soon. Don't let problems fester between you and your child."

For more specific suggestions, send for the free booklet, *Anger—Plain Talk About Dealing with the Angry Child* (ADM-92078), available from the Information Resources and Inquiries Branch, National Institutes of Mental Health, 5600 Fishers Lane, Room 15C-05, Rockville, MD 20857.

Faced with drastic cutbacks that affect their lifestyle, teenagers may react with the same shock, disappointment, and anger that you experienced when you lost your job. Their greatest concern at this point is how the struggle for popularity through clothes and other status symbols will be affected by a change in family economics. Try not to view this as a shallow response. Remember they live in a much narrower world, mostly controlled by you.

Teenagers are only a few years away from having to deal with the ups and downs in the workplace themselves. Take this opportunity to share insights with them to prepare them for their future. Your experience could put a damper on their perceptions of their prospects for "getting ahead in the world." Emphasize that they are an integral part of the solution, not the problem. Keeping all channels of communication open is crucial.

> In the last few weeks, Laura's son Matthew has been spending more time away from home with his friends. Fitting in with his group appears to provide a needed substitute for his absentee father. Although she misses Matthew's help, Laura realizes that he has already assumed more responsibility than she had at his age. She feels guilty about having foisted the "man of the family" role on him since her divorce and more so since her advertising agency failed.
>
> Laura is aware that Matthew is also seeking alternative methods for approval and acceptance by his peer group to compensate for his inability to compete financially. Her guilt and their estrangement now that he's hardly home prevent her, however, from confronting him about his change in behavior. The warning bells are ringing, but at this point not loud enough to spur Laura into action.

Stress in a household where a parent is unemployed can drive teenagers to seek escape from perpetual arguments over money or induce steely silence. Escape is a natural impulse, so don't take it personally. Attacking your teen for what you perceive as insensitivity will only exacerbate an already delicate situation. Talk it out calmly. Encourage friendships that provide an outlet for frustrations with the family. Let your teen know you are there when you are needed, but understand her or his need for some extra space during these trying times.

CHILD POWER

Find tasks for your children that demonstrate the need for their help. Begin with a level of participation that makes it easy to contribute. Make your own list, and then confer with your children for other suggestions.

If possible, give your child an allowance to cover some of the expenses you normally would pay for. Seeing firsthand how money must be stretched and budgeted to meet obligations provides the best lesson on economics and evokes a greater understanding of the financial difficulties you are faced with.

Older children should be encouraged to earn money to pay for such items as clothing, cosmetics, and records, and to make their own budget. Allow them to make their own mistakes without saying "I told you so." Just don't bail them out when they don't have the money for what they really need. They will soon learn they will have to make their own adjustments to accommodate their income. This is not to say that you shouldn't offer the benefit of your greater experience. Show them that few people can buy anything they want. Suggest alternatives for buying every latest toy that is advertised on the Saturday morning cartoons. Help form a neighborhood cooperative to swap toys on the first weekend of each month. Videos, music cassettes, and books are other items that can be traded.

Help your child develop a savings chart showing how much needs to be put aside each week for a desired purchase. Place a star next to the amount when banked to show progress.

PULLING TOGETHER

A family is interdependent, a team that must work together for the greater good. Every team needs a captain (or captains) to provide the necessary leadership to emerge victorious. If the captain stumbles, the team suffers.

In the case of a two-parent household, cohesiveness and mutual support between the mates are critical for keeping the team viable. When one is unemployed, a united effort in the search for a new job is an important element in holding the team together. Assistance may not, however, win immediate acceptance. Your mate may perceive your rewriting of a résumé as criticism and your inquiries about the job search as meddling or nagging. Explain that you need to do something useful, that letting you help reduces the anxiety you feel. Depending on your areas of expertise, specific tasks you might contribute include:

- Researching companies where your partner intends to interview.
- Networking through your social contacts to turn up job leads.
- Editing letters and résumés.
- Tracking progress and organizing information from the job search.
- Gathering job openings from classified ads or other sources.

Try not to take charge. *Assist* is the key word here. Despite your anxiety, think twice about urging your mate to take a job where you know he or she will be unhappy.

Respect your partner's style of doing things. That includes everything from how the job search is conducted to how a dish is washed. *How* he or she approaches a task is not nearly as important as getting it done.

COMMON GROUND

Resilient families rise to the occasion when misfortune hits. Values are put into perspective, the important separated from the unimportant. They ask themselves, "What is the good I can take away from this experience?"

Unemployment is one of those unexpected calamities, but it presents the opportunity to identify priorities for your family. Discuss family goals with your mate to lay a foundation for future decisions. By agreeing on what you want to achieve, you establish guidelines for exploring resolutions to future problems.

The most frustrating aspect of problem solving is the disagreement over how to reach the solution. The difficulties stem from differing styles of discussion and views of the situation. For the sake of illustration, think of the proverbial manure pile.

If you woke up and discovered a pile of manure in your driveway, would you:

  a. Start cursing about how long it's going to take to clear away this mess?
  b. Dive in and start digging, because there's got to be a pony in there somewhere?
  c. Find out how the manure got in the driveway in the first place?
  d. Turn around and leave, hoping someone else will clean up the mess before you need to get your car out of the garage?

If you and your partner chose different answers, would you argue about who was right? Each answer makes a logical point. How then would you reach a decision about what to do with the pile?

Begin by identifying which items you can agree on. In the case of the manure, you could safely agree that there is a big pile in the driveway. Certainly you will agree that it can't stay there. Finding humor in the situation helps (is there really a pony in the pile?). From that point, brainstorming about what to do about it is much easier. By establishing common ground, you can proceed to discuss options for a problem's solution without undue arguments.

If you and your partner are having frequent arguments about who is right, both of you are losing every time. You both win when you work together to identify a solution you can both agree on.

Before you can discuss goals and share ideas for alternatives to reach them, you must feel free to confront your mate with something that is bothering you. An argument may ensue, but avoiding issues can destroy the problem-solving process and ultimately damage the relationship even more. Confrontation means a face-to-face meeting but needn't result in conflict with the right approach and attitude.

It's a wise person who doesn't look for an argument, but constantly changing the subject to a "safer" topic, pretending nothing is wrong, physically leaving the scene, and acting complacent create roadblocks that can become insurmountable.

Stored resentments can build to irrational proportions, sometimes culminating in vengeful actions such as making outrageous purchases or withholding sex. Placing all the blame squarely on your mate, punishing him or her by telling confidential secrets to others outside the family, withholding something of value to the partner, even sabotaging any efforts toward conciliation are other examples of destructive behavior. The more you attack, the more defensive your partner becomes and the less likely you will ever resolve your differences. Avoid avoidances. Overcome these barriers by learning to speak frankly on the issues without placing blame.

Focus on arriving at the most effective and satisfying solution. Respect your partner's views as legitimate and sensible. The concern of who is right should never come up.

As soon as you focus on who's right or who's wrong, you are engaged in a power struggle. "Understanding a point of view is more important than who is right or wrong," stresses Liberty Kovacs, Ph.D., MFCC (Marriage, Family, and Child Counselor), who heads up the Center for Marriage and Family Therapy in Sacramento, California. Dr. Kovacs advises clients to consider differences in opinion as "a matter of 'differentness.' Each has their own view and way of looking at the world. Understanding and acceptance is the key."

Before you talk with your partner about something that's bothering you, do your homework:

1. Identify what you believe to be the problem.
2. Consider alternatives you think might remedy the situation.
3. Decide what you want or need from your partner. Identify *why* it is important to you.
4. Above all, be flexible. Be open to compromise. You've got to give a little to get a little.

Your first step toward harmony may be in determining as a couple what you don't want. Agreement is easier to reach on what you don't want. Narrowing your options helps you to zero in on what is really important and reduces topics ripe for disagreement.

Dealing with someone whose reason for being is being right becomes a major life skill. Every discussion or confrontation is a struggle, and real issues are never addressed.

In this case the more flexible partner has to appeal to the other on the basis of what is important to him or her without getting caught up in explanations. Reasons don't matter—it just is. If there is affection and caring in the relationship, the one can bend to the other, raison d'être intact.

A video titled "Marriage: The Six Steps," produced by Dr. Kovacs, is available for $39.95. Write to Today's Marriage: The Six Stages, 455 University Ave., Suite 250, Sacramento, CA 95825, or call 916-646-0212.

CHANGING TIMES

Change creates stress, especially when coupled with uncertainty. By setting boundaries on change, you can function more productively. Plan for the worst-case scenario and know what actions you will take.

Pretend you had a vision that you will not find a job for the next fourteen months. What decisions will you make? Map out survival and job search strategies—plans A, B, and C with scheduled dates for implementation. Once a month have a family meeting to evaluate the effectiveness of those strategies.

Take a serious look at your prospects for finding work that will sustain your present lifestyle. Can you find a job in your geographical area before severance and unemployment benefits run out? On what date will you expand your job search to other states? How long can you continue to make house payments? When will you have to decide whether or not you need to move?

Identify those decisions you can control, and take action. Even making the decision to do nothing until forced can relieve stress. For example, you and your partner agree you can afford to make house payments for only another six months before you suffer serious financial damage. Both of you want to do everything you can to keep the house you worked so hard to buy, but you don't want to go bankrupt trying to hold on to it and then lose the house anyway. Plan A may call for no change for five months while you concentrate on finding a new job. If you are successful, moving will not be necessary. At the start of month six, if you haven't found a job, you may decide that the family will have to rent the house to enable you to continue mortgage payments and move to less expensive quarters (plan B). When all else fails, you may have to implement plan C—sell the house.

A master plan will save you time and energy. Your efforts can be directed toward more productive areas like your job search. Include an alternative course of action to allow you to change direction without missing a beat. To make your plan work, you and your partner must be in agreement. Determining survival strategies together may incite some arguments, but the resulting united stance makes the few confrontations worthwhile.

GREAT EXPECTATIONS

Often one member of the partnership assumes the sole responsibility for making the other one happy. That is an unrealistic burden to place on oneself. You should be able to depend on each other for comfort during a bout with the blues. Just be aware that your sympathy and efforts to help may be rebuffed.

Barbara can't understand why Joe doesn't pull himself together. She has always respected Joe's ability to handle difficult situations. In the beginning she gave him her complete sympathy. When Joe became sloppy in his dress, refused to call on friends, or to get out of the house at all, she became irritated with him. He was voluntarily dismantling the man she had respected and admired, leaving a stranger in his place.

She wonders if he is sick and wants him to see a doctor, but Joe refuses. She feels responsible for turning Joe around but doesn't know how. All of her efforts are met with resentment and resistance. He belittles her work at the gift shop, openly envious that her schedule has changed so little when his has changed so much.

Barbara continues to urge him to accompany her on visits to the kids or to the movies, to no avail. What is most alarming to her is his utter lack of interest in sex. A sensual man, Joe has always been very receptive to her advances in the past. Nothing, not even sex, prods Joe into action. She's certain that if he genuinely loved her, he would bring back the Joe she had been married to for so long.

Meeting continual rejection from her husband, Barbara eventually gives up trying. She spends more time with friends and works longer hours at the gift shop. She finds that getting out more gives her new perspective and enables her to be less critical of Joe when she's home.

A period of adjustment to a new status is to be expected. Out of sync with what has become normal routine, your partner may have difficulty seeing everyone else continue with their schedules when his or hers has been virtually aborted. Your mate's restlessness and hostilities may trigger your need to get away. Follow your instincts. Separate activities give you a breather and help you to deal more compassionately with what your mate is going through. Encourage your mate to do the same. In this case, extended family, friends, and support groups may have more influence than you do.

If your partner appears to be sinking further into depression, don't try to cope by yourself. Urge him or her to seek counseling. Go yourself if your mate refuses. If nothing else, you will have an outlet for your frustration and will get some guidance in dealing with the situation.

BEING THERE

Sometimes you can help the most by serving as a sounding board as your partner works through emotions or ideas. Offering advice interferes with the process at this point and could provoke a debate. Just listen! In a sense, your mate is using you to argue both sides of the issue. Ask questions to keep him or her talking. Talking is cathartic and often the first step toward insight. Let your partner know that at times, you too will need this type of discourse.

Put yourself in your mate's place. By embracing the other's perspective, you broaden your understanding of one another and strengthen your problem-solving abilities as a team. No mind reading, though. Playing psychic gets you both into trouble. Encourage your partner to express ideas and feelings so you don't misread them. Candid conversations can help your partner and you stay grounded in reality instead of panicking under the influence of projected fears.

Learn to offer support that bolsters confidence. While it's okay to offer sympathy, feeling too sorry only confirms fears about his or her ability to cope with problems. Talk about past accomplishments. Point out personal strengths. Allude to the job loss as only a temporary setback. Remind him or her that the traits that caused you to fall in love haven't changed.

Your partner may have a difficult time turning away from the stress of the job search at the end of the day. A person under stress often loses the ability to initiate action and needs help getting started. You should encourage him/her to enjoy leisure time. Devise activities that involve the whole family.

FRIENDLY PERSUASION

You may have to intervene to ensure that your mate maintains contact with friends. Similar to divorce, unemployment often makes friends feels awkward and unsure how to respond. On the other hand, the one who is unemployed is often too embarrassed to face old friends.

> Anne runs into one of Richard's old buddies. Normally effusive, he has little to say except that he hasn't seen Richard (her husband) in quite a while and has been meaning to call. In a flash, Anne realizes that these two friends have been avoiding each other for all the wrong reasons.
>
> Anne invites him and his wife over the following Saturday night. Later, she invites some of Richard's other friends as well. A little hesitant at first, most accept with offers to bring some snacks or wine.
>
> Once they are assembled and enjoying each other as they had in the past, Richard realizes he has done his friends an injustice by not trusting them to stick with him during the hard times as well as the good. His friends see that Richard is the same old Richard, not some basket case or a yuppie panhandler who would hit them up for a loan. They are embarrassed for having avoided him.

THE FACTS OF LIFE

Physical intimacy between partners usually changes during unemployment. You and your mate haven't lost your sex drive, you've just misplaced it.

Financial hardships and rejected job applications would shrivel anyone's regular hormonal urges. The one who lost the job may even feel unworthy of sex, while the mate's desire is abated by the partner's continual melancholy.

The absence of grand passion does not indicate that your partner no longer finds you attractive or sexy, so don't take it as one more blow to your already bruised ego. Your intimacy can be expressed in other ways that, ironically, can bring you closer together than at any other time in your relationship.

Confide in your partner. Share hopes and fears you don't share with anyone else. Maintain connection by exchanging trivial incidents from your day, including daydreams. And don't overlook romantic gestures. A love note under the toast at breakfast, a bouquet of garden flowers, a touch, a glance, a compliment, all reinforce affection.

THE BEST THINGS IN LIFE ARE FREE

Don't let financial worries distract you from the gifts your family has to offer one another. What price can you put on tucking your child in at night? On discovering a bird's nest together? On holding your grandchild for the first time? Adversity should not deprive you of the enjoyment from those blessings that money can't buy.

AM I BLUE?
How to Recognize When You Need Outside Help

U nemployment robs you of control over your life. Your future is uncertain, the present turned inside out. An unpredictable emotional ride and the lack of regular income magnifies preexisting problems within the family. If rage at the injustices of unemployment is driving you to extremes, partially or completely incapacitating you, you need assistance.

In your search for employment, rectifying family difficulties lays a stronger foundation for success. Just as you cannot leave all your problems at home when you go to work, you cannot leave unbearable stress behind when you go on a job interview. Family problems may even have factored into your job loss, especially if you were fired. Take action now. Avoidance makes a situation worse.

> Joe finally gets out to teach classes on fly-fishing and seems to feel better, but he still has many periods of despair. A couple of times he hints to Barbara that his life is over. Since he lost his job, his weight has increased. Joe's sleep schedule is all turned around, sleeping until noon and staying up long past midnight. Barbara can't under-

stand why Joe doesn't pick himself up and snap out of it.

Concerned about her husband, she first tries cajoling him, to no avail. Later she notices that he has started drinking scotch before bed to help him sleep. She isn't sure exactly how much he's drinking, because she falls asleep long before he goes to bed.

She pleads with Joe to get help, and even though he makes promises that he will, weeks pass without his taking action. In desperation, Barbara calls the family physician and explains the situation. The doctor suggests that Barbara schedule an appointment and accompany Joe on the visit.

During the appointment, Joe describes how worthless he has felt since he lost his job. Getting up in the morning requires a monumental effort, and he isn't sure it's worth it anymore. Alcohol temporarily relieves his pain, but Joe wakes up to the same rotten feelings the next day.

After listening carefully and giving Joe a complete physical evaluation, the doctor asks if Joe has had thoughts of suicide. Joe doesn't answer. Further conversation reveals that Joe has recently started to have problems with forgetfulness and that he can't make decisions anymore.

The doctor explains to Joe that his symptoms are typical of depression. Major changes in life patterns can trigger depressive episodes, but Joe doesn't have to continue to suffer with the symptoms. The doctor instructs Joe to stop drinking, since it only compounds the problem. He prescribes an antidepressant medication and suggests several sources to consult for counseling. The promise of help and relief from his symptoms offers Joe a glimmer of hope for the future, the first he has felt in months.

UNDERSTANDING DEPRESSION

Depressive disorders are widely misunderstood. According to the National Institute of Mental Health (NIMH), "A depressive disorder is a 'body' illness, involving your body, mood, and thoughts. . . . A depressive disorder is *not* the same as a passing blue mood. It is *not* a sign of personal weakness or a condition that can be willed or wished away." If you or a loved one suffers from depression, you may not recognize that you have a treatable illness. Symptoms can last for years without appropriate treatment.

Whether or not a person is likely to experience a depressive episode depends on several factors. Genetic, psychological, and environmental elements combine to trigger depression. Any unwelcome change in your life—such as unemployment—can leave you vulnerable to the onset of depression.

Depression is a serious illness. People die from it. Know the signs of serious depression and learn to recognize it in yourself or in loved ones.

Signs of Depression

- Persistent sad, anxious, or "empty" moods
- Feelings of hopelessness or pessimism
- Feelings of guilt, worthlessness, helplessness
- Loss of interest or pleasure in hobbies and activities that were once enjoyed, including sex
- Insomnia, early-morning awakening, or oversleeping
- Appetite and/or weight loss or overeating and weight gain
- Decreased energy, fatigue, feeling "slowed down"
- Thoughts of death or suicide; suicide attempts
- Restlessness, irritability
- Difficulty concentrating, remembering, making decisions
- Persistent physical symptoms that do not respond to treatment, such as headaches, digestive disorders, and chronic pain

A counterpart to one type of depressive disorder involves not only periods of lows but cycles of euphoria as well. During such a mood upswing, a person may feel better than at any other time of his/her life. This manic high can affect a person's judgment and social behavior in ways that cause serious problems. Indiscretions such as spending sprees, casual sexual encounters, and substance abuse are common.

Signs of Mania

- Inappropriate elation
- Inappropriate irritability
- Severe insomnia
- Grandiose notions
- Increased talking
- Disconnected or racing thoughts
- Increased sexual desire
- Markedly increased energy
- Poor judgment
- Inappropriate social behavior

MY BROTHER'S KEEPER

To determine if you or a member of your family has a depressive disorder, first get a complete physical and psychological evaluation. A physician will learn whether possible medical conditions or medication side effects have caused mood problems. Should the doctor diagnose a depressive disorder, he or she will recommend appropriate treatment. Depending on your diagnosis and severity of symptoms, you may need medication and/or one of the forms of therapy that have proven effective for depression.

A person suffering from depression may not recognize the symptoms and may need your intervention to get an appropriate diagnosis and treatment. This could require making an appointment and accompanying the person to the doctor. Any mention of suicidal thoughts should spur you to seek outside help *immediately*.

Contact your community health center, or call one of the hot lines listed in appendix B for a referral to someone who can help. For more information on depressive disorders, including the free brochure *Helping the Depressed Person Get Treatment* (ADM 90-1675), contact the Information Resources & Inquiries Branch, National Institutes of Mental Health, 5600 Fishers Lane, Room 15C-05, Rockville, MD 20857.

BROKEN AND BEATEN

Unemployment can leave you filled with anger and resentment. Financial problems strain your nerves to the breaking point. Screaming matches with your mate go in circles without resolution, and the silent treatment that follows is worse than the screaming. Those eggshells under your feet grow more fragile by the minute.

In a confusing tangle of frustration and fear, family members turn against one another. Isolation from friends and relatives can leave you nowhere to go for help. As any police department can tell you, domestic violence calls increase during periods of high unemployment.

No matter what the excuse, it is a crime to beat anyone, including a family member. You deserve to feel safe in your own home. According to NIMH, a woman who is a victim of abuse should have a plan for emergency action:

> A woman can do a number of things to protect herself. She can hide extra money, car keys, and important documents somewhere safe so that she can get to them in a hurry. The phone number of the police department should be handy. She should have a place to go, such as an emergency shelter, a social service agency, or the home of a friend or trusted relative.
>
> During an actual attack, the woman should defend herself as best she can. As soon as she is able, she should call the police and get their names and badge numbers in case she needs a record of the attack. Most important, she should leave the house and take her children with her. She may need medical attention, too, because she

might be hurt more severely than she realizes. Having a record of her injuries, including photographs, can protect her legally should she decide to press charges.

Long-range plans require identifying sources of support. Avenues to investigate include women's organizations, social service agencies, community mental health centers, and hospital emergency rooms. Confiding in a trusted friend or family member may help you determine your best course of action for your future. Should you require emergency counseling or need suggestions on how to take the first steps out of an abusive situation, call the National Coalition for Domestic Violence hot line at 1-800-333-SAFE.

Even if your relationship hasn't reached the point of domestic violence, you may need mediation to resolve conflicts. If you cannot convince your mate to seek help with you, consider going alone. Locate qualified counselors through your community mental health center or religious organization. The American Association for Marriage and Family Therapy is a national organization that offers assistance in finding therapists in your area and can be contacted at 1717 K St., N.W., Washington, DC 20006, tel. 202-429-1825.

THE WONDER YEARS

One of the worst parts of unemployment is giving up your fantasies of sending your teenager away to military school. Raising children is never easy, but coping with an adolescent under your roof when you're out of work is nearly impossible.

Laura, a divorced mother of two boys, has been having problems with her elder son, Matthew. He has lost respect for her position as head of the household since she was forced to close her advertising agency and has not been able to find a job. His every move and look says "What makes you think you're the boss?" He's hanging out with the wrong crowd. The smell of cigarettes permeates his clothes, and Laura suspects he is drinking as well. She confronts him with her suspicions, but he indignantly denies everything. She fears he is involved with drugs but she doesn't dare ask. Communication between them has completely broken down.

After much floor pacing, Laura contacts the Family Resource Coalition for information on family support services in her area, and she is referred to a local chapter of Families Anonymous. There she meets other parents who have children with behavior and substance abuse problems. From them, Laura gets suggestions and the support she needs to reach out to her son. She patiently encourages him to open up to her and, in time, learns that her fears for her son were magnified by her own anxiety about the family's financial problems. She considers herself lucky this time but knows that she must maintain a constant state of awareness for signs of developing problems.

The best way to help your kids, according to professionals, is to help yourself first. It's easy to get so wrapped up in your own problems that you no longer recognize your children's emotional needs. Learn to identify early warning signs of anxiety in your children and in yourself.

At Children's Hospital in Boston, doctors see an increase in child abuse as the unemployment rate rises. Typically, reports involve a despondent, out-of-work, often white-collar father thrust into the role of caregiver with little preparation. Such a situation can erupt into anger and violence.

In any situation where you can no longer cope with your kids, call an abuse prevention hot line. Child Help U.S.A. maintains a toll-free twenty-four-hour hot line at 1-800-422-4453 (1-800-352-0386 in California), where counseling is available for crises. Another source of support may be found through chapters of Parents Anonymous, listed in local phone directories.

When Anne became pregnant, she and Richard were overjoyed. Anne looked forward to becoming a full-time mother, and Richard was delighted that Anne made that decision rather than pursue her career as a women's fashion buyer. His salary as a graphic artist with a printing company would have been sufficient to support the growing family.

By the time Anne delivers her baby, however, Richard is out of a job, and her plans for full-time motherhood must be placed on hold. She has to return to work. Burdened with these pressures as well as the anxieties that many women suffer after the birth of a child, Anne experiences severe postpartum depression. Although Richard is understanding and patient, Anne shuns his efforts to help, because inwardly she is jealous that he is the one home with the baby, not she. She experiences unpredictable, volatile mood swings.

Even the baby seems to sense something is wrong, stiffening and crying when Anne holds her. This only exacerbates Anne's envy of her husband. Overwhelmed with despair, Anne cannot reconcile her dual role as wage earner and mother. She feels she is failing at both.

Anne's mother urges her to attend a meeting of a postpartum support group. The other mothers help Anne through her difficult transition, offering advice on how to deal with the guilt she feels for "abandoning" her baby and giving her assurance that she is a good mother despite the demands of her job.

CHILDREN HELPING PARENTS

If your children are grown and out of the nest, taking care of your aging parents may be a main concern. Thanks to a strong lobby, impressive voting records, and a rejuvenated spirit of volunteerism, senior citizens have many avenues of support services available. The Council on Aging and your local senior center are good starting places for up-to-date information about programs, discounts, activities, organizations, and agencies.

If you are in the unfortunate position of having to decide on long-term care options for your parents, you will want to read *How to Protect Your Life Savings from Catastrophic Illness and Nursing Homes: A Handbook for Financial Survival*, by Harley Gordon with Jane Daniel (Financial Planning Institute, 1991), or *Avoiding the Medicaid Trap: How to Beat the Catastrophic Costs of Nursing Home Care* (revised edition), by Armond D. Budish (Henry Holt and Company, 1990). The information in these books will also help you to prepare your family financially for your own care in the future.

FINDING RESOURCES

You might worry that you can't afford help when you don't have a job. Even though family intervention is critical, you are trying to tough things out on your own. But many sources of effective and inexpensive help are available to families in crisis. There are mutual self-help groups to guide you through almost every imaginable human problem.

Self-help groups that disseminate current information to those who need it are set up around the country. All mutual self-help groups have the same underlying purpose: to provide emotional support and practical help in dealing with a problem common to all members. A list of self-help organizations appears in appendix B. An organization's national headquarters can point you toward a group in your area or provide information on how to start a new one.

Check with your reference librarian for names and addresses of other types of support groups in your area, or get a local referral through a self-help clearinghouse. The American Self-Help Clearinghouse publishes *The Self-Help Sourcebook*, which contains information on finding or forming mutual self-help groups. If your library doesn't have a copy in the reference section, you can order the book by sending $8.00 (plus $1.00 for first-class shipping) to the American Self-Help Clearinghouse, Saint Clares–Riverside Medical Center, Denville, NJ 07834.

If you're not a group-type person, investigate private counseling options through your community mental health center. Local clinics often provide counseling on a sliding-fee basis. If you still have health insurance, many plans cover mental health care.

Don't forget the time-honored source for assistance: your clergy. Churches and synagogues are centers of many kinds of strength.

If you need outside assistance to cope with family problems, get it. Don't let anything stop you. The price you pay for not seeking appropriate help may be the life of a loved one, or even your own. Pick up the phone and talk to someone about your situation. Remember that people who work and participate in these support organizations understand what you are going through.

ONE DAY AT A TIME

In *A Certain Slant of Light* (Seaview Books, 1979), author Margaret Bonanno wrote, "It is only possible to live happily ever after on a day-to-day basis." Deal with today and the tomorrows are bound to get better.

FRIEND OR FOE?
Extended Family

Your extended family can be a great ally when you are unemployed. The family you grew up in knows your personality traits and background, and can draw on your past to help guide you through the present and into the future.

BLOOD MATCH

Your extended family is also affected by your unemployment. Parents and siblings feel your pain but are unsure about how much they should intervene. They feel powerless to change the situation—after all, what can they do? Reticent to step in where they may not be welcome, they feel impotent. How could this happen to someone they care about? Their concept of how the world is supposed to work has been shaken.

Parents are often confused as well. They were raised in a time when almost everyone they knew was employed by the same company until retirement. Unemployment is incomprehensible to them, almost unacceptable. They may even feel as if they have failed. If they had raised you "right," you would have been able to hold on to your job; ergo, they weren't good parents. Fearing your job loss may reflect badly on them, they keep it secret from friends.

Awareness of your parents' guilt and shame may make you feel inadequate. Mistaking your parents' feelings as criticism of you, you become defensive, driving them farther away. Rebuked, the extended family stands off, powerless even when explosive situations threaten safety within your household.

THE BUDDY SYSTEM

Shutting out your extended family cuts off a great potential source of comfort and support. They can expand your networking scope. If they live in other cities, they can yield concrete leads for employment by keeping an eye out for job opportunities in their newspapers. If they live nearby, they can take your kids out for a special day or invite you to dinner once a week, which may be the first step toward freeing you from self-imposed isolation. They can provide you with the praise you need for the things you do well, at a time when your self-esteem is low.

Doing something for them will also reinforce your sense of worth. Should you need help for drug or alcohol abuse, depression, abusive treatment of your immediate family, or other problems that may require intervention, this intimacy you've established increases the likelihood that you will reach out to them for help.

One of the best ways your extended family can help is by spending more time with your kids. Getting the kids out of the house is good for them and for you. The children need a break from the pervasive tension of the household, and you need the time to regroup. Many parents fear they are losing their own identity when overwhelmed with the never-ending responsibilities of parenthood, particularly those who have become full-time parents through unemployment.

The extended family also benefits. They get the opportunity to cultivate a closer relationship with your kids, while taking an active role in assisting you. Just their baby-sitting services during a job interview would be a great help, but they may be willing to sit while you have a badly needed night out or even to pay for the kids' piano lessons or to buy their school clothes.

THE OTHER SIDE OF THE COIN

Some parents and siblings who have never experienced unemployment have difficulties understanding the volatility of the current job market. This could result in their unwillingness to become involved in your problems. Even worse, they could become your biggest critics. Instead of compassion, you will get a litany of your shortcomings. Instead of support, you will be urged to "stand on your own two feet."

Parents may resent you for not living up to their expectations. "We sacrificed to educate you and you failed us" may be implicit in their attitude toward you, even verbalized.

Parents can manifest their disapproval in a variety of ways, unheedful of the havoc they may be wreaking. They may interfere with the relationship between you and your spouse or between you and your children. They may offer money with strings attached, informing anyone who will listen that you couldn't have made it without them. Their ultimate weapon might be trying to resurrect the power they had over you when you were growing up.

If other members of your extended family are also out of work, your unemployment may add to their bleak view of the future. They may avoid you because they "have troubles enough of their own." In this situation, misery may not love company. As one in a similar position, you should understand their motive if not their methods.

Accepting these attitudes from those you felt you could depend on may be the hardest thing you've ever done, but possibly the wisest. Adding to a breach that can never again be bridged can deprive you of a lifetime of other benefits your extended family can provide you—and especially your kids—once the hard times are behind you.

Holding a grudge can be more damaging to you than to those against whom it's directed. Think about the Thanksgiving and Christmas dinners and all the other family reunions you and your children will miss if you alienate yourself. Think about the guilt you may have to live with when your parents pass on. Does an honest difference of opinion or perspective justify all that? Only you can answer those questions, but think long and hard before you do.

Don't assume your family doesn't love you when they don't respond to your predicament as you feel they should. Maintain contact, but choose safe topics. Listen to their advice without arguing. They probably feel their blood ties give them the right to advise you whether or not you ask for their input. Family meddling is a clearer indication of affection than indifference.

While some families may not overtly offer advice, they nevertheless can't resist dropping hints here and there. Others lapse into steely silence. You would do well to solicit their opinions. Not only do you honor them by asking, you will ease a strained relationship by allowing them to speak frankly.

If your extended family is driving you to distraction, try not to vent your anger on your mate. On the other hand, if your mate is a source of irritation to you, try not to complain about that to your family. The irritation may be only temporary, but the effects of taking your complaints about him/her to your family are long range. Your family may store up resentments that will be hard to shrug off when life is back on track again.

FOR BETTER OR WORSE

Sometimes intervention by the mate who is coping better can reestablish ties with the extended family. One may be too immobilized, too ashamed to reach out, putting the onus on the other to bring everyone together.

> Tony feels as though his family has abandoned him when he needs them most. He still hasn't found a job, and his daughter needs surgery. Yet none of his siblings have called or visited. Becoming more adamant and irate as each day passes without hearing from his sisters and brother, he refuses to call them first.
>
> Tony's wife, Susan, can see that if she doesn't intercede, Tony and his family could be estranged forever. She calls his sister Claire to ask why no one in the family has been in touch. Susan reminds Claire about Tony's stubborn pride and the terrible strain he's been under since he lost his job. She tells Claire that despite his failure to call, he loves his family and needs them more now than ever.
>
> Claire confesses that she and the rest of the family got all the wrong signals from Tony's demeanor. Keenly aware of Tony's pride, they assumed that he preferred to be left alone to work out his problems. They believed their contact would be considered an intrusion on his privacy. Claire assured Susan that she would rectify this appraisal with the rest of the family and all would be in touch with Tony by the end of the week.

ANGELS IN THE OUTFIELD

When the entire financial world has slammed its door in your face, your extended family may be your only economic lifeline.

Discuss the eventuality of financial help before you need it. If assistance is impossible, you'll have time to seek alternatives. Also, you may be less embarrassed to accept the money before you're in desperate straits. Accepting help early can also save you from getting into serious financial trouble down the road.

If your parents offer money even though you don't need

it, let them know how much you appreciate their concern. Ask them if you can take a rain check on the offer should you run short in the future. If and when that time comes, don't hesitate to go back to them. Offering repayment with interest may make the task more palatable to you.

Don't let your pride prevent you from accepting financial assistance from your family. Try not to view your family's support as "charity." Their offer is an expression of love and may be the only way they feel they can help. "Pride cometh before a fall" may be a cliché, but it is all too true.

Borrowing from anyone, even your family, should be kept strictly business. Spell out in writing the terms of the loan and scheduled payback. Everyone has heard stories about money loaned to family members that was never paid back or returned too slowly. Don't jeopardize future family relationships by leaving the terms of the loan arbitrary, subject to interpretation later.

Make the terms as easy on yourself as is acceptable to all parties. Take into consideration that months may go by before you are working again. More months may pass before you can catch up well enough to begin repayment. If everyone is satisfied with the arrangement now, no one can call you to account later unless you fail to comply.

HOME SWEET HOME

Many young families move back to their childhood home when unemployed. Living with parents assures a roof over your head and food to eat, saving you money and reducing the stress that comes from worrying whether you will be able to afford the basic necessities of life.

While there are pluses, there are also minuses to moving back under your parents' roof. Loss of independence, living by someone else's set of rules, interference by grandparents in how you discipline your children, and loss of privacy are some of the risks you have to take in exchange for economic solvency and peace of mind.

When Anne and Richard moved in with her parents shortly after their daughter was born, she had great difficulty in adjusting to her return to the family home. She cried easily and often. Richard's job loss and his inability to find another filled her with angst. She swung between resentment toward him and guilt for feeling that way. Her mother immediately assumed almost total care of her new granddaughter, Hannah, shutting Richard out. Although Anne managed to function at her job, she willingly abdicated domestic and maternal responsibility to her mother.

Anne's parents were beside themselves because they didn't know how to help their daughter. They blamed Richard for everything—for getting "fired" (although he was laid off) and for not getting a new job, exacerbating Anne's condition. Richard was convinced that if the newspaper arrived late one morning, he would be blamed for that too.

With no other alternative for living arrangements, and in view of Anne's delicate psyche, Richard knew he had to try to assuage his in-laws as best he could. He recognized that their criticism stemmed not from malice but from concern for their daughter. His willingness to help around the house, his pleasant demeanor in the face of adversity, and his obvious love for his wife and daughter eventually softened his in-laws' antagonism toward him and secured him a more relaxed, if somewhat delicate, status as a legitimate member of the family.

At a time when your self-esteem is at its lowest, moving home again can trigger regression to adolescence in the presence of parents. You become defensive about your "inadequacies" and overly sensitive to any criticism. This scenario may be your mind's own creation. You have to remind yourself constantly that you are not still a child but an adult in control of your own destiny.

What you may not have any control over is the loss of your family autonomy, which can get absorbed into the established traditions of the host family. Holiday observances, mealtimes, the programs you watch on television, bathroom schedules, and other routines will be governed by the household in which you reside.

Living with another family under one roof is challenge enough, but when the families are so closely related, total harmony may be a fantasy. Mutual respect and understanding are vital. While those who own the home have a right to expect the guest family to adhere to their routines, they should not interfere with their lives.

Interference, however, works both ways. Stay out of your parents' relationship. Don't try to solve what you think are their problems. They have been married for a long time and have worked out their own way of doing things. Diplomatically demonstrate to them that you are entitled to the same consideration.

Recognize your parents' good intentions and anxieties. Keep an open mind. Accepting advice when it's good is a sign of maturity, not your parents' dominance over you. Neither should you feel guilty when you reject a suggestion as inappropriate for you. Everyone has to make moves to meet halfway, the most reasonable destination for all concerned.

DON'T TELL MOTHER

In an article in the *San Francisco Chronicle*, Charles Pierce stated, "I'd rather be black than gay because when you're black, you don't have to tell your mother." Parental approval is often a motivating force in our lives. Fear of disappointing them could prevent soliciting your parents' help when you most need it. More than likely, they would be disappointed and hurt if you didn't seek their guidance.

16

IS THE PARTY OVER?
Inexpensive Ways to Socialize

S o you've made a new budget, adopted a new lifestyle, left
the entertainment line blank in your master plan because
it's just too frivolous to consider during times like these.
Right? Wrong! Money doesn't necessarily buy joie de vivre,
so lack thereof shouldn't take it away.

LET THE FUN BEGIN

"Eat, drink, and be merry" is a phrase taken much too
literally. Our leisure time is too often linked to eating, drinking, and smoking in restaurants and bars because we have
been conditioned to think of this as a common ground for
getting together with friends. Besides being expensive, this
kind of entertainment is not necessarily relaxing. Alcohol or
other addictive escapes (for some, that includes food), can
leave us even more anxious and desperate once the effects
have worn off. Also, lack of variety in routine can result in
restlessness and dissatisfaction.

Having fun is a very personal matter. What entertains one
may be boring for another. Others' disapproval of or disdain
for your choice of leisure activities should not prevent you

from pursuing them. Nor should criticism. If you are enjoying tennis but have yet to sustain a decent volley, don't let sneers and groans scare you away. The important thing is getting off the sidelines and into the game.

ARE WE HAVING FUN YET?

Roller skating has come back into fashion. (Remember that treasured roller skate key you wore around your neck when you were a kid?) Roller-skating rinks generally charge anywhere from $2.50 to $5.00, including skate rentals. For that, you can skate to your heart's content (and, unlike ice skating, stay warm and dry in the process). Group lessons are usually offered for around $2.50 each. Some rinks make up only one part of an entertainment center that also includes bowling alleys, another relatively inexpensive activity for the whole family.

Most communities offer free or low-cost use of tennis courts, playing fields, ice skating rinks (if only a pond), and swimming pools. Gather some friends and arrange a tennis, swimming, or skating party, a softball or soccer game. These activities need not take place only during the day, since most facilities have night lighting.

If some are reluctant to join in for lack of prowess in the activity planned, say to them, "Try it, you might like it," and assure them that dexterity is not a prerequisite. Do not press too hard, however. Remember, fun is a personal choice. What's good for you as the gander may not be sauce to the other geese.

Wherever you live, there is bound to be within a reasonable number of miles any number of other fun and educational activities that cost little or nothing. If you've never been to a museum or an art gallery, you don't know what you've been missing. There is no admission charge to most art galleries, while most museums offer days or certain hours when entrance is free. Others have a "suggested donation." For example, the Metropolitan Museum of Art in New York City has a pay-as-you-wish program for those who cannot afford regular admission. Los Angeles County Art Museum offers every other Tuesday free all day. Whatever the focus—art, history, science—the experience can be exhilarating. The beauty, the history, the ethnic cultures of the world, indeed the entire universe, reach out and encompass you.

Try being a tourist in your own town. Swing by any hotel or tourist information center and pick up one of those "what's-doing-around-town" magazines. If visitors use this as a guide for having a great time, why shouldn't you? Take a city tour bus or trolley for around $3 to $5. Bet you haven't really seen at least half of the points of interest on the tour bus route.

Keep your eyes open for city festivals. Several communities throughout the country have "First Night" festivals, for example, held on New Year's Eve. Just $5 or $10 buys you entrance to an array of exciting events, indoors and out, that start mid-afternoon on December 31st and go on until after midnight. (Most of the outdoor activities require no fee at all.) Other festivals may be planned for mid-February to fight the mid-winter doldrums, or at the beginning and end of summer to usher in or bade fond farewell to the lazy, hazy days.

Then there's the three *p*'s—picnics, potluck suppers, and politics. Politics? Why not! Pick a candidate you believe in and volunteer to work on the campaign. It's a great way to meet new people, socialize, and eat free. (Eager candidates, with the help of their more affluent supporters, give great parties that campaign workers generally get to go to free.) Picnics and potluck suppers speak for themselves—a great way to get together with family and friends without fuss and for little cost. As long as we are talking volunteering here, look into joining committees for special events sponsored by charitable organizations. As a member of the working inner circle, you may earn your glass slipper for free admission to the ball.

If you like to shop but are afraid to hit the malls because your version of window shopping is buying a window, try yard or garage sales and flea markets. Make an excursion out of it by lining up several sales within the same area, invite someone who shares your enthusiasm to go along, and pack a picnic lunch that can be eaten in the car en route or in some pretty spot during a break. Bring with you only what you can afford to spend (no credit cards), and spend it only on what you really need. The fun here is the browsing. Poking through someone's belongings is like reading someone's diary with permission.

Eerie as it may sound, outings to old cemeteries are educational and entertaining. Some of the epitaphs could provide a stand-up comic with material for a year. Others are beautiful or poignant, often relating little pieces of lost history. Bring paper and charcoal to make headstone rubbings of the most impressive. Framed and hung, the rubbings make interesting and unique additions to your decor.

CURTAIN GOING UP

If you prefer more structured entertainment, volunteer as an usher at theatrical productions, both amateur and professional. Check out all possibilities, and don't be scared off by what appears to be too prestigious. Even in rural areas, small repertory production companies and community theaters can be found. College theater groups probably use only students to usher, but tickets are inexpensive and productions are surprisingly professional. Grade and drama school productions that feature children may not be as professional, but their enthusiasm is contagious. It may not be Broadway, but it's entertaining and stimulating nevertheless.

Large cities, of course, offer a much richer and more diverse selection. For example, cities such as Chicago, New York, San Francisco, Los Angeles, St. Louis, Miami, and Atlanta all have professional companies featuring seasoned actors in tried-and-true productions or new plays. Many of these cities may have as many as six companies, perhaps even more. Numerous amateur productions go on as well throughout the year.

Requirements for ushering are minimal. Call in advance to volunteer. Show up about an hour prior to performance. Direct patrons to their seats and pass out programs. A few minutes after the show begins, when you are confident that everyone is seated, grab an empty seat and enjoy. You will also be asked to stay after the performance to help clean up— a small price to pay for a great evening out.

FOOTLOOSE AND SOMETIMES FANCY FREE

Almost every major newspaper in the country publishes a once-a-week listing of events. Among them you will find an array of lectures, concerts, exhibits, classic film festivals, and other regional and ethnic events, many free and others for modest cost. Your library (where you will generally find the classic film festivals) is a treasure trove of entertainment for adults and children alike.

Your local center for adult education may seem an unlikely place for having a good time, but the walls reverberate with the sounds of laughter and dancing feet. Each one varies, of course, but many offer swing dance parties (around $5), hosted by the dance teacher who is happy to give tips on how to move two left feet.

An eight-week, once-a-week dance course costs around $75, which breaks down to a little over $9 a week for the most fun you'll have in leather-soled shoes (suggested footwear for the course). Pick your own tempo—jazz, swing, ballet, tap, ballroom, modern, folk, square, or belly dancing.

If your interests lie in more intellectual pursuits, adult education centers offer myriad courses from art appreciation to yoga, all for under $100 for up to eight-week courses. At some centers your tuition will be discounted in exchange for volunteer work. Those over 65 may enroll for half the regular tuition. Scholarships are available based on financial need.

Anne and Richard want to go out dancing to celebrate their third anniversary, but with no new job in sight for

Richard, they can't spare the money. Their anniversary falls in the spring around high school prom time. They volunteer as chaperons at the senior graduation dance and have more fun than the kids. An evening of dancing, refreshments, and romance costs them nothing. Baby-sitting is provided free of charge by Mom.

Now that Anne and Richard have reignited their terp-sichorean tendencies (and their moms have indicated they would baby-sit on occasion) they look into other free or low-cost places they can go to dance. They discover that virtually every fraternal or veterans' organization and union that maintains a hall sponsors dances on a regular basis. This includes the Elks, Amvets, VFW, Masons, American Legion, and Odd Fellows. Some offer live music, others offer disk jockeys, and the variety ranges from ballroom to rap dancing. Entrance is rarely more than $5; membership is not a requirement, and guests are often allowed to bring their own refreshments.

I WALK ALONE

Enjoying yourself does not always require company. Solitary activities are also satisfying, rewarding, and even cleansing. Try your hand at writing. Even Hemingway had to start somewhere. Recording your innermost thoughts while unleashing your imagination can relieve you of some of your pent-up emotions. Biking, jogging, or walking gives you physical release of tensions. Spend some time each week in the library for some peaceful reading or writing—even poetry. Rod McKuen may not consider your verse a threat, but you can often say something in rhyme or prose that you can't express in any other way. Try sketching. That, too, could open up a whole new vista for you. Any or all of these suggestions afford you the opportunity to get outside of yourself, not a bad place to be for a while, particularly during stressful times.

ANOTHER SEASON

Limited budgets need not take the fun out of holidays. Rather, they can add to it. Just let your creative juices start to flow. Encourage the rest of the family to do the same. With a little ingenuity, you could complete your Christmas gift list on a shoestring and still make everyone happy, particularly the kids.

How often have you heard someone complain that the kid pushed away an expensive gift to play with the box it came in? You could make such a kid deliriously happy with a giant-sized moving or appliance box. Cut out a door, add some windows, and decorate, and voilà, you have a playhouse, fort, or store.

If you know which end of the hammer to hold, you probably can build a bird feeder to give to some lucky kid. (It would also make a thoughtful gift for an adult.) According to the United States Fish and Wildlife Service, 82.5 million Americans regularly feed wild birds and love it. It's inexpensive, educational, and endlessly entertaining.

Set the feeder a short distance from the house for better viewing, preferably near a big bush or tree that provides cover for the birds as they come and go. In bad weather when kids are confined to the house, they can get a terrific show watching the birds, a great way to pry them away from the television set for a while. The National Bird Feeding Society recommends using a good quality commercial wild bird mix and urges consistency in feeding. Send a self-addressed, stamped envelope to the National Bird Feeding Society, 1163 Shermer Road, Northbrook, IL 60062 for more information on bird feeding.

For the future actresses on your list, collect "dress-up clothes"—cast-off dresses, sweaters, shirts, shawls, shoes, hats, purses, jewelry, scarves, and more. Find a large box to use as a "trunk" and decorate with stars, theatrical posters, and names of exotic cities in which your budding Sarah Bernhardt may some day perform. Complete the picture by stenciling on the name of your "star." Someday, your potential thespian may be thanking you for that gift from behind the footlights.

For your future engineer or mechanic (over 10 years old), collect broken small appliances and present them with a mini toolbox that holds a screwdriver and pliers. Taking the appliances apart and trying to put them back together can provide hours of fun and satisfy some natural curiosity about "what's inside?" as well. Be sure to cut off the power cord from the appliances before giving them to the child, to prevent him or her from trying to plug them in.

For stocking stuffers, buy a package of cotton T-shirts in a discount store (around $5) and give one to each kid with the appropriate materials to decorate or tie-dye; make pencil containers from soup cans covered with felt, contact paper, or yarn; decorate coffee cans or oatmeal containers to use as containers for trinkets. Fill with marbles, a deck of cards, hair ornaments, or the like. Craft books found in abundance at your public library can give you enough ideas for the next twenty Christmases.

Give "gift certificates" to the adults on your list. For example, ten hours of baby-sitting; mowing the lawn for any four weeks; free labor for painting a room (or rooms), knitting a sweater or making a dress (materials provided by the giftee). A romantic candlelight dinner for two, catered by you, would require some outlay of cash, but the $15 or $20 expenditure for a good, nutritious meal would be much more appreciated than a tie or a scarf that would cost the same. The old standby brownies or Christmas pie would also be more appreciated than a store-bought item of equal cost.

Kids, too, can get into the spirit with their own handicrafts. Getting a picture of a baby cousin and making a frame for it out of decorated popsicle sticks, with a magnet on the back for easy mounting on a refrigerator, would make a perfect gift for an aunt or uncle. A paperweight made from a baby food jar containing a rubber aquatic animal swimming in glitter water would make a lovely gift for Mom or Dad, as would small bowls made from air-dried clay decorated and sprayed with an acrylic finish.

Homemade tree decorations can be a family affair and cost virtually nothing. Snowmen can be made by sticking together two sizes of styrofoam balls (found in any craft shop) and using buttons for eyes and felt for nose, a strip of material glued on as a scarf, and twigs as limbs. Toilet paper rolls can be magically converted to a variety of decorations with a little imagination and inexpensive materials found in any dime store or craft shop—glitter, sequins, ribbon, felt, and more. Holiday craft books are loaded with suggestions, but get to your library early in the season. More and more people are recapturing the joys of a homegrown Christmas.

I LOVE YOU TRULY

Romance is not something that just happens. You have to make it happen, but it needn't take a major investment. Eat your heart out, roses, but a flowering potted plant grown from cuttings from an existing plant sends the same message. Homemade chocolates still say "sweets for the sweet." A picnic in a special, private spot can show more love than a chichi dinner in an expensive restaurant.

Any token gift can shine like a jewel when wrapped as a kiss—a Hershey kiss, that is. Make a cardboard circle larger than the item to set the gift on, wrap in tissue paper in an upward swirl, cover in aluminum foil, and run a piece of paper, secured with tape, out of the top for a name tag. Be prepared to pucker up upon presentation.

Send your Valentine card via Valentine, Arizona; Valentine, Nebraska; or Loveland, Colorado. Your postmaster will provide the postmark if you send him or her the stamped, addressed card in an envelope with written instructions for location. (There's also Christmas Valley, Oregon, and Santa, Idaho, for Yuletime cards and at least one town for almost all other holidays.) Call your main post office for more information.

Make your own Valentine card. Use a roll of construction paper to cut out the words "I love you" in one piece. Hold the banner in front of you and get someone to take your picture. Blow it up to 11″ × 14″ and mount it. It will cost less than a box of candy or a bouquet of flowers, but the sentiment and effort will make it that much dearer.

Mom and the kids could make a "smooch card" for Dad by applying vivid red lipstick and "kissing" a plain piece of paper. ("Guess whose lips these are, Dad.") A dime-store frame completes the picture. While you've got the lipstick out, use it to write a Valentine message on the bathroom mirror before your lover wakes up. That may be the one day that shaving or applying makeup is a pleasure, not a chore.

Get to the heart of the day with a homemade expression of your love. Fashion a heart from any red-patterned remnant material and stuff it with old panty hose or a discarded baby quilt. A lace border would give it even more pizzazz. One could be used as a pin cushion. Two or three attached to a pretty wide ribbon could make a beautiful wall hanging to display a pin collection.

Tony and Susan have a birthday party for Nick, using a pirate theme. Tony dresses up as Captain Hook, complete with makeup, to entertain the kids, who are all given bandannas and eye patches to wear. A huge cardboard box turned on its side and set under a tree is converted to a ship. The sails (sheets hanging from an overhead branch) billow in the breeze.

Guests are provided with sheets of construction paper and crayons to draw treasure maps. Tony helps them to cover their creations with clear contact paper for use as place mats during the party and as souvenirs to take home. Two dollars in pennies are buried in the sandbox for the treasure hunt. Total cost for the refreshments and props is $12.

HAVE IMAGINATION, WILL TRAVEL

With a little ingenuity and direction, vacations may still be within the realm of possibility. If you are a single man over 50, you qualify for consideration in the "host program" initiated a few years ago by the Royal Cruise Line and now being adopted by other cruise lines. Any man in that category lucky enough to be chosen gets a free cruise in exchange for entertaining and dancing with the single women passengers.

Your talents or expertise could also qualify you for a free cruise. Most ships offer seminars and classes to their passengers as part of the cruise activities. Subjects may include saving on taxes, drawing your own will, beating inflation, protecting your investments, yoga, diet- and health-related topics, stress control, wines, art appreciation, or art history. Any topic that is informative and stimulating would be considered.

Given the competition for these free rides, your proposal must be that much more interesting, professional, and unique. Before applying, draft a course prospectus outlining your subject and how you would present it. Send an inquiry to every cruise line for which you can find an address. You can probably find a list in your local library or cajole a travel agent into sharing this information with you on the promise that you and your family will book all future trips with him or her. Keep in mind that you are usually responsible for your fare to and from the ship, so you may want to solicit only those cruise lines whose embarkation ports are closest to where you live.

ON A WING AND A SHOESTRING

If mal de mer is de rigueur for you, there is a way you can wing to foreign lands for as little as $150 round trip (from Boston to Milan, Italy)—as a free-lance courier. Because security restrictions do not allow unaccompanied baggage on passenger flights, courier companies will sell tickets at a greatly reduced price to passengers who are willing to accompany their freight.

The more flexible your travel dates, the cheaper the ticket, but you usually have to survive for a week or two on as much as you can cram in one carry-on piece of luggage. Your baggage allowance is usually used up by the cargo you accompany.

Couriers may be asked to escort boxes of business documents, photographs, medical supplies, or the like that must be delivered in hours. It's a good idea to be informed about the contents, to appease customs officials who have little patience with travelers who don't know the answer to "What's in that case?" Also, always get a local contact in the cities where you will be traveling in case you have inadequate information to pass a customs search.

Another possible downside, besides a potential customs hassle, is that you may be bumped from your trip at the last minute in favor of an in-house employee. You could also get caught in the bind of missed connections, resulting in an additional outlay if you opt not to spend the night in an airport. All possibilities are fairly remote, but forewarned is forearmed.

The Air Courier's Handbook, by Jennifer Bayse (Big City Books, P.O. Box 19667, Sacramento, CA 95819), is a great guide for where to go and what to do to sate a wanderlust on a limited budget. The book includes a listing of air courier companies to contact. Other sources for cheap trips are "bargain-basement" travel agencies that offer greatly reduced rates, mostly for charter trips, to travelers who can pack up and go with very little notice. Maintain a current passport. The opportunities reach to the four corners of the world.

POSTCARDS FROM THE EDGE

Volunteering to work in a national park could earn you a "free" vacation. You pay only for the cost of getting there and back and, in a few cases, for groceries. (Some programs cover meals or offer stipends for groceries.) In 1990 approximately 67,000 volunteers gave time to the National Park Service. Another 9,000 worked for the Fish and Wildlife Service, and more are signing up every day.

You don't need any special skills to qualify, but those with special talents may get the more plum jobs, which range from computers to library science to photography. Your best chance of acceptance, however, is when you are flexible on both job assignment and time of year. If you're not above picking up litter, banding birds, or feeding fish and are willing to go during the less-requested spring and fall seasons, you will probably have one of the most memorable experiences of your life.

Some of the locations available are Lake Powell in Arizona's Glen Canyon National Park (on a 44-foot houseboat); Assateague National Seashore in Virginia; Sequoia National Forest and Mendocino National Forest, both in California; Alaska's Togiak Wildlife Refuge; and Yellowstone National Park. Volunteers who come with their own RVs or camping equipment are more welcome than those who need housing, but limited housing is available for those who commit to a regular schedule for at least a week or two. For those who bring their own digs, the park provides hookups and campsites and pays for all utilities.

If you want to volunteer, decide on a region where you would like to go and list the skill(s) you have to offer. Send this information to one or all of the three agencies that administer national public lands—the National Forest Service, which is part of the Department of Agriculture; and the Fish and Wildlife Service and the National Park Service, both part of the Department of the Interior. Each has regional offices that are listed in your phone book. Some of the regional offices issue bulletins listing positions; others will circulate your application among their parks or refer you directly to a particular location. Apply well in advance of the time you would prefer to go.

PARTY LINE

Before the Soviet Union disintegrated, comedian Yakov Smirnoff quipped, "In America you can always find a party. In Russia the party always finds you." Unlike in Russia, the party is not over. All you have to do is go out and look for it.

THE PURSUIT OF CHANGE:
Investments in Your Future

America has always been a nation of pioneers. Thousands of early Americans drove their covered wagons across barren lands looking for greener pastures despite the uncertainties and dangers they knew they would encounter.

Once again we are challenged to reignite that pioneer spirit for a different kind of homesteading—carving out new places in a business wilderness that has left some 9 million jobless with no end in sight.

OPEN FOR BUSINESS

From the time our forefathers set foot on Plymouth Rock, the "little guy" was the backbone of the country's economy. Mom-and-Pop ventures proliferated but ultimately died when conglomeration became synonymous with better. But so many of the mighty have fallen, leaving niches for a new breed of little guys who have the benefit of history to prepare them for the future.

Some 1.3 million new businesses opened in 1991. More than half were sole proprietorships or microbusinesses with only one or two employees. A large percentage of these are conducted in basements, garages, or converted bedrooms. If you can't find a job, make one.

Hard as it is to believe, recessions have a bright side, at least for those with entrepreneurial aspirations. Hot on the heels of retreating corporate employers are the enterprising itinerant professionals who are providing companies the services formerly done in-house. Small businesses are mushrooming to capitalize on the markets no longer considered feasible or profitable by dissipating corporate giants.

THE GREENING OF A BUSINESS

Adequate financing is the big *IF* when trying to become one's own boss. Nearly two out of every three new businesses fail for lack of sufficient capital. Businesses that require more blood, sweat, and tears than money have a better chance for survival.

A home-based service business needs little more than a desk, a telephone, and office supplies to get started. To compete in our highly competitive world, however, a computer, fax machine, and copier are required. Even secondhand equipment could add up to around $5,000.

Any business that can't be conducted at home is going to take a great deal more money to get started—anywhere from $50,000 up, depending on the business. For someone without a job, never mind a track record, obtaining financing is a near impossibility, but *near* is the key word here. The most determined are giving new meaning to the expression "Where there's a will, there's a way."

Turned down by financial institutions that are having troubles of their own, new business owners are taking desperate measures to find financing. *Time* magazine reported on just such a determined former sales executive of Polish extraction who couldn't borrow one zloty for her East European restaurant through traditional channels. Undaunted, she made calls to every doctor and lawyer in her city's phone book whose last name ended in -*ski* and -*cz*. She raised all the money she needed to start the restaurant and keep going until it began to pay off. In addition to the expectation of repayment with interest, her Polish investors had a great place to go for meals like mother used to make.

Two states, Washington and Massachusetts, initiated pilot programs in the early nineties to help the jobless fund start-up businesses. Known as Self-Employment and Enterprise Development (SEED), Washington's program allows unemployment benefit recipients one lump-sum, up-front payment instead of the biweekly check for six months.

Massachusetts began its Enterprise Project in 1991, which offers ten weeks of small business instruction and bank financing. Unemployment checks, however, are still doled out as usual over a twenty-four-week period.

TO BE OR NOT TO BE?

Given the state of the economy and the high failure rate of new businesses, aspiring entrepreneurs are asking themselves if starting a new business is such a great idea. It's not a bad idea, say the experts, if you can find one within your area of expertise that's in demand but not widely available.

According to surveyors of mercantile movements, the businesses that boasted the healthiest increases during the first two years of the nineties when the recession was at its peak were those that reflected the back-to-basics approach. Among them are home entertainment outlets, inexpensive restaurants, auto parts stores, home improvement centers, local tourism, and retailers who gave rock-bottom discounts.

The recession accelerated a trend toward prudence in spending patterns that economists predict will prevail when the crunch is alleviated. The new businesses, therefore, that embrace this fundamental concept probably have the best chance to survive and thrive. Dedication to top customer service and value is vital in the Spartan nineties.

By putting a new twist on applying a technical skill or an acquired talent, some new-wave businesses are thriving. For example, peripatetic mechanics are discovering that many car owners are willing, indeed happy, to pay extra for getting an oil change at home or at work by appointment. More and more personal shoppers for anything from food to computers are making comfortable livings serving busy people who can afford to pay surcharges to make their lives easier.

Up until the time Tony lost his job, he worked steadily in banking from the time he graduated from college, veering off somewhat from his college major—accounting. Because of his expertise in that field, however, he was constantly called upon by his family to help them prepare their tax returns. Thus he kept up with new tax laws and practices to ensure that everyone (particularly the IRS) would get a fair shake. Drawing on this knowledge, he initiates a tax service with a perk that H&R Block doesn't offer: he makes himself available to go to the client's home to accommodate varying schedules. Promoting fees commensurate with those charged by large tax-service agencies and the extra inducement of home visits, Tony develops a clientele that could spur him on to a new, year-round, home-operated business.

While Tony is delighted with his newfound source of income, his wife is not as enthusiastic. The money he earns is very much needed, Susan concedes, but given Natalie's condition, she would prefer that Tony use his time to find another job that would provide the family with health insurance benefits. The tension between them mounts when Tony is unwilling to give up a somewhat stable means of immediate income for the uncertainties of full-time job hunting.

The age of home product parties has returned, offering much more than the traditional housewares. Cosmetics and lingerie are among the most popular wares today. A mini-craft fair in your living room selling your and your friend's creations is a unique way to make some money and get instant gratification.

One woman with no previous experience or artistic bent learned how to hand-paint T-shirts, which she sells to boutiques at a hefty profit. Her designs yield her $50 to $60 each and ultimately sell retail for around $100. Some home-grown enterprises can graduate to pushcarts in malls or other busy shopping areas. Start-up costs usually range from $3,000 to $5,000. Sticking to one theme, such as "romance," is generally advisable at the beginning.

I AM WOMAN

Each decade generates its own language. One of the big new coined words in the nineties is "mom-preneurship." In 1991 almost 10 million women were running businesses at home, up around 9 percent from the prior year. Around half are mothers. Although many are still typing, baking, and sewing to pay the bills, less traditional, higher-income-bearing services provided by women at home are on the rise.

Reflecting the growing trend, America's consummate housewife, Blondie, the comic strip character, operates a catering business from her kitchen. She does so against the objections of her husband, Dagwood, who has a big problem with her newly divided loyalties. Fiction (even the comics), of course, mirrors real life. Spouses and children often have trouble coping with a business conducted in what they consider to be their private space.

Home businesses operated by women are as diverse as their talents, including public relations agencies (often just a single practitioner or with one part-time assistant), party-planning services, graphic design, desktop publishing, catalogue sales, temporary-employment agencies, free-lance writers, even TV and magazine production.

"Mom-preneurs" generally agree that staying home for the bacon allows them to be better, more available parents, averting some of the problems that beset latchkey kids. The flip side is the constant interruption by the kids when Mom is trying to conduct business. Home workers also face two other challenges—getting motivated to start in the morning, and knowing when to quit in the evening. The worst problem with working in the home is the isolation. Days can go by before Mom has contact with another adult except by phone.

In keeping with our indomitable enterprising nature, new trends invariably give rise to new support groups, including The Mothers Home Business Network in East Meadow, New York, tel. 516-997-7394.

When Laura's business was thriving and money was not an issue, she was the consummate shopper whether she needed something or not. Her taste, her style, and her ability to zero in on the best buy in the store became legendary among her friends, who would beg her to go shopping with them.

Laura decided her unique prowess could be marketed. Where she once shopped for fun, she would now do it for profit. She contacted everyone she knew to offer the benefit of her expertise, at a price. She also placed an ad in her local newspaper. Geared for busy people who have more money than time, her services include shopping for clothing, other personal items, and gifts; coordinating and weeding out wardrobes; and setting up closets and drawers for easier access and efficiency.

She charges $25 an hour plus expenses. At eight hours a day, five days a week, her potential weekly earnings are $1,000. At this point, she says, she will settle for making half that much. With two clients already signed up (friends of hers), she is convinced she will succeed.

In the process of her newfound vocation, Laura becomes a willing, pro bono resource for her friends and family who are also having hard times making ends meet.

She tips them off about great sales and bargains she finds in the course of conducting her business and even picks out something for someone who has expressed a need for that particular item when the price is too good to pass up. Her refrigerator and cookie jar are filled with tokens of appreciation for her favors.

GETTING A JUMP START

Rather than starting a business from the beginning, you may want to consider buying a franchise. The failure rate of franchises is twice as low as other start-ups, mostly because the parent company provides the complete business organizational plan and advertising support.

One former advertising executive used his severance pay to buy a franchise pet shop. His knowledge of the field was limited to the ownership of a dog, but this was something he had always wanted to do. Thanks to the marketing handholding provided by the parent company, thirteen-hour days, and his family's on-the-job support, he now owns three successful shops.

THE LEARNING CURVE

Research must be an integral part of starting a business. The library is the best place to start. Find out everything you can about your business's target area. Most chambers of commerce offer (or can give information on) seminars that are helpful in establishing businesses. Talking to anyone who will listen to you is also a good way to test reaction to your business plan.

Most state small business agencies offer where-to-go guides for assistance in solving business problems, as well as printed materials giving basic facts on how to start a new business. Other helpful publications include:

- *How to Run Your Own Business*, Coralee Smith Kern and Tammara Hoffman Wolfgram (Lincolnwood, IL: VGM Career Horizons, 1990)
- *Working Together: Entrepreneurial Couples*, Frank and Sharon Barnett (Berkeley, CA: Ten Speed Press, 1988)
- *Inc. Magazine's Guide to Small Business Success*, supplement to *Inc.* magazine, 1979
- *Women in Their Own Business*, Katherine Oana (Lincolnwood, IL: VGM Career Horizons, 1982)
- *Starting from Scratch*, Joe Sutherland Gould (New York: John Wiley & Sons, 1987)
- *Starting and Operating a Home-Based Business*, David R. Eyler (New York: John Wiley & Sons, 1990)
- *Guerilla Marketing Attack*, Jay Conrad Levinson (Boston: Houghton Mifflin, 1989)
- *Making It on Your Own* (1991), *Working from Home* (1990), *The Best Home Businesses for the 90's* (1991), and *Getting Business to Come to You* (1991), Sarah and Paul Edwards (Los Angeles: Jeremy P. Tarcher)

Several national organizations offer assistance as well to the new business owner. Among the most helpful are:

- Office of Women's Business Ownership, Small Business Administration, Washington, DC 20416
- Small Business Development Center, Small Business Administration, 1441 L St., N.W., Washington, DC 20416
- American Entrepreneurs Association, 2311 Pontius Ave., Los Angeles, CA 90064
- National Association of Women Business Owners, 500 N. Michigan Ave., Suite 1400, Chicago, IL 60611
- Women Entrepreneurs, 2030 Union St., Suite 310, San Francisco, CA 94123
- Office of Minority Business Development Agency, U.S.

Department of Commerce, 14th St. and Constitution Ave., N.W., Washington, DC 20230
- National Association of Black Women Entrepreneurs, P.O. Box 1375, Detroit, MI 48231

WORKER BEES

Not everyone can or wants to be the queen of the hive. (Getting fertilized by drones and constantly procreating may not be your lifelong ambition.) If bosshood is not for you, you must hone your job-seeking techniques to a leading edge. Adopt the posture of the self-employed out to sell your skills and products to a series of clients who will benefit from your wares.

Getting a job is increasingly determined by the variety of skills you can offer. Developing what is known as a "portfolio career" is the best ammunition for meeting the current and future job markets head-on. Possessing myriad skills gives you the mobility to fit into a number of divisions, companies, or even industries.

The paterfamilias corporation that provided a lifetime of security is a thing of the past. Anyone beginning a career in this decade should expect to work for at least five employers before retiring. Constantly assembling and acquiring new skills with each new job is critical for staying at the head of the pack. Straddling two careers is good insurance too. With two directions to go in, down time should be cut in half.

Stop thinking of yourself as the teacher, banker, geologist, retail buyer (etc., etc., etc.) you used to be. Too narrow a focus on your potential in the job market could be the kiss of death. Ask yourself what else you can do that people would pay for. Almost everyone has latent skills.

Find yours by doing an evaluation of all your personal and professional assets. Don't be modest, but be honest with yourself. This is for your eyes only. In addition to your professional credentials, look to your hobbies, your non-work-related interests, your likes and dislikes, your education (including courses just for fun), knowledge of a second language, your innate qualities (artistic, technical, etc.), your community and volunteer work, travels, personality, or anything of this nature to give you clues to your hidden talents.

CHANGE OF LIFE

Whether and when to make a change in career direction is a decision only you can make. The inability to find a job in your field may be the tip-off. The current health and potential of the field in which you have been working are two more clues. If the future looks bleak in your market area, a new route is probably advisable.

Now that you have completed your evaluation and know how good and diverse you are, why not investigate other fields where your background and expertise may fit in? Look into the functions of the jobs in those fields that will enable you to make best use of your assets. Keep thinking far and wide. For example, if writing is your bent, don't restrict yourself to newspapers, magazines, and publishing houses. Also look into industrial companies that self-publish newsletters, annual reports, employee handbooks, and a variety of self-help booklets for their workers through their human services departments.

If you speak, write, and read another language fluently (often thanks to parents or grandparents who perpetuated their ethnic origins in the home), look into the growing opportunities for translators in the international market. Companies eager to do business in foreign countries (Russia is the new hot spot) must have the ability to communicate in the appropriate language. The medical and legal fields, too, are increasingly in need of translators.

Your knowledge of another language could also be the beginning of a cottage industry for you. You could specialize in translating documents and could do it from the comfort and convenience of your own home. If your proficiency in the language is just short of marketable, consider taking a twelve-week intensive course to bring you to the required level.

If you have always wanted to teach but are not certified, you may still qualify. Even if you speak only English, you could get a job in one of the hundreds of American schools scattered through Europe, Asia, and Africa. For example, English-language schools are currently the rage in Japan, and almost any native English speaker can qualify for a job.

Look into retraining programs and other services offered under the federal Job Training Partnership Act (JTPA), which can assist you with job search and relocation funds and with individual counseling and assessment as well as retraining. Look for a JTPA office in your area or inquire through your local unemployment or job service office. JTPA is administered by the Employment and Training Administration of the U.S. Department of Labor, 200 Constitution Ave., N.W., Washington, DC 20210. Call its office of Public Affairs at 202-219-6871 for more information.

Other helpful publications include *The Occupational Outlook Handbook* (Superintendent of Documents, U.S. Government Printing Office, Washington, DC 20402, tel. 202-783-3238) and up-to-date brochures on careers and businesses from the Consumer Information Center, P.O. Box 100, Pueblo, CO 81002.

PICTURE PERFECT

Whether you decide to stick with your old field or go on to another, you should reorganize your résumé. A résumé is generally your first contact with an employer, so you'd better make the most of it if you want to get beyond the dreaded circular file marked "W" for wastebasket. Your résumé should give a panoramic picture of you. Stress personal attributes and describe former duties in detail rather than making vague references. Translate your past achievements into dollars and cents. Let them know at the outset that you are a potential boiling teapot of a profit center just waiting to whistle for them.

For example, don't just mention that you reorganized a department. Outline how you did it. If you doubled productivity with 25 percent less staff, or headed a project that decreased costs while increasing profits, or won an award for a design that was created in a minimal amount of time and resulted in a boost of sales, say so. The one who reviews your résumé should be impressed enough to at least invite you in for an initial interview.

The way you arrange your résumé should depend on where your strengths are. If your experience is your ace in the hole, play that card first. If you are achievement oriented, go for that first. This could also give you the chance to fit into a wider variety of jobs available within the company besides the one for which you are applying.

Whatever unorthodox format you choose, stick with the traditional presentation—no photographs, colored or outsized paper, unusual typefaces, or other cutesy gimmicks. Forget the videotape. Not everyone has a VCR handy, and few want to put a dent into their daily schedules by sitting in front of a TV for an hour (the idea is neither original nor unique). Also, keep your résumé short, no more than two pages.

A plethora of books and pamphlets are available to help your prepare your résumé. Check your local unemployment office, your branch office of the U.S. Department of Labor, and, of course, your old reliable library. For a fee, you can also consult a résumé-writing service that will provide you with a very professional-looking document but not necessarily one that presents the information in the order you prefer. Unless you are specific, you will probably end up with the cookie-cutter approach.

Send your résumé with a cover letter written individually for each company. Direct the letter to the person who would do the hiring. The letter should be short and to the point, and *must* be typed without errors. Exhibit your knowledge of the company and indicate how you can benefit the company. Request an interview. The letter should be compelling from the first word to capture the employer's attention. Talk about the company first, mentioning awards or projects that you have read about, then talk about yourself. If you have a mutual contact who suggested that you apply, mention the name (if you have permission to do so).

GET OUT THE NET

Think of job hunting and the steps that prepare you for your search as building a pyramid. You begin with a solid foundation of self-evaluation, expansion of scope, and determination of marketability in areas you hadn't considered before. Your next plateau is preparation of the tools you need for your search—résumé, letters of introduction, etc. Then you are ready for the third stage, structuring your professional support base, otherwise known as networking.

Identify everyone who could direct or help you in your job search. This includes friends, friends of friends, family, colleagues, former coworkers, former clients or customers, old school buddies, your doctor, your lawyer, your dentist, even your postman. Consider every passing acquaintance as a potential contact. Collect their business cards, noting on the back how and when you met, and file (by category or company if you have trouble remembering names of individuals).

If you haven't done so already, pick out some mentor figures in your field whom you can approach to assist you in job seeking and/or getting you involved with some professional organization activity. You may find mentors among your former professors, career-related supervisors, colleagues, or policy makers in your community. The mentor system has been used effectively for generations and should be perpetuated even after you find a new job.

Get out and meet new people. Join support groups and

professional organizations; volunteer for parent activities in your children's school or at your church; join your local amateur baseball league or a health club (many executives find this a good way to relieve stress). If there are no support groups or job clubs in your area, start one.

Seek a committee appointment in a professional organization, preferably on an ad hoc committee that makes policy recommendations to the board. This gives you greater visibility than as one of the herd of no-voice members. Choose a committee related to your area of expertise. This is another situation where your mentor can assist you by recommending you for membership.

Familiarize yourself with *Robert's Rules of Order*, the most definitive explanation of parliamentary procedure, to become most effective in business and committee meetings. Once you have established yourself on a committee, you could seek an elective position on the organization's board, which is bound to bring you in contact with some of the more influential members of your business community.

Networking is essential and should be a permanent element of professional life, whether you are out of a job or employed. Networking groups comprise both the employed and unemployed, the ones with jobs helping those without, knowing full well that in this economy the positions could be reversed with a slip of the pink. These groups are a great way to trade information, experiences, and leads. They also provide counseling, ideas on new ways to market yourself, and feedback on improving appearance, speech patterns, and interviewing skills.

If you are intimidated by large groups, you can network by computer. Exec-U-Net is a nationwide networking organization for managers and professionals that provides members (at $300 a year) with a computer data base of jobs with salaries of $75,000 or over. Monthly meetings are held for professions in general management, finance, management information systems, sales, marketing, law, and operations. Call 1-800-637-3126 for more information.

Call or write everyone you have identified as possible contacts and tell them you are looking for a new job. Inquire if they are aware of any openings or know anyone in any position that may be of assistance to you. Record comments from each and dates called, and mark your diary to call them back again in a reasonable amount of time.

ON WITH THE HUNT

Employment professionals insist that contrary to the gloom-and-doom reports, there are plenty of solid job opportunities. The trick is knowing where to look. Focus on small- and medium-sized companies. Many of these companies continue to grow despite the recession and need all levels of staff to keep up with the expansion.

Use active as well as passive job strategies. You are doing less than half the job if you are applying only for known openings. Specialists estimate that 80 percent of available jobs are never advertised. This is what is known as the "hidden job market." Contact 50 to 100 companies you would like to work for and where you believe you would fit in. Try sending your résumé to venture capital firms in hopes that you will be referred to one of their portfolio companies that may be looking for someone with your credentials.

Anticipate opportunities by reading the business sections of newspapers and magazines. If a business is opening a branch office in your area, expanding, or changing, new positions will become available. Check out the names of department or division managers and send in your résumé with a cover letter explaining that the news report indicated to you that they may have an immediate or near-future need for additional staff. Describe what you can contribute to their organization. Be sure to follow up your letter with a phone call. You will be one step ahead of the competition, and your initiative may be the one factor that will make you stand out among the crowd.

Don't ignore the traditional methods in your quest for originality. Answer ads in newspapers and trade and professional journals. Register with employment agencies. Talk to head-hunters who specialize in your profession. Check notices on bulletin boards of personnel offices.

The most difficult part of your job-searching process is dealing with the inevitable rejection, but it's in your best interest to prevent your disappointment from affecting your outlook. Employers are quick to detect negativity and lack of confidence. Few are willing to hire those who are down on themselves and the world at large. Try not to take rejections personally. More often than not you were passed over for reasons beyond your control. As the song says, "Pick yourself up, dust yourself off, and start all over again."

NEW HORIZONS

In the wake of the recession, certain industries rise above the rubble. Health care continues to offer the most potential, including manufacturers of medical instruments, diagnostic equipment, and drugs; biotech companies; and home health care delivery services. Of the ten fastest-growing occupations in Massachusetts, four are in the field of health care.

Some of the other fields offering the greatest opportunities are in software sales and technology, environmental and safety technology, electrical engineering, marketing, tax services, and financial planning. Geographically, the Pacific Northwest is booming by comparison to other locales. Several new companies in Atlanta, Georgia, one of the fastest-growing business capitals, have opened up new job vistas there, while the many food companies based in the Midwest have kept the economy there on an even keel and show good potential for growing.

Ohio and Kentucky are luring such plum companies as Toyota, H. J. Heinz, and Star-Kist Foods by offering aggressive relocation incentives and have gone from among the highest jobless rates in the country to below the national average. Other revitalized business centers are Omaha, Seattle, and Pittsburgh. Don't overlook opportunities in small towns. Salaries, though often lower, go much farther in smaller communities than in larger cities.

SCHOOL DAZE

Going back to school may be the long-range answer to protecting your professional future. The field you ultimately want to be in may require specific skills you don't have. Of course, going from teacher to computer scientist requires more than just a few crash courses to rise above the low-level jobs.

Boston University's Metropolitan College reports that at least 60 percent of its students in the evening program are looking to change careers. At Northeastern University, where one-third of the entire student body of 15,000 are hoping to move on to new careers through education, intensive programs have been developed to accelerate the process. Teachers, nurses, psychologists, businesspeople, artists, and other professionals may take a 2½-year program in computer applications and graduate with a master of science degree from the university's School of Engineering. Other schools throughout the country are responding similarly.

Long-term, high-cost training is not always necessary to make lateral moves within the same industry or into one that is somewhat compatible with your educational background. Some brushing up or additional courses may be all you need. You may be losing out to other candidates because you haven't finished your degree, even though you qualify better in every other way.

If you need, say, 100 hours to complete your degree, you don't necessarily have to spend 100 hours in the classroom to do so. Colleges and universities are giving credits for life and on-the-job experiences and are offering equivalency exams in lieu of taking certain courses if you pass. This could cut your time and your cost in half.

There are many scholarships and loans available through the state and federal governments as well as from private sources, most of which are as accessible to the older student as to the high school graduate going on to college. Most public library systems have a higher education information center where guides to existing programs and financial aid are listed. (See chapter 7, "School Maze," for more information.)

A graphic artist, Richard conducts an exhaustive search for a new position in his field. With so few opportunities and so much competition for the few, Richard comes to the conclusion that this marketplace is glutted and just might not have room for him anymore.

Now that he and Anne, his wife, and the baby have moved in with his in-laws, the family's financial strain has been alleviated somewhat, so he looks into going back to school to study product design, a growing field. With his background and prior education, he can probably complete his retraining within a year, depending on the number of courses he can manage within that time frame.

Anne agrees with his plan but is concerned about the cost. Her salary will be their only source of income when Richard's unemployment benefits run out in two months. After looking into available loan programs, they find that they can qualify for a low-interest education loan that they won't have to begin to repay for at least nine months after Richard graduates. Confident that his new skills will yield a job before the repayment schedule begins, he signs up for the program and the loan to finance it.

LOWERING THE BOOM

A longtime tradition known as "booming out," dormant during good times, has been reactivated with a vengeance. Generally practiced by construction workers who go where the jobs are, "booming out" is drawing a new breed of migrant worker. Unable to find work in their own areas, corporate executives and middle management are on the move, leaving their families behind for weeks, even months depending on the distance.

Dictated by necessity and desperate times, this arrangement is less than desirable for most but allows the family to protect their lifestyle. For the most part the jobs are temporary, and moving the family from place to place is too impractical (and generally unacceptable to most of the members). With real estate values plummeting, moving the family could also result in the loss of thousands of dollars on the sale of their home. Economics and practicality invariably win out, and the family stays behind.

Commuting puts an enormous strain on everyone but could provide the life preserver for staying afloat in choppy waters. Many workers, particularly in the more distressed areas of the country, feel they have no other option. There is always the chance that the temporary job will turn out to be permanent, and most feel that's a chance worth taking.

PEOPLE HELPING PEOPLE

Staying active is very important when you are unemployed. Anyone who was used to the routine imposed by a job is bound to have withdrawal symptoms when unemployed. Volunteering will get you up and out and give you something else to add to your résumé in the process.

Some misanthropic job counselors advise against volunteering because it distracts from job hunting. Others say it's a way to gain new experience, investigate career changes, and network. It also fills in the gap on your résumé. While growing and learning in a volunteer capacity, you can feel good about yourself, and that positive attitude helps when you interview for a job.

For some, volunteer jobs have been parlayed into full-time positions, but the cost could be a year without salary. Joining a board of directors or working free for a start-up company could also reap rewards down the road.

For extensive material on volunteerism, contact the ACTION Resource Center, 806 Connecticut Ave., N.W., Rm. M-205, Washington, DC 20525.

A BLESSING IN DISGUISE

No one can discount the trauma and financial strain resulting from the loss of a job. Burnout aside, few are prepared and the blow is staggering. The experience, however, is not without its value. Forced unemployment provides the mid-career break you probably needed but would never take on your own. It's a time to recharge, rebuild skills, and improve credentials. The silver lining may well be a more satisfactory and secure future.

ARE WE THERE YET?
Putting Your Life Back Together

Getting out of debt will probably take longer than it took you to get into it. Fixing your credit should be your first order of business as soon as you restore your income on a regular basis.

GETTING YOUR REPORT CARD SIGNED

The first step toward resolving your credit difficulties is to check your credit report. Check for errors. Often these reports contain incorrect information. Also be aware that information exchanges between credit offices are not always reciprocal. One report may differ from the other.

Try to soften negative information as much as possible by adding a statement to your credit file outlining any extenuating circumstances, like unemployment. Future reports on you must include at least a summary of your statement. If you report a mistake, the credit bureau must investigate. If the bureau disputes your claim, add another brief statement noting the dispute. If your claim is justified, the bureau is obliged to notify your creditors of corrections and changes. You can get a free report once a year from TRW Information Services by writing to TRW Complimentary Report Request, P.O. Box 2350, Chatsworth, CA 91313-2350. No phone requests are processed, but information on what is required may be obtained by calling 1-800-392-1122. Additional copies within the same year may be obtained for $7.50 plus applicable state tax by writing to TRW at P.O. Box 749029, Dallas, TX 75374, tel. 213-254-6871.

If you have been rejected for credit, you are also entitled to a free report from Trans Union Corp, P.O. Box 7000, North Olmstead, OH 44070, tel. 312-408-1400, and from Equifax, Inc, P.O. Box 740241, Atlanta, GA 30374-0241, tel. 1-800-685-1111. Vermont residents, too, are exempted from fees normally charged by Equifax, whether rejected for credit or not. For all others, Trans Union charges $15 for a single report, $20 for a joint. Equifax, which allows a phone order and payment by credit card, charges from $3 to $8 depending on the state where you reside.

When applying for a report, be sure to include your full name, spouse's first name, correct address and zip and all previous addresses for the past five years, social security number, year and date of birth, photocopy of a billing statement or a utility bill or other document that confirms your name and the address to which the report should be mailed. It's a good idea to phone first to check on changes in charges or requirements for application.

You can expect to find the following information on your credit report:

- Any data on any outstanding debts, including balances on auto loans, lines of credit, credit cards, government/ student loans, and small business loans.
- A record of your payment schedule—prompt, slow, late—shown either by recording payments or by a grade assigned to you by the creditor.
- Public court records relevant to your creditworthiness.
- Bankruptcy filings.
- Legal judgments.

- Tax liens.
- Divorce settlements.
- Name of your employer.
- Your salary.

A report may not contain information about every account and *should not* contain any judgment about your overall credit-worthiness. Nor should it contain any information on your bank accounts, any criminal record, race, sex, religion, or any other information of a highly personal nature.

For information on the Fair Credit Reporting Act, write to the Office of Consumer Affairs, Federal Deposit Insurance Corporation, 550 17th St., N.W., Washington, DC 20429.

STARTING OVER

Getting out of debt isn't easy, but it's possible. A good place to start is by using the charts in Appendix A to guide you in balancing your budget as you are increasing your income. You will need to add or increase payments to satisfy your debts. (Many experts advise keeping credit payments below 10 to 15 percent of annual income after taxes and housing expenses.)

You should notify each creditor of your new status when you are again employed. Contact anyone with whom there may have been a problem, such as utilities, mortgage companies, schools, or department stores. (See the sample letters on pages 235 to 237.) If you have been making only token payments to your creditors, begin to dig out by arranging your payment plan to reflect your current earning capacity. Ask each creditor to confirm your arrangement by letter. Request that they send a copy to the credit bureaus to which they report. You, too, should notify the credit bureau of any new arrangements.

Your letters to creditors should include your name, ad-

FOLLOW-UP LETTER TO CREDITORS, UTILITIES, MORTGAGE COMPANY, AND LANDLORD

(Date)

(Name of contact person)
(Title)
(Name of company)
(Street address)
(City, state, ZIP code)

RE: Account # (your number)

Dear (contact person):

- describe situation

I am happy to inform you that I have found a new job. Therefore I should be able to resume regular payments of (amount) next month.

- outline suggested schedule for payments & verification to credit agencies

I am aware that my outstanding balance is (amount). In addition to current monthly charges, would you accept (amount) each month until the balance is paid in full? Should this arrangement be acceptable, I would appreciate a written memo, one to me and one to the credit agency to which you report, verifying your acceptance.

- express appreciation

Thank you for your patience and cooperation over these last months.

Sincerely,

(Your name)
(Your address)
(Your city, state, ZIP code)
(Your telephone number)

---

dress, home and work telephone numbers, and account number. Make your letter brief and to the point, specifying all the important facts about the agreement, including the date and the name of the person with whom you have made the arrangements. State exactly what you can do to resolve the situation and how much time you will need. Be reasonable and realistic. Type your letter if possible. If it is handwritten,

FOLLOW-UP LETTER TO
<u>DAY CARE OR PRESCHOOL</u>

(Date)

(Name of contact person)
(Title)
(Name of school or day care)
(Street address)
(City, state, ZIP code)

Dear (contact person):

- describe situation

Thank you for your assistance on Nicholas's behalf. We are pleased to inform you Tony has a new job that will enable us to resume regular tuition payments for Nicholas.

- outline significance of keeping service

We appreciated your consideration of our financial situation during the last several months. Nicholas's continued participation in school gave him a constructive outlet for his boundless energy while continuing his education without interruption.

- renew tuition and express appreciation

We are enclosing a check to cover current tuition. In addition, you will find a check to apply toward the fund that helped Nicholas stay in school, or toward educational toys for the classroom.

Once again, thank you for your understanding.

Sincerely,

(Your name)
(Your address)
(Your city, state, ZIP code)
(Your telephone number)

make sure it is legible. Keep copies of all correspondence, checks, and payments. It's also a good idea to keep a log noting any personal or telephone contact.

If you are fighting a losing battle trying to pay off a particularly problematic bill, you may want (or need) to urge your creditor to accept a write-off agreement, stressing that half

FOLLOW-UP LETTER TO SCHOOL

(Date)

(Name of contact person)
(Title)
(Name of school)
(Street address)
(City, state, ZIP code)

Dear (contact person):

- describe situation

I am happy to inform you that I have found a job that should alleviate the strain, both financially and emotionally, my family has experienced during the period I was unemployed.

- outline significance of keeping service

I greatly appreciate your support of my son Matthew during a very difficult time for him. I am convinced that his continued participation in his extracurricular activities at school was most significant in keeping him on track while I was temporarily derailed.

- express appreciation

I can now resume paying for Matthew's activities fees. Also, please apply the enclosed check to the fund that helped Matthew when he needed it most.

Sincerely,

(Your name)
(Your address)
(Your city, state, ZIP code)
(Your telephone number)

the pie is better than none. The creditor may be willing to accept a lesser amount as payment in full to write off the debt rather than go through the cost and hassle of initiating collection activities against you.

You will need to come up with the entire amount of the settlement, since partial payments are usually not accepted in this arrangement, and a deadline for payment will be imposed. As part of the deal, try to convince your creditor to send a "paid in full" notice to the credit bureau and not a "write-off" that adds another negative item to your report. Be sure to confirm any arrangement in writing.

PULLING IT ALL TOGETHER

Consolidating all your debts may ease some of the anxiety that comes with the barrage of bills you have to face each month. Accessing a home equity loan, if you are already approved, is one way to do that.

A debt management plan, administered by an attorney or by your local office of the Consumer Credit Counseling Service, sets up reduced monthly payments to unsecured creditors. Amounts sent to creditors are based on your available income and distributed proportionately.

Rolling all of your bank credit cards into one is another option. This service is being offered at reduced interest rates by some major credit card companies such as Citibank, which has assumed many of the Visa and MasterCard accounts from failed financial institutions or smaller ones that can no longer service these accounts.

Qualification may hinge on whether your accounts are current or in the process of being brought up to date. Call 1-800-843-0777 for Classic card information and 1-800-645-9565 for preferred cards. Also check with Bankcard Holders of America, 560 Herndon Parkway, Suite 120, Herndon, VA 22070, tel. 1-800-553-8025 or 703-481-1110. See chapter 10, "Obscene Phone Calls," for more information on debt consolidation.

Seek outside help from a credit counselor if managing your own credit becomes too overwhelming. Many banks or credit unions offer debt counseling free as part of their services. Family service agencies and civic organizations such as the American Red Cross may also offer assistance or can refer you to appropriate sources. Elders may find help on debt management (as well as on investing wisely) through the area agency on aging listed in the white pages of local telephone books. Assistance is also available through Debtors Anonymous, a mutual-help program that helps members achieve financial solvency. To locate a chapter near you contact Debtors Anonymous, P.O. Box 20322, New York, NY 10025-9992 or call 212-642-8222.

The Consumer Credit Counseling Service charges $25 for a budget and money management counseling session. The enrollment fee for an ongoing debt management plan is generally $35 and from $5 to $35 per month. Information on home purchasing, maintenance, and tenant-landlord relations is also available. CCCS is a nonprofit financial counseling service with approximately 180 offices in the United States, Puerto Rico, and Canada. For more information call 1-800-388-2227.

A RAINY DAY

Make a savings plan you can live with to hold you over in case of future unemployment or crisis, or to make major purchases. Get into the savings habit by starting with a piggy bank, if necessary. Put a dollar a day away and/or stash the change from your pockets. This small effort could easily yield $300 to $600 in less than a year.

Stick to your unemployment budget as closely as you can, even when you are working again, and you may have enough left from your salary to start a savings plan almost immediately. With something tucked away for emergencies, you are on your way to a debt-free life.

To become a good saver, you must be a wise spender. Develop a written spending plan and assign priorities. The goal here is to get out of old debt without incurring new debt. Continue to question every item on your expense list. Can it be reduced? Is it really a priority or just a whim? Stick to the Mutual Assistance Programs you have developed. Continue to look for ways to save money through sales, couponing, and rebates.

Your goal for savings should be at least 10 percent of your after-tax income. Try to build an account equal to three to six months' income. If your new company offers savings payroll deductions, consider enrolling. A designated amount is deducted each pay period and automatically deposited to your savings account. Out of sight, out of mind!

The slew of bank failures that rocked the country may have made many people wonder if they should go back to hiding money under their mattresses, but the FDIC, though troubled, remains viable. Depositors who saved at failed banks were protected by the FDIC up to the $100,000 insurance ceiling. The banking system prevails, but it's a good idea to play it safe nonetheless.

If you intend to bank most of your liquid assets, you should investigate your bank's status as carefully and completely as you would a mutual fund. Find out about FDIC coverage as it applies to every type of account you open at your bank. Check the bank's annual report and its level of capital (there should be at least a 6 percent ratio of capital to assets according to financial experts). Don't be lured by banks offering rates much higher than others without checking further. This could indicate trouble that the bank hopes to offset by quickly bringing in new depositors. Write to the Office of Consumer Affairs, FDIC, 550 17th St., N.W., Washington, DC 20429.

IN YOUR OWN BEST INTEREST

When the interest on CDs declined and money market mutual funds plummeted, investors rediscovered U.S. Savings Bonds. The savings bond rate is adjusted by the Treasury Department each November 1 and May 1 to 85 percent of the average yield on five-year Treasury securities in the previous six months. If you own a bond five years or more, you get the average of the semiannual rate in effect while you owned it. No matter how low general interest rates go, the

Treasury guarantees a minimum of 6 percent if held five years. When interest rates fall as drastically as they did in early 1992, that 6 percent looks mighty good.

Also, interest on savings bonds is free from state tax. You don't pay federal tax on the interest until you cash in the bonds. Interest is paid for thirty years. Interest on bonds bought after 1989 is tax-exempt if they are cashed in to pay for a child's college education. To qualify for the tax exemption, your income must meet the criteria in the year you cash the bonds. The amount is adjusted each year for inflation. For instance, in 1991 interest was tax-free for single filers earning less than $41,950 but only partially tax-free if income was between $41,950 and $57,700. Joint filers qualified for full exemption if combined income was below $62,900.

Savings bonds can be purchased for as little as $25 through your bank or credit union. If you are planning to buy a bond for a gift and need it for a particular day, check with your bank a week or two in advance. Often there is a delay between the time you order the bond and when you will receive it.

The financial world is a maze. Without formal education in the field or acquired knowledge, you could be going around in circles trying to find the best way out. Even if you have only $100 a month to invest, you want maximum return for minimum risk and to keep your investment at least in line with inflation. Consider working with a financial adviser to get you on the right track to a more secure future. With the right planner and a little luck, your money tree will grow tall and green.

A planner should be able to answer all the questions you've ever had about investing but were afraid (or couldn't afford) to ask. She or he will explain the pros and cons of tax-exempt investments, money markets, mutual funds, stocks, bonds, how to get the most out of IRAs and Keoghs, whether you should be thinking long-term to cover your children's education and retirement or short-term if you're older and want to reap benefits while you can still enjoy them.

Look for a planner who specializes in helping families that

can only invest minimal funds initially. The best referrals come from friends and family who have had a good experience with a planner. Your Consumer Credit Counseling Service office should also have a list of recommended planners.

NO QUICK FIX

After experiencing financial disaster personally in 1980, Bob Throckmorton started the Consumer Fresh Start Association (CFSA), a nonprofit organization dedicated to helping consumers restore their credit. He assures people that reestablishing credit can be done, but slowly and methodically. "It can't be done overnight," he warns. "There is no such thing as a quick fix." In fact, his watchdog agency is always on the lookout for the new quick-fix scams that proliferate in this type of economy.

Signing up for CFSA costs $40 per household, per year. Members receive a quarterly newsletter, clinical counseling, and an opportunity to apply for a secured credit card. CFSA plans to add new services to the program, such as a legal service plan. Call 815-875-4078 for more information.

Qualifying for new credit may be iffy until you establish some indication that you have turned yourself around financially. Start by depositing money in a bank or credit union and request a debit card. Try not to charge more than you can pay off each month. You should avoid applying for credit that is likely to be refused. Rejections are also reported to credit agencies. Call around to your local department stores to determine which appear to be the most lenient in granting credit.

Try contacting the manager of the credit department where you are intending to apply. Explain your situation and that you are trying to restore your credit. He or she can probably tell you if your chances are good or bad for a new card. When making your application, list your gross income and be sure to include your job title if it implies responsibility and sounds impressive. Don't lie; just polish the truth a bit.

When you apply for a new major credit card, look for one with no annual membership fee and a low interest rate. *Money* magazine publishes a monthly list of credit card companies and terms, or contact Bankcard Holders of America at 1-800-553-8025 for its list. *The Consumer Handbook to Credit Protection Laws* would be a good addition to your resource library. For a copy, write to the Board of Governors of the Federal Reserve System, Washington, DC 20551.

BACK TO THE FUTURE

Recessions do end, but millions of people will feel the effects for months, even years, after. For every one who emerges without debt, hundreds will stay buried. Keep reminding yourself that you are not alone while you rebuild your life. Regaining and maintaining financial security requires patience, good sense, and vigilance.

Periodically review this checklist:

- Resist temptation. Don't let the thrill of post-recession excitement entice you to add to your debt.
- Maintain your restored credit standing. You didn't clear up one mess to make room for another.
- Establish an emergency fund. Ideally, your minimum should be enough to cover at least three months' worth of living expenses.
- Evaluate discretionary expenses. Now that your financial outlook is improving, continue to look at the big picture. You may now decide that you can't postpone major repairs any longer, but you should think twice about buying that new appliance or gadget you've been wanting. If you lived comfortably without them up to now, you probably can do without them for a while longer.
- Be realistic. Financial troubles happen almost overnight, but recovery takes time. Try not to let the process get you down. Take each step one day at a time. You can make progress every day by forgoing an expense, looking for

ways to improve your job performance, putting a few dollars away, or finding another source for additional income, all of which puts you on a positive route toward financial security.

- Be nice to yourself. Times have been tough, and you wondered whether or not you would make it. If you have gotten this far in this book and followed the suggestions, congratulations: you have survived. You and your family should take the time now to do something to reward yourselves. It need not be expensive, but whatever you do, don't put it on a credit card. By now you are aware that there are any number of wonderful activities and trips you can take that are not costly but are fun, and provide the setting for enjoying one another without the strain of day-to-day pressures. The trip can also authenticate for you your new lifestyle, now self-imposed rather than financially motivated. No matter how you choose to celebrate, pat yourselves on the back. You have survived unemployment.

THE IMPORTANCE OF BEING EARNEST

You are back to work and have made a good beginning on straightening out your finances and credit record. Now is the time to prepare for new crises. Use your last experience as a gauge for the future.

Beef up your loan capacity while you qualify. Set up a program whereby you can automatically access money when you need it but don't pay interest until you do, such as a home equity loan. If you are contemplating a career change or suspect you are about to be laid off again, you may want to apply for a personal loan while you can still get it.

Try not to use the loan money. Bank it or make a safe investment. Granted, you will probably not earn as much interest as you will have to pay, but you will have the security of "something to fall back on" when all other assets are exhausted.

Apply for new credit cards. By now you've probably learned your lesson and will use these for necessary purchases and emergencies only.

If you own your home, try to refinance for a lower interest rate while you have the income to justify a new mortgage. A lower monthly payment is welcome in good times as well as in bad. If you rent, consider looking for a new apartment now that you can pass a new landlord's financial scrutiny. You may find one equal in standard to where you are now living but for less rent.

The experience you've just come out of could be a dress rehearsal for future recessions and unemployment. If you conduct your financial life accordingly, you will join the elite ranks of realists. The next time, you will be prepared. Keep all your records organized, maintain adequate insurance coverage, participate in retirement plans, and borrow only for worthwhile purposes. And, of course, spend wisely and save, save, save.

MENDING BRIDGES

Money (or the lack thereof) is the greatest source of controversy between mates, creating tension for the entire family. If you're itching for an argument, bring up the subject of money. Bingo! You've got the fight you were looking for. Good times will not eliminate all heated discussions about money, but the lean times should have given you a better handle on how some disputes can be avoided and confrontations resolved without spending the night in separate bedrooms.

If you have come this far together, you are obviously a good team. Now that your financial picture is looking brighter, try not to forget how you and your mate, indeed the whole family, pulled together to get through the hard times. Keep that teamwork intact and look for new ways to minimize money-related stress.

One method is to schedule monthly family budget meetings. Now that the kids have, we hope, been cured of the "gimmes" (give me this; give me that), their input will help to set priorities that are acceptable to them and reinforce their sense of family.

Make separate dates with your mate to review the family meetings and develop a budget that everyone can live with. Also make long-range plans—a new car in a year? repaint the house in six months? a new refrigerator? Determining together how and when the money should be spent eliminates the friction and resentment that come from unilateral decisions.

KEEP YOUR GUARD UP

Employment professionals warn that someone beginning professional life in the nineties should expect to have from five to eight jobs before retiring. LIFO (Last In, First Out) is not a ghost of jobs past; it's a fact of your professional life.

The keys to career success are commitment to learning and flexibility. Your skills must be constantly updated to establish your value to the point of indispensability. This may require additional education. Take advantage of study grants and fellowships that may be offered by colleges and universities, or businesses. Become the company "jack-of-all-trades" by knowing every part of the project you work on (not just your own), by familiarizing yourself with the other jobs in your department as well as with the responsibilities of other departments.

Career-related ambidexterity is another safeguard against unemployment. Acquire knowledge about a field other than the one in which you work. If one industry dries up and starts to shed its leaves, you will not be as likely to get raked into the compost pile. You will be ready to make your move without missing a beat.

IT ALL ADDS UP

The late Senator Everett Dirksen once remarked, "A billion here, a billion there, and pretty soon you're talking about real money." Real money is the hottest topic of conversation during any economic descent. The dilemma of where to get it and how to hold on to it long enough to do some good has the same elements as a new jigsaw puzzle. All the pieces are there; you just need some time and patience to put them all together.

COMES THE REVOLUTION

In his *Tale of Two Cities*, Charles Dickens wrote about the French Revolution, "It was the best of times, it was the worst of times." Contradictory as that may sound, his observation was right on the mark. The worst of times can bring out the best in us. It tests our mettle to the limit and makes us summon up all of our reserves. The lessons we learn in the worst of times make the best of times even better.

APPENDIX A

Charts and Worksheets

SEVERANCE PACKAGE CHECKLIST

- Severance pay.

- Compensation for earned vacation days.

- Continued use of company car during period covered by severance.

- Continued use of perks such as answering machines, computers, mobile phones, club memberships, etc.

- Profit sharing.

- Pension fund.

- Outplacement counseling.

- Continued insurance & medical coverage during severance period (covering insurance payments before activating COBRA).

- Maintenance of company-sponsored day care for the duration of your job search or until conclusion of your severance package term.

- An office from which to conduct a job search.

- Staff support, such as taking your phone calls, providing secretaries.

- Letter of recommendation.

ACTIONS TO TAKE WHEN YOU LOSE A JOB

- Tell your family you will need to find a new job.

- File for unemployment compensation. If you can do it on the same day you lose your job, you get an unpleasant task out of the way and shorten your waiting period for eligibility.

- Assess your financial situation. (See chapter 2, "Charting Your Course," for details.)

- Contact your children's school to let them know you are unemployed. They can provide counseling if appropriate. (See the letter on page 83.)

- Make sure you have a library card. In large metropolitan areas, check out several libraries to learn which ones have the best reference and magazine sections. Some cities have libraries that specialize in business materials. Don't forget to check local university libraries or university career centers for materials.

- Get business cards printed. Think of yourself as a consultant and of your cards as mini-résumés. List your skills to remind potential employers or clients which talents you offer. At the very least, a calling card printed with your name and address is helpful.

- Identify job networking groups or unemployment support groups in your area. The unemployment office, churches, synagogues, community centers, or libraries should be able to supply you with information.

- Begin to update your résumé. Listing your strengths and career accomplishments is a therapeutic process.

- After you have updated your résumé, inform friends you are looking for work.

- Notify creditors of your situation. (See chapter 2.)

HOW TO COPE WITH
A BUREAUCRATIC MAZE

Dealing with Agencies:

- Call ahead for directions. Make sure you're headed to the right place. Find out who will be able to help you when you get there. Learn what documentation you will need to have with you.

- Carry proof of identification, your Social Security card, proof of residence, and any documentation required by the office you intend to visit.

- Take something to do while you wait.

- Write down the name of the person you talk to. Note what they tell you in case you need to refer to it later.

- Ask questions to get the information you need.

- Be pleasant. Most people really do want to help. Make it easy for them, and they are likely to go an extra mile for you. Make it difficult, and they are likely to terminate the discussion.

- Keep copies of all letters and documentation you receive from agencies or through the mail. Never ignore them. Make sure you understand what they mean and what action you should take. If you're not sure, contact the agency or business and ask to have the document explained in terms you understand. If necessary, get advice from an appropriate source about what options you might have.

Tracking Down Information via the Phone:

- Find a starting point through the phone book, *Information U.S.A.*, or a reference librarian.

- Have something to write with, a notebook, and any necessary documentation ready before you call.

- Use a gracious tone and be respectful of those to whom you speak.

- Get a name and note it. Names are useful when making referrals or follow-up phone calls.

- Ask your questions. If the person can't help you, see if they have suggestions of other people to call.

- Be persistent if you don't get the help you require. When dealing with major companies, it sometimes helps to call back later. You may get a different, more knowledgeable customer service person next time.

SPENDING YOUR LIFE ON HOLD

When unemployed, you can expect to spend an exorbitant amount of time waiting: on the phone, in agency lines, and for appointments. Lessen the aggravation of waiting by planning activities that help you relax and/or spend your time productively. Here are just a few suggestions.

When Waiting Away from Home:

- Read a book
- Write letters/thank-you notes
- Read want ads
- Read newspapers/magazines, especially trade-related journals
- Design something (garden, woodworking project, circuit board, business idea, creative daydreaming, etc.)
- Listen to Walkman/tapes (motivational, foreign language, management, books on tape)
- Clip coupons
- Work on craft projects for gifts, such as knitting
- Mend clothes

When Waiting on Hold at Home:

- Fix meals
- Fold clothes
- Go through mail
- Anything from the "away from home" list

<u>CURRENT ASSETS</u>

Cash on Hand

checking accounts   _____

savings accounts   _____

government bonds   _____

certificates of deposit   _____

money market mutual funds   _____

life insurance cash value   _____

retirement accounts cash value, e.g., IRAs,
   Keoghs, vested benefits   _____

Working Assets

loans receivable (owed to you)   _____

real estate equity (current market value
   minus mortgage)   _____

market value of business interests   _____

market value of cars, trucks, boats, etc.
   (less loan amount)   _____

market value of household goods, e.g.,
   furnishings, appliances, entertainment
   centers (less any loan amounts)   _____

market value of personal investments, e.g.,
   jewelry, paintings, Persian rugs, coins, etc.   _____

                           Total Current Assets   _____

PROJECTED INCOME

	This Month	6-Month Estimate
Monthly Income		
salary/wages		
unemployment compensation		
child support/alimony		
investment income		
pension/annuities		
Social Security/disability benefits		
other		
Additional Income Sources		
severance pay		
profit sharing		
interest		
trust fund		
gifts		
sales of assets		
capital gains		
tax refunds		
sideline business		
Total 6-Month Income		_____
Divide total estimated 6-month income by 6 to project:		
Average Monthly Income		_____

<u>BUDGET WORKSHEET</u>

	Previous Month	*New Target*
Fixed Expenses		
housing		
rent	_____	_____
mortgage	_____	_____
property taxes	_____	_____
condo fees	_____	_____
insurance premiums		
life	_____	_____
disability	_____	_____
health	_____	_____
auto	_____	_____
home	_____	_____
debt payments		
auto loans	_____	_____
installment loans	_____	_____
credit cards	_____	_____
other	_____	_____
child support/alimony	_____	_____
other	_____	_____
Variable Expenses		
utilities		
gas or oil	_____	_____
electricity	_____	_____
local telephone	_____	_____
long-distance telephone	_____	_____
water	_____	_____
sewer	_____	_____
trash collection	_____	_____
home maintenance		
repairs	_____	_____
home improvement	_____	_____
cleaning	_____	_____

	Previous Month	*New Target*
Variable Expenses (cont'd)		
landscaping & lawn service	_____	_____
gardening	_____	_____
medical care		
doctors	_____	_____
dentists	_____	_____
therapists	_____	_____
medications	_____	_____
transportation		
gasoline	_____	_____
auto repairs/ maintenance	_____	_____
public transportation fares	_____	_____
food		
groceries	_____	_____
school meals	_____	_____
work meals	_____	_____
clothing		
adult purchases	_____	_____
children's purchases	_____	_____
shoes/boots/coats	_____	_____
dry cleaning and laundry	_____	_____
tailoring or repairs	_____	_____
uniforms/costumes	_____	_____
personal care		
hair care	_____	_____
manicure	_____	_____
toiletries	_____	_____
child care		
day care	_____	_____
baby-sitting	_____	_____
diapers/formula	_____	_____
education		
tuition	_____	_____

	Previous Month	*New Target*
Variable Expenses (cont'd)		
special fees		
books		
supplies		
lessons/ extracurricular activities		
pets		
food		
grooming		
veterinary care		
other		
savings/investments		
membership/dues		
bank service charges		
taxes		
federal		
state		
city		
excise		
job search expenses		
Discretionary Expenses		
entertainment/recreation		
cable TV		
restaurants		
movies/theater		
sporting events		
hobbies		
other		
vacations		
subscriptions		
books		
magazines		
newspapers		
alcohol and tobacco		

	Previous Month	*New Target*
Discretionary Expenses (cont'd)		
mail		
postage	_____	_____
stationery	_____	_____
cards	_____	_____
gifts		
holiday	_____	_____
birthday	_____	_____
anniversary	_____	_____
other	_____	_____
contributions	_____	_____
pocket money		
adults	_____	_____
children (allowance)	_____	_____
Total Monthly Expenses	_____	_____

KID'S BUDGET PLAN

	Previous Month	*New Target*
Expenses		
clothing		
snacks		
entertainment		
hobbies		
Total Monthly Expenses		
Income		
allowance		
recycling		
newspaper		
bottles		
cans		
other _____		
work		
part-time employment		
newspaper route		
baby-sitting or mother's helper		
lawn & garden service		
snow shoveling		
housecleaning		
car wash		
animal care		
other _____		
sales		
garage sale of old toys		
lemonade & cookie stand		
garden vegetables stand		
cash gifts		
interest on savings		
Total Monthly Income		

WHAT TO TAKE TO
THE UNEMPLOYMENT OFFICE

- Proper identification; call your local unemployment office to find out what they will accept.
- Your Social Security number.
- Proof of salary or wages, such as a W-2 form or pay stub.
- Names and addresses of all employers you worked for during the fifty-two weeks prior to filling your claim.
- Documentation of dependent child(ren).
- Something to do while you wait.

EMERGENCY LARDER

For an emergency larder, the Department of Agriculture recommends choosing canned or sealed package foods that will store at room temperature. In addition to being useful in an economic emergency, these larder items come in handy during natural disasters such as hurricanes or earthquakes. Particularly convenient are those foods that do not require cooking or refrigeration.

Suggested Items for an Emergency Larder

Milk:
- evaporated milk
- nonfat dry or whole dry milk, in airtight container

Canned Meat, Poultry, Fish:
- Meat, poultry
- Fish
- Mixtures of meats, vegetables, cereal products
- Condensed meat-and-vegetable soups & stews

Fruits and Vegetables:
- Berries and cherries, canned
- Citrus fruit juices, canned
- Other fruits and fruit juices, canned
- Dried fruit in airtight containers
- Tomatoes or sauerkraut, canned

- Other vegetables, canned
- Dry beans, peas & lentils in airtight containers

Shortening and Oil:
- Hydrogenated shortening
- Vegetable oil
- Salad dressing

Cereals and Baked Goods:
- Ready-to-eat cereals in airtight containers
- Uncooked cereal (quick-cooking or instant) in airtight containers
- Crackers or cookies
- White flour
- Pasta in airtight containers

Sweets and Nuts:
- Sugar
- Nuts, canned
- Peanut butter
- Instant pudding
- Fruit gelatin

Miscellaneous:
- Coffee, tea, cocoa (instant)
- Artificial cream products, dry
- bouillon cubes
- Flavored beverage powders
- Salt
- Flavorings, spices

- Baking soda, baking powder

Baby Supplies:
- Formula
- Baby food

Pet Foods:
- Dog or cat food, dry

Shelf Life of Stored Foods:
- Frozen butter lasts up to one year
- Evaporated milk lasts up to one year
- Dry milk stored in the refrigerator lasts up to one year
- Frozen eggs last one year
- Dried eggs stored in the refrigerator last up to one year
- Frozen meats and fish, with the exception of lamb and beef, which last longer, generally last only 6 months
- Frozen vegetables and fruits last up to one year, except processed french fries, which last only up to 6 months
- Meatless substitutes, beans, and nuts last 1–3 years
- Frozen baked products last up to 9 months
- Uncooked pasta will be good for at least one year
- Uncooked rice lasts 2 years
- Dried legumes last up to 2 years
- White flour lasts up to one year, whole-grain flours only 2 months
- White sugar lasts indefinitely
- Refrigerated jams last up to one year
- Canned meat, poultry, fish, and most fruits and vegetables last about 18 months
- Canned tomatoes and sauerkraut last 6 months
- Canned citrus fruits and juices last 6 months
- Canned berries and cherries last 6 months

CREATING A SCHEDULE

- Make time to look for work. Don't let anything interfere with that time.
- Don't fall into the household routine without a plan. Although it's okay to get involved with the housework and errands, make sure it is written into your schedule rather than allowed to happen randomly.
- Limit the amount of time you are allowed to spend on a job search, and your time will be more productive. (Remember the old adage that a busy person gets things done.)
- Try to have a place to go first thing in the morning when you conduct your job search: the library, an outplacement center, etc.
- Set realistic job-search goals for the day, such as X number of letters or follow-up phone calls, obtaining a list of X contacts, X appointments, etc.
- When you're not actively looking for work in the daytime, create activities that will alleviate boredom and depression.
- Every evening, make a list of things to do the next day. Assign tasks to your subconscious to work on overnight. The next morning you won't spin your wheels trying to figure out how to get started.
- Reserve time to do nothing. This will help you avoid stalling on tasks that are scheduled.
- Plan successes in your life. Schedule time away from your job search so you can continue to value those aspects of yourself that aren't part of your occupation.
- Set goals: What do you wish to accomplish? When can you do it? Remain flexible in goals and reassess them as necessary.
- If you haven't had time for exercise, begin now. Exercise improves your morale, your capacity to cope with problems, and your physical health. You don't have to train for the triathlon to see the benefit reflected in your medi-

cal bills. Even a ten-minute walk three times a day makes a difference in your health and in your outlook.

- Plan time to daydream. Daydreaming is a great way to relax and reduce stress. Activities like woodworking, knitting, painting, and walking offer wonderful opportunities to exercise your imagination.

- Pick something to look forward to and write it into your schedule every morning. You might choose breakfast with your kids, a walk around the park, or a danish smothered in butter with a hot cup of coffee.

- Use a daily planner like the one on page 269 to help you custom-tailor your own schedule. Consider making copies for the kids to work out their own.

- When scheduling activities, your goal is to create a balance between family, work, play, exercise, and rest. No one component is less important than another. Think of these activities as the legs on a table: remove just one, and the table collapses.

- Take advantage of your circadian rhythms to maximize peak performance times. Peak times may vary according to whether an individual tends to be a "morning" or "evening" person. According to Jane Wegscheider Hyman in *The Light Book* (Jeremy P. Tarcher, 1990), your natural body clock operates on a timetable:

6:00–8:00	Transition from night to day. Wake up, shower, dress, get kids ready for school, eat breakfast, read news, walk dog, etc.
8:00–12:00	Immediate memory or verbal reasoning tasks. A good time to compose letters for a job search or place follow-up phone calls. If possible, schedule job interviews before lunch.
12:00–5:00	Physical tasks. A good time to schedule errands away from a desk, including exercise and sports.

4:00–8:00   Repetitive tasks requiring manual dexter-
                 ity. Use this period for activities like piano
                 practice, typing, collating résumés, and
                 food preparation.

7:00–11:00   Long-term memorization tasks. A good
                 time to review information related to your
                 professional field or learn about a com-
                 pany for an upcoming interview.

DAILY SCHEDULE

<table>
<tr><td>**WEEKDAYS**</td><td>**WEEKENDS**</td></tr>
<tr><td>Morning:</td><td>Morning:</td></tr>
<tr><td>6:00 _____</td><td>6:00 _____</td></tr>
<tr><td>7:00 _____</td><td>7:00 _____</td></tr>
<tr><td>8:00 _____</td><td>8:00 _____</td></tr>
<tr><td>9:00 _____</td><td>9:00 _____</td></tr>
<tr><td>10:00 _____</td><td>10:00 _____</td></tr>
<tr><td>11:00 _____</td><td>11:00 _____</td></tr>
<tr><td>Afternoon:</td><td>Afternoon:</td></tr>
<tr><td>12:00 _____</td><td>12:00 _____</td></tr>
<tr><td>1:00 _____</td><td>1:00 _____</td></tr>
<tr><td>2:00 _____</td><td>2:00 _____</td></tr>
<tr><td>3:00 _____</td><td>3:00 _____</td></tr>
<tr><td>4:00 _____</td><td>4:00 _____</td></tr>
<tr><td>5:00 _____</td><td>5:00 _____</td></tr>
<tr><td>6:00 _____</td><td>6:00 _____</td></tr>
<tr><td>Evening:</td><td>Evening:</td></tr>
<tr><td>7:00 _____</td><td>7:00 _____</td></tr>
<tr><td>8:00 _____</td><td>8:00 _____</td></tr>
<tr><td>9:00 _____</td><td>9:00 _____</td></tr>
<tr><td>10:00 _____</td><td>10:00 _____</td></tr>
<tr><td>11:00 _____</td><td>11:00 _____</td></tr>
</table>

HE SAYS, SHE SAYS

How Your Focus on Feelings Directs a Conversation

What a Person Thinks and Says if Focused on Internal Feelings:	What a Person Says if Focused on Partner's Feelings:
She thinks: *Even though I planned carefully, groceries cost more than I budgeted. Shopping is frustrating, and I feel so bad afterward!* She says: "I ran out of money. At this rate, we won't be able to afford the bare necessities."	She could have said: "I didn't have enough money for everything on my list. I put some things back."
He thinks: *I feel responsible for supporting my family, but it's not my fault we don't have an income. I knock myself out every day looking for a job.* He says: "What did you do, buy caviar and champagne? There was plenty of money in that budget when we set it up."	He could have said: "It must have been hard to put things back. You've done a good job sticking to our budget, and I'm proud of you."
She thinks: *I worked hard to stretch every penny, and he thinks I'm extravagant!* She says: "You think it's so easy doing the shopping? Fine! You do it from now on. It's not as if you're contributing to anything else around here."	She could have said: "I guess when we set the budget up, we expected money to go farther. But this is what we agreed on and I'm determined to stick with it."
He thinks: *See? She blames me for not finding a job. There is no work out there!* He says: "I have enough to worry about looking for a job without doing your work around the house!"	He could have said: "We agreed not to let anything interfere with my job search. I know shopping is difficult when the budget is so tight."

APPENDIX B

Resources

RESOURCES

Business and Careers

The Complete Job Search Handbook, by Howard Figler, Ph.D. (New York: Henry Holt and Company, 1988).

For information about career opportunities in science and technology request *Employment Roadmaps* from:
Congressional Caucus for Science and Technology
House Annex Building #2, H2-226
2nd and D Sts., S.W.
Washington, DC 20515

How to Win the Job You Really Want, by Janice Weinberg (New York: Henry Holt and Company, 1989).

Parting Company: How to Survive the Loss of a Job and Find Another Successfully, by William J. Morin and James C. Cabrera (New York: Harcourt Brace Jovanovich, 1991).

The Professional Image (1984) and *The Professional Presence* (1991), by Susan Bixler (New York: Putnam).

Second Careers: New Ways to Work After Fifty, by Caroline Bird (Boston: Little, Brown & Company, 1992). Explores career possibilities for those who want to change fields. Excellent resource section at the end of the book.

Thoughtline: The Intelligent Writer's Companion, by Xpercom. An interactive MS-DOS software program for brainstorming and writing that belongs on the desk of every businessperson who uses a PC. An add-on program includes *Job Search: The Total Interview*, codeveloped with Dawson & Dawson Management Consultants in Houston. With *Job Search*, the user rehearses interviews and develops solid responses to questions. Highly recommended. For current pricing and information, write to:
Xpercom
3605 Luallen
Carrollton, TX 75007

What Color Is Your Parachute?, Richard Nelson Bolles (Berkeley, CA: Ten Speed Press, published annually). Resource section filled with leads to helpful organizations and books to uncover job leads.

Wishcraft: How to Get What You Really Want, by Barbara Sher with Annie Gottlieb (New York: Ballantine, 1986). Recommended especially for individuals interested in nontraditional career choices.

The Woman's Guide to Starting a Business, by Claudia Jessup and Genie Chipps (New York: Henry Holt and Company, 1991).

Finances

Conquer Your Debt: How to Solve Your Credit Problems, by William Kent Brunette (New York: Prentice Hall, 1990).

Earning Money Without a Job (1991) and *555 Ways to Earn Extra Money* (1991), by Jay Conrad Levinson (New York: Henry Holt and Company).

How to Protect Your Life Savings, by Harley Gordon and Jane Daniel (Boston: Financial Planning Institute, 1991).

Food and Gardening

From the Consumer Information Center, P.O. Box 100, Pueblo, CO 81002:

> *Making Food Dollars Count.* Includes information and recipes to help the shopper on a limited budget meet nutritional needs.
>
> *How to Buy Economically: A Food Buyer's Guide.* Gives advice on cutting grocery costs, including which months offer the best buys on fruits and vegetables.

To locate a community garden near you, inquire at your county extension service, town hall, local garden club, or garden center. If you want information on how to establish a community garden in your neighborhood, write to:

American Community Gardening Association
325 Walnut St.
Philadelphia, PA 19106

To locate farms that offer low-cost pick-your-own fruit or vegetables contact your county extension service.

Free/Low-cost Gifts and Activities

Free boating lessons. Contact your local U.S. Coast Guard office or write:

Commandant (G-BAU-1)
U.S. Coast Guard
Washington, DC 20592

Free coloring book, *Charlie Brown Cleans the Air*, contact:
Environmental Protection Agency
Public Information Center
820 Quincy St., N.W.
Washington, DC 20011

Free comic books about money, including *The Story of Money, The Story of Banks*, and *The Story of Inflation*, contact:
Federal Reserve Bank of New York
Publications Section
33 Liberty St.
New York, NY 10045

Free firewood for personal use is available for the cutting at national forests. For more information, contact your local Forest Service office.

Free maps for biking and hiking:
U.S. Department of the Interior
18th and C Sts., N.W., Room 1013
Washington, DC 20240

Free publications on space and aerospace. For a current listing, contact:
NASA Educational Publications
NASA Headquarters, Code LEP
Washington, DC 20546

Free youth group accommodations and airplane rides. Write to the U.S. Air Force installation nearest you:
Base Commander
(Appropriate name) Air Force Base
State, Zip
Attn: Youth Organization Project Officer

For $1.00 you can cut your own Christmas tree if you live near federal land in one of ten western states. Contact your local Bureau of Land Management office or write:
Division of Forestry
Bureau of Land Management
Department of the Interior, Room 901, Premier Bldg.
1725 I St., N.W.
Washington, DC 20240

The U.S. Department of Agriculture offers business loans for children and teenagers. These loans are usually made in conjunction with youth groups and require parental consent. Write to:

Production Loan Division
Farmers Home Administration
Department of Agriculture
Washington, DC 20250

General Resources

Find It Fast: How to Uncover Expert Information on Any Subject, by Robert I. Berkman (New York: Harper & Row, 1990). Explains how to locate information on topics ranging from economic forecasts to health news. An invaluable guide for finding resources during unemployment and for honing job-hunting skills that require networking for information.

Information U.S.A., by Matthew Lesko (New York: Viking Penguin Books, 1986). A massive reference guide to services and publications offered by the federal government.

Legal References

You and the Law, by the American Bar Association (New York: Signet, 1991). Written in a question-and-answer format, this reference explains legal issues in plain English. It also lists resources to contact for further information or assistance.

Your Rights in the Workplace, by Dan Lacey (Berkeley, CA: Nolo Press, 1991).

Your Rights at Work, by Darien McWhirter (New York: John Wiley & Sons, 1989).

Retirement and Relocation

Henry Holt Retirement Sourcebook: An Information Guide for Planning and Managing Your Affairs, by Wilbur Cross (New York: Henry Holt and Company, 1991).

Over Fifty: The Resource Book for the Better Half of Your Life, by Tom and Nancy Biracree (New York: Harper Perennial, 1991).

Places Rated Almanac (1989) and *Retirement Places Rated* (1990), by Richard Boyer and David Savageau (New York: Prentice Hall).

Support for Individuals and Families

The American Self-Help Clearinghouse publishes *The Self-Help Source Book*, which contains information on finding or forming mutual self-help groups. If your library doesn't have a copy in the reference section, you can order the book by sending $8 (plus $1 for first-class shipping) to the American Self-Help Clearinghouse, Saint Clares–Riverside Medical Center, Denville, NJ 07834.

Integrity International is an organization that provides support to whistle-blowers and their families. Integrity International gives advice on effective steps to take before blowing the whistle and suggestions on how to minimize damage afterward. For information contact:

Dr. Donald Soeken
6215 Greenbelt Rd.
College Park, MD 20740
301-474-7358

The Light Book: How Natural and Artificial Light Affect Our Health, Mood, and Behavior, by Jane Wegscheider Hyman (Los Angeles: Jeremy P. Tarcher, 1990). Shows how light regulates our biological rhythms involved in concentration, dexterity, mood, health, and sleep. Information may be useful in setting up schedules that maximize personal productivity and pleasure.

Everything You Need to Know When a Parent Is Out of Work, by Stephanie St. Pierre (New York: The Rosen Publishing Group, 1991). An excellent book for children up through the early teen years. It may also help parents of young children to simplify explanations about unemployment.

When Bad Things Happen to Good People, by Harold Kushner (New York: Avon, 1983).

You Mean I Don't HAVE to Feel This Way? New Help for Depression, Anxiety, and Addiction, by Colette Dowling (New York: Charles Scribner's Sons, 1991). Interesting, up-to-date information on effective treatment of affective disorders. Highly recommended, not only for those who endure depression or related problems, but also for their families.

800 Numbers

AT&T's "800" Directory Assistance 1-800-555-1212

Financial
American Small Business Association. . . . 1-800-235-2398
Bankcard Holders of America 1-800-553-8025
Citibank
   Classic card information 1-800-843-0777
   Preferred card information. 1-800-645-9565
Consumer Credit Counseling Service. . . . 1-800-388-2227
Equifax, Inc 1-800-685-1111
Exec-U-Net 1-800-637-3126
Federal Deposit Insurance Corporation
   Office of Consumer Affairs 1-800-424-5488
Help-You-Sell Real Estate. 1-800-526-2625
IRS Tax Forms 1-800-TAX-FORM
IRS Information Line. 1-800-829-1040
National Barter Corporation 1-800-523-2047
Re/Max, Barry Nystedt 1-800-821-5270
Time Solutions, MedSure. 1-800-552-3302
TRW Information Services 1-800-392-1122

Health
American Association of Retired Persons . 1-800-523-5800
Department of Health and Human Services
   (Hill-Burton) National Hotline 1-800-638-0742
   (Maryland residents) 1-800-492-0359

Insurance
American Council of Life Insurance 1-800-423-8000
Insurance Information Institute 1-800-942-4242

Nutrition
Alabama University Nutrition Information Service . . . . .
. . . . .1-800-231-DIET
American Dietetic Association 1-800-366-1655

Scholarships

College Resource Materials 1-800-545-8616
Federal Department of Education, Inspector General's
    Office 1-800-MIS-USED
Federal Student Aid Information Center 1-800-4-FED-AID

HOTLINES AND MUTUAL HELP GROUPS

AIDS REFERRAL
The U.S. Conference of Mayors publishes a brochure, *Local AIDS-Related Services National Directory*, a listing of over 2,000 AIDS groups.
1620 I St., N.W.
Washington, DC 20006
202-293-7330

AIDS INFORMATION CLEARINGHOUSE
(Centers for Disease Control) For people who want referral information about AIDS services and programs, or who want to know how to talk to family members about AIDS.
1-800-458-5231

AL-ANON FAMILY GROUP HEADQUARTERS
For relatives and friends of persons with alcohol problems. Includes ALATEEN.
1372 Broadway
New York, NY 10018
1-800-245-4656
(In NY call 212-302-7240)

ALCOHOLICS ANONYMOUS
For men and women who share the common problems of alcoholism.
P.O. Box 459
Grand Central Station
New York, NY 10163
212-686-1100

ALZHEIMER'S DISEASE AND RELATED DISORDERS ASSOCIATION
Offers assistance and information to Alzheimer's families through its 188 chapters nationwide.
P.O. Box 5675
Department PXI
Chicago, IL 60680
1-800-621-0379
In Illinois call 1-800-572-6037

AMERICAN ASSOCIATION OF SUICIDOLOGY
For those who have experienced the suicide of someone close.
2459 South Ash
Denver, CO 80222

THE COMPASSIONATE
FRIENDS
For bereaved parents: peer
support.
P.O. Box 3696
Oak Brook, IL 60522-3696
312-990-0010

DEPRESSION AFTER
DELIVERY
For women experiencing
postpartum depression.
P.O. Box 1282
Morrisville, PA 19067
215-295-3994

EMOTIONS ANONYMOUS
For persons with emotional
problems: a twelve-step program
adapted from the Alcoholics
Anonymous program.
P.O. Box 4245
St. Paul, MN 55104
612-647-9712

FAMILIES ANONYMOUS
For concerned relatives and
friends of youth with drug abuse
or related behavior problems.
P.O. Box 528
Van Nuys, CA 91408
818-989-7841

GAMBLERS ANONYMOUS
For those with compulsive
gambling problems.
P.O. Box 17173
Los Angeles, CA 90017
213-386-8789

NARCOTICS ANONYMOUS
For narcotic addicts: peer
support for recovered addicts.
P.O. Box 9999
Van Nuys, CA 91409
818-780-3951

THE NATIONAL ALLIANCE
FOR THE MENTALLY ILL
For families and friends of
seriously mentally ill individuals.
2101 Wilson Blvd.
Suite 302
Arlington, VA 22201
703-524-7600

NATIONAL ASSOCIATION
OF ANOREXIA NERVOSA
AND ASSOCIATED
DISORDERS
Offers assistance to anorexics/
bulimics and their families.
Box 7
Highland Park, IL 60035
312-831-3438

NATIONAL CHILD ABUSE
HOTLINE
A crisis information and referral
service for child abuse issues.
Child Help U.S.A.
P.O. Box 630
Hollywood, CA 90028
1-800-4-A-CHILD (1-800-422-
4453)
(In California call 1-800-352-
0386)

NATIONAL COALITION
AGAINST DOMESTIC
VIOLENCE
National organization of shelters
and support services for battered
women and their children.
P.O. Box 15127
Washington, DC 20003-0127
1-800-333-SAFE (1-800-333-7233)

NATIONAL DEPRESSIVE
AND MANIC DEPRESSIVE
ASSOCIATION
For depressed persons and their
families.
Merchandise Mart
P.O. Box 3395
Chicago, IL 60654
312-939-2442

NATIONAL FOUNDATION
FOR DEPRESSIVE ILLNESSES,
INC.
Provides referrals to support
groups.
P.O. Box 2257
New York, NY 10116
212-620-0098
1-800-248-4344

NATIONAL MENTAL
HEALTH ASSOCIATION
Citizens' advocacy group
concerned with all aspects of
mental health and mental illness.
1021 Prince St.
Alexandria, VA 22314-2971
703-643-7722

PARENTS ANONYMOUS
Provides referrals to local
chapters.
6733 South Sepulveda Blvd.
Suite 270
Los Angeles, CA 90045
1-800-421-0353

PARENTS UNITED
For abused children and for
adults who were abused as
children.
P.O. Box 952
San Jose, CA 95108
408-280-5055

PHOBIA SOCIETY OF
AMERICA
For people who suffer from
phobia and panic attacks.
133 Rollins Ave.
Suite 4B
Rockville, MD 20852
301-231-9350

RECOVERY, INC.
For former mental patients: peer
support.
802 North Dearborn St.
Chicago, IL 60610
312-337-5661

SUICIDE HOTLINE*
For suicide prevention.
1-800-333-4444

*Call the National Suicide Hotline at 1-800-333-4444 from anywhere in the
U.S. You will get a recording, but *a person will call you back*, usually within half
an hour. If you're suicidal, you will need to be in a safe place. Arrangements can
be made for a drug or detox program if necessary. Do not worry about your
ability to pay for treatment. If you cannot pay the deductible, programs are
available to accept only the amount insurance will cover.

Emergency Action

The National Institute of Mental Health recommends the following emergency tactics if a person is completely out of control or tries to commit suicide:

- In a dangerous crisis, call the police. Often the police are the best equipped, most available resource when there is a strong possibility that the person may do physical injury to himself or herself, or to others.
- In a nonviolent crisis, calling the police may be a poor choice. Depending on the situation, you can contact a physician, mental health specialist, member of the clergy, or crisis hotline for help.

INDEX